TANNA TIMES

Tanna Times

Islanders in the World

Lamont Lindstrom

UNIVERSITY OF HAWAI'I PRESS

HONOLULU

University of Hawai'i Press books are printed on acid-free paper
and meet the guidelines for permanence and durability
of the Council on Library Resources.

Library of Congress Cataloging-in-Publication Data

Names: Lindstrom, Lamont, author.
Title: Tanna times : islanders in the world / Lamont Lindstrom.
Description: Honolulu : University of Hawai'i Press, 2021 |
Includes bibliographical references and index.
Identifiers: LCCN 2020021086 | ISBN 9780824886660 (hardcover) |
ISBN 9780824886677 (paperback) | ISBN 9780824886684 (adobe pdf) |
ISBN 9780824886691 (epub) | ISBN 9780824888619 (kindle edition)
Subjects: LCSH: Tanna Island (Vanuatu)—History. |
Tanna Island (Vanuatu)—Biography.
Classification: LCC DU760 .L545 2021 | DDC 995.95—dc23
LC record available at https://lccn.loc.gov/2020021086

Cover photo: Women and girls at a boy's circumcision exchange,
Ikurup village, 2010. Photo by the author.

for Katiri, Maui, and Nora Rika

Woe to those who are at ease in Zion
and to those who feel secure
on the mountain of Samaria. (Amos 6:1)

And he must needs go through Samaria. (John 4:4)

CONTENTS

PREFACE

In 1978, I found my way to Tanna Island in what was then the New Hebrides, and Vanuatu today. My proposal to study differential success with economic development as informed by religious affiliation soon morphed into a series of better conceived and more fruitful projects. Then and now, the generous people of Samaria village put me up and put up with me. Over the years, I have come to know Samaria and its neighboring villages located within southeast Tanna's Nafe language area. Although I write of Tanna as a whole, this is shameless ethnographic license that commonly takes one particular place as representative of some encompassing culture, society, and history. Tanna is a remarkable and complex island, and stories from a single village or area never adequately capture its larger truths.

Anthropologists like to tell other people's stories but local experts tell them even better. Tanna offers a rich and profuse narrative archive and Islanders keep this vital with recurrent retellings of Tanna's times. I draw on island narratives to present the life stories of a dozen island personalities, situating these exemplar heroes and heroines within their cultural and historical worlds. Personal names, on Tanna, are tricky economic and family resources. The stories presented here introduce Islanders with their given names until we reach the present day. I re-name people who share our own times, asking their forgiveness for thus partly shadowing their persons.

In addition to the many island stories told to me over four decades on Tanna, to understand these lives and their times I draw on the writings of explorers, missionaries, traders, administrators, reporters, and anthropologists who found their way to the island, beginning in 1774. For those who might want to pursue a particular life story or an ethnographic theme, I provide suggestions for further reading at the end of each chapter. This literature, selected from a larger canon that has informed my research and writing, offers additional, detailed ethnographic and historical information about Tanna and its people.

ACKNOWLEDGMENTS

Passing years have decidedly lengthened the list of my benefactors and supporters, on Tanna and elsewhere. This book draws upon 250 years of island history and forty years of my own. As it may be my last, I must thank many friends and colleagues, some sadly missed. These include professional mentors including Margaret Mackenzie, Bob Tonkinson, and Roger Keesing; departmental colleagues at the University of Tulsa; research hosts and island companions Ken and Anne Calvert, Gordon MacFarlane, Bob Paul, Cynthia Frazer; Kirk Huffman, Ralph Regenvanu, Marcellin Abong, Richard Shing, Jacob Kapere, Jean-Pascal Wahe, and Joel Iau from the Vanuatu Cultural Centre/National Museum; and fellow scholars of Vanuatu's many cultures and languages whose research has informed mine and whose books fill my shelves, including Michael Allen, Lissant Bolton, Joël Bonnemaison, Terry Crowley, Annelin Eriksen, Ellen Facey, James Flexner, Haidy Geismar, Jean Guiart, James Gwero, Sabine Hess, Bergmans Iati, Margaret Jolly, Janet Dixon Keller, Thorgeir Kolshus, Daniela Kraemer, Joan Larcom, Vincent Lebot, Jeremy MacClancy, Carlos Mondragon, Anna Naupa, Ken Nehrbass, Mary Patterson, Jean-Marc Philibert, Knut Rio, Margaret and William Rodman, Benedicta Rousseau, Rachel Smith, Matthew Spriggs, Marc Tabani, John Taylor, Darrell Tryon, Chelsea Wentworth, and Alexandra Widmer, with much appreciation to Howard Van Trease, John Lynch, Robert Early, and Nettie Moerman for many entertaining and illuminating conversations in Port Vila's kava bars.

The University of Tulsa's Office of Research, the Henry Kendall College of Arts and Sciences Dean's Office, and the Department of Anthropology partly supported open access publication. I also thank University of Hawai'i Press editor Emma Ching and her colleagues at the Press for transforming text and photos into a tangible book—a book I offer to my island friends in return for many years of welcome and hospitality. Samaria is propitiously named and I owe most gratitude to the families I first met there in 1978, extending now to the children, grandchildren, and great-grandchildren of Rapi and Iati, Iau and Sakrai, Vani and Kasaia, Kieri and Jacobeth, Nakutan and Neiporo, Kamti Asori, Kauke Asori, and Sarei, generous and good Samaritans all. And I thank many other storytellers in neighboring villages. All are expert raconteurs of island lives and times, and I am much obliged that my own story has joined Tanna's narrative flow.

CHAPTER I

Ipare

WE MIGHT LIKE TO think that we live in a most hectic age, buffeted by epic global flows of people, of things, of ideas. But our times are not extraordinary. We might like to think we inhabit the world's hub, the global core. But our place is not special. We might like to think we set the human standard, that everyone else desires naturally to emulate our ways. But we are not exemplary. Gaze out into the world and we can find global networks established millennia before the Old World met the New World (or first remembered so doing) in 1492. These intensifying grids and channels have continued to proliferate. Globalization reaches us all. But within our interconnected world, despite this worldwide intercourse, we also find myriad forms of local exceptionalism, going strong and underway.

Global Island

Come to Tanna, an island in the southern reaches of Vanuatu, a Y-shaped archipelago in the southwestern Pacific, 750 miles west of Fiji and 1,200 miles east of Australia (map). Strangers from abroad found their way to Tanna in 1774 following the glow of its volcano, Iasur, which reddened the horizon. British explorer James Cook and his crew, on the sailing ship *Resolution*, were atypical visitors but not exceptional in that Islanders themselves sailed about Vanuatu's southern islands and beyond to the Loyalties and New Caledonia. Their oceangoing ancestors had canoed in from the north about three thousand years previously.

Cook needed to replenish his ship's supplies of water and firewood and he also wanted to explore. Johann Forster, the expedition's natural scientist, with his son Georg ventured forth into island hamlets located around a bay that Cook named Port Resolution, after his ship. The Forsters reconnoitered and chatted with the locals whom they called Indians, a residue label from even earlier global encounters. They reported back to Cook that *Resolution* had landed on Tanna. This word, though, means ground or soil. An anthropologist in the 1920s would

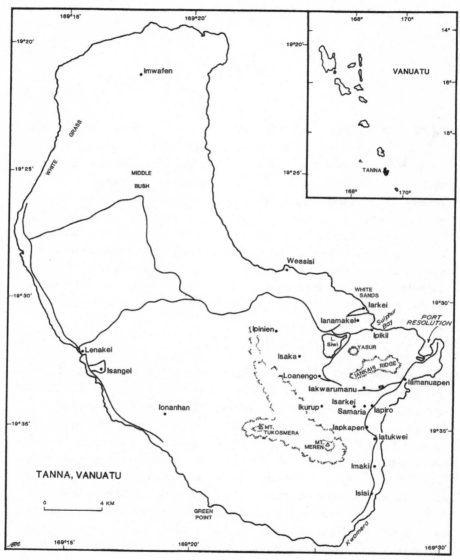

Tanna map. Created by author.

joke that Cook, searching for the island's name, pointed downward: "What do you call this?" he asked. "Why, we call it dirt."[1]

This may be just an amusing yarn as the Forsters provided few details of that linguistic encounter. Tanna might already have been the island's established name, as it has since become. Some suggest that the island's true name is Tanauta, which means something like "land of wealth," and people on neighboring Futuna Island call Tanna *Hgauta*. Nomenclatural claims are muddled although Tanna is most recognized. The long archipelago has also shifted identity. Captain Pedro Fernandes de Queirós, in 1606, landed on its largest island that he dubbed Austrialia del Espiritu Santo. A century and a half later, in 1767, French explorer Louis Antoine de Bougainville sailed through northern Vanuatu, pausing to rename the islands the Grand Cyclades, having in mind a smaller archipelago in the Aegean Sea. Cook, who was likewise inclined to bestow new place names, renamed these islands the New Hebrides after some mostly treeless islands off Scotland's west coast. Leaving behind his newly identified Tanna and the New Hebrides, he sailed south next to find a facsimile of Scotland, a long narrow island that he christened New Caledonia. When Vanuatu in 1980 achieved its independence from France and Great Britain, the nation's new leaders sloughed away a number of these colonial appellatives and discarded New Hebrides for Vanuatu, an invented toponym built on *vanua* that means "land" in many island languages.

Back on Tanna, if Cook and crew had probed further they would have discerned that their new island acquaintances also called their home Ipare. This is both a name and a direction. *Ipare* means "inland, toward the land." It pairs with *iperaha* (seaward) and it parallels *pesu* (clockwise along the shore) and *prahi* (counterclockwise along the shore). These names, and directions, encode mobility. They chart peoples' comings and goings, heading inland or keeping seaward. Islanders in motion evoke these directions to account for their journeys. "Where are you going?" they like to ask. "I'm off to sea." Or, "I'm climbing toward Ipare, going home."

Travelers move around Tanna in these four directions and they also have left island shores for parts and places abroad, increasingly so after 1774. Although surrounded by tropical seas and ocean trenches, Tanna with its red volcanic radiance was never isolated since Austronesian-speaking settlers first came ashore three millennia ago. After Cook marked Tanna on the map, overseas arrivals and departures briskly escalated. Some Islanders traveled far. Williamu, from Aneityum Island to Tanna's south, was in London in 1860 assisting missionary John Inglis' Bible translation efforts. Many others, beginning in the 1860s, left Tanna for plantation work in Australia, Fiji, Samoa, and New Caledonia. Others joined ships' crews. In turn, whaling vessels, ocean traders seeking sandalwood, dried sea slugs, pearl shell, and coconut oil or meat, sundry explorers, European naval vessels, missionaries, and even some early tourists found their way to Port Resolution. So did more singular global wanderers including Rangi, a nineteenth-century sandalwood trader from Malaysia, and at least one African American refugee from the US Civil War.

More formidable arrivistes included British and French colonial administrators. After neither power could agree which would occupy the archipelago, they together proclaimed a peculiar jointly governed Condominium of the New Hebrides in 1906. Although the British positioned an administrator on Tanna in 1912, he soon left to fight the First World War. Administration of the colony, which was never notably effective, was significantly delayed until after the armistice of 1918. Two decades later, from 1942 to 1946, several hundred thousand American servicemen steamed into the colony, some to staff Pacific War military bases there and others passing through on their way to battle the Japanese.

This brief American occupation left powerful memories and souvenirs that continue to reverberate, particularly on Tanna. Wartime experience shaped the liturgy and rituals of an island social movement that ignited in the late 1930s. John Frum, a shadowy figure, materialized with the message that Islanders should revive their abandoned traditions and return to home grounds. In 1941, John Frum's preaching spread rapidly and island churches and chapels emptied out for a number of years. John Frum continues to visit Tanna, spectrally or in people's dreams. I come and go, too, always staying in Samaria village that lies up the mountain from Port Resolution, and south of Iasur Volcano (figure 1).

Tanna Island is high and volcanic, its southern mountains rising to over three thousand feet. Just west of Port Resolution, the stratovolcano Iasur continues every few minutes to erupt with lava bomb explosions and dark plumes of volcanic ash. Although surrounded by warm seas, most Islanders, including my Samaria friends, are farmers. Volcanic ash annoys, as it contributes to acid rain that can harm or even destroy crops, but volcanic ash also rains down potassium, magnesium, and other chemicals that contribute to soil fertility. Every year, Tanna's diligent farmers plant abundant gardens of yam, taro, banana, breadfruit, sugarcane, island cabbage (edible hibiscus leaves), kava, and other cultigens that arrived on ancient canoes along with more recently introduced crops including manioc, sweet potato, mango, papaya, watermelon, corn, carrots and other vegetables, and tobacco. People tend pigs and chickens that arrived with early canoe voyagers, and also the cattle, horses, dogs, and cats that followed Captain Cook to the island.

FIGURE I. Samaria village, 1979. Photo by author.

When I first came to Tanna in 1978, people then earned a little money by selling copra to passing trading ships. They produced this by chopping open coconuts, scooping out and smoke drying the meat. Most since have given this up as too labor intensive. Instead, many follow money by leaving Tanna to work in Port Vila, Vanuatu's capital town. Around thirty thousand Islanders call Tanna home, but several thousand more have moved up to Port Vila's urban settlements on Efate Island, or live elsewhere in the country. Many seek new opportunities to profit from Tanna's budding tourist flows, catering to overseas visitors who come mostly to sightsee the volcano.

Iasur attracts visitors, but so do Tanna's regular festive exchanges and dances. People use the Bislama word *kastom* (custom) to label these festivals, along with any traditional or local practice, style, or belief. Bislama, a onetime Pidgin language that has evolved into a creole among children born in Port Vila, is Vanuatu's lingua franca. A lingua franca is essential in that linguists keep finding more and more distinct languages in these islands. The count is up to more than 130 different languages, and these are kept current by a national population of fewer than 300,000 ni-Vanuatu, the local term for citizen. On Tanna, Islanders speak five or six languages depending on how one draws dialect versus language boundaries. In Samaria and other mountain and valley villages south of the volcano, the language is Nafe (What). Missionaries called it Kwamera.

Nafe's language area stretches east to Port Resolution, and then down the coast to Kwamera near Tanna's southern tip, and then round to Green Point in the southwest. (Nafe has six vowels [a, e, i, o, u, and mid-central i]. For ease of reading, I use other vowel symbols for this latter. To represent the nasal velar (as in *singer*) I use [g]. Nasals [m, n, and g] and liquid [r] are sometimes devoiced, represented orthographically as mh, nh, gh, or rh.)

Many have come to Tanna, or left the island, since 1774 when Cook cast an anchor in Port Resolution's rocky bottom. In years since, many have gone abroad looking for work, while others from across the seas have come to Tanna, entranced by its volcanic nature and culture. These voyagers who came to Tanna, or who left their island home behind, followed the world's coiled routes and networks that have deepened and multiplied during the past two centuries and a half. I follow the stories of a dozen mobile heroes and heroines whose lives exemplify the travels of many others, blown away to near or distant parts by strengthening global winds. Their stories reveal essential aspects of Tanna's culture, society, and history that the following chapters explore.

Beyond this ethnographic and historical detail, these twelve island lives demonstrate that people everywhere, even those living on seemingly out-of-the-way Pacific Islands, for many years have been firmly linked into the world's networks. Concurrently, as an attendant effect of their travel and experience abroad, Islanders continue to maintain resilient bonds with Tanna, their island home, and they fiercely protect their island identity. These twelve lives, through the years, also track changes in patterns of island leadership, personhood, and gender. Women, in particular, through travel, education, and other opportunities have found ways to have a greater say over their life choices. Their ability to do so recently has strengthened with the advent of mobile telephones and social media, by which women can create digital spaces and connections that partly escape the oversight of men. Although each of these twelve lives is distinctive and remarkable, each also tells broader human stories of cultural continuities and change.

Memory

Literate explorers, missionaries, and anthropologists recorded bits and pieces of island biographies, and I rummage through this archive to share some of the hills and valleys of these lives. I also draw on anthropological fieldwork on Tanna, which included recording village friends' life histories. Tanna's cultural and biographical memories perpetuate themselves orally. Until nineteenth-century missionaries arrived to school new converts, orality rather than literacy was the main medium of knowledge transmission, and it remains fundamental today.

Oral cultures cultivate and encourage expert and tenacious memory, much longer than that which typically pertains in the literate world where writing and books allow people to forget. Socrates, from another discursively focused society, was no fan of letters. He produced no writing so far as we know, although Plato transcribed his dialogues. In one exchange with Phraedrus, Socrates disdained literacy. Writing, he said,

> will create forgetfulness in the learners' souls, because they will not use their memories; they will trust to the external written characters and not remember of themselves . . . they will be hearers of many things and will have learned nothing; they will appear to be omniscient and will generally know nothing; they will be tiresome company, having the show of wisdom without the reality.[2]

On the other hand, cultural memory in oral systems can be supple and pliant insofar as stories, and *kastom,* are neither written nor codified. People may amend memory to fit the present. This flexibility keeps *kastom* current and functional, whatever circumstance may come to pass.

On Tanna, I was a hearer of many things and, as anthropologists should, I wrote everything down, or at least everything that then seemed a thing. This included beguiling stories of island lives and times. Peoples' excellent memories keep alive the past. Their transcribed stories, I hope, offer more than Socrates' tiresome company or wisdom without reality.

There is ample presentism within Tanna's culture. This works to sustain its essentials. Although Islanders eagerly follow roads leading away to novel experience, they also firmly cultivate island home ground, keeping *kastom* going across the years. Tanna time fixes on a persistent center. Island temporal categories presume an unmoving island that is centered within a circling sea of time. Moving from today or from now into the future, one passes through tomorrow. Moving back a day into the past comes yesterday. But, then, the day-after-tomorrow is the same word as for the day-before-yesterday, and the word for indefinite future is the same for the indefinite past. *Kurira,* which means "behind," is also "next" situating the present as the center point with past/future as its horizon. *Nari kurira* is either something located behind one or is something following or next-in-line, that is, *nuk kurira* being the following (future) yam harvest/ year. Facing inward toward the present, people keep their backs to the future and also to the past.

Western progressive, developmental time concepts overlap the island's centered cyclicity. Many Islanders, unless attentively schooled, don't care to structure their life stories chronologically or progressively, organized as some developmental line that runs from infancy, through adulthood, to seniority. Larger
island history, too, isn't progressively organized and conceived. Today is yesterday and also tomorrow. Island personal names repeat, generation to generation,
so that the personages of the past are likely animated today as they will again
be tomorrow. The ancestors, *ris* (a word also used for seed yams), established
Tanna's fixed nomenclatural infrastructure. We might say that they did so "long
ago," but ancestral spirits remain always present. As do yams every year, island
personages persistently return.

I present a dozen of these personages in chronological chapters, beginning
with Pavegen and James Cook in 1774 and ending with my young friend Reuben
who teaches on Tanna today. Echoing island cyclical time sensibility, however, in
these chapters I turn from past to present and back to capture both the swirling
and the steady essentials of island history. Despite Socratic and island appreci-
ations of literacy, orality, memory, and time, I offer these dozen Tanna stories
attending to our own written ways of sharing knowledge, and perhaps wisdom.
Emulating Tanna time sensibilities, I revive these island travelers, inviting them
back into our own times, so that their lives, past and present, continue to reso-
nate and inform. Let's begin with a pair of sharks.

Notes

1. C. B. Humphreys, *The Southern New Hebrides: An Ethnological Record* (Cambridge:
Cambridge University Press, 1926), xv.
2. Plato, *Phaedrus,* trans. W. C. Helmbold and W. G. Rabinowitz (Cabin John, MD:
Wildside Press, 2017), 68.

Further Readings

Vanuatu Prehistory Including Voyaging

Bedford, Stuart. *Pieces of the Vanuatu Puzzle: Archaeology of the North, South and Centre.* Canberra: Pandanus Books, 2006.
Spriggs, Matthew. *The Island Melanesians.* Oxford: Blackwell Publishers, 1997.

Vanuatu History

MacClancy, Jeremy. *To Kill a Bird with Two Stones: A Short History of Vanuatu*. Port Vila: Vanuatu Cultural Centre, 1980.

Island Agriculture

Weightman, Barry. *Agriculture in Vanuatu: A Historical Review*. Cheam, Surrey: British Friends of Vanuatu, 1989.

Tanna Culture and History

Adams, Ron. *In the Land of Strangers: A Century of European Contact with Tanna, 1774–1874*. Pacific Research Monograph no. 9. Canberra: Australian National University, 1984.

Bonnemaison, Joël. *The Tree and the Canoe: History and Ethnogeography of Tanna*. Honolulu: University of Hawai'i Press, 1994.

Guiart, Jean. *Un siècle et demi de contacts culturels à Tanna, Nouvelles-Hébrides*. Paris: Musée de l'Homme, 1956.

Lindstrom, Lamont. *Knowledge and Power in a South Pacific Society*. Washington, DC: Smithsonian Institution Press, 1990.

Plommée, Gérard. *Tanna, Kwérya, Itonga: Histoires Océaniennes au Vanuatu*. Paris: l'Harmattan, 2012.

Tabani, Marc. *Une pirogue pour le Paradis*. Paris: Éditions de la Maison des Sciences de l'Homme, 2008.

Nafe (Kwamera) Language

Lindstrom, Lamont, and John Lynch. *Kwamera*. Munich: Lincom Europa, 1994.

CHAPTER 2

Sharks

THE OLD MAN WATCHED the strange and large canoe sail closer and
closer to Ipare. It moved steadily toward the land, his island. It is early
August 1774. To follow the vessel's movements, the watcher stood on
the eastern headland of a snug bay. Island ancestors had named this triangular
peninsula the "tail of the fish." Looking down at the harbor and peninsula from
the interior mountain uplands, the fishtail looks ready to thrash. The land is a
fish, and the old man is a shark—*Pavegen.* He carries one of the island's fixed
personal names that fathers, or other name-givers, must bestow upon their sons.
Some, like Pavegen the shark, also are animal, fish, or tree names.

   That extraordinary canoe is HMS *Resolution,* a 110-foot-long sloop, a onetime coal transport refitted by the British Navy for oceanic exploration; her
captain the explorer James Cook on his second circumnavigation and survey of
southern Pacific islands. Cook sailed with more than one hundred crew members onboard, including roving scientists Johann Forster and his twenty-year old
son Georg (or George), Swedish naturalist Anders Sparrman who embarked at
Cape Town, and expeditionary artist William Hodges. Cook was looking for a
harbor to fill his water tanks and his larder with fresh food. The previous day, he
had moored *Resolution* in a bay on the eastern side of Erromango, the island due
north of Tanna, where dealings with people quickly soured. Cook himself, with
a boat's crew, beat a rapid retreat back out to *Resolution* when hostile Islanders
hurled spears, arrows, and slingshot. In his haste, Cook left behind a pair of oars
and a few new place names, as was his habit. Naming celebrated discovery, and
Cook liked to rebrand many of his ports of call. On Erromango, this allowed
him to grumble: "the promontory, or peninsula, which disjoins these two bays, I
named Traitor's Head, from the treacherous behaviour of its inhabitants."[1] And
the bay, where he anchored and then fled, is now Cook's Bay.

   Resolution cut southeast to have a quick look at Aniwa, a low, small coralline
atoll, and then headed down toward Tanna. A red, volcanic glow marked the
horizon. This was Iasur volcano, soon to become famous as the "lighthouse of

the Pacific." Wary of another hostile welcome like that from Erromango's "traitors," Cook hove to outside a beautiful bay that cuts into the island, just east of the smoking volcano. He sent two boats, well armed, into the harbor to sound both its bottom and the temperament of its people who, in increasing numbers, gathered on shore, or set out in their own canoes, shadowing *Resolution*'s two boats. Satisfied of safer harbor, Cook warped *Resolution* into the bay.

Cook and party anchored here for two weeks, taking on water, wood, and a little food, and reconnoitering island resources and people. Pavegen, standing at the fishtail's tip, would have been among many who watched *Resolution* close in, looming larger and larger as it approached from the north. He, too, hurried down to the bayshore to commence dealings with the alien visitors, be they human or spirit. That first day, two or three owls flew over Cook's ship. Tannese gathered on shore shouted and some threw stones at them. One landed in the water and men in a canoe grabbed her and delivered her to the British. Owls, who hunt at night, are a sign that spirits are stirring.

Cook, better secured than on Erromango, resumed his promiscuous renaming practice. Although he had collected the harbor's Nafe language name, Iuea, he rechristened it Port Resolution in honor of his ship. Ironically, Cook and others onboard, including astronomer William Wales and young draughtsman and scientist Georg Forster, all described the Tannese themselves as they gathered nervously around the bay, to be "irresolute." This island irresolution might better be understood as part watchfulness, part friendliness. Local mildness encouraged Cook to secure his anchors for two weeks of refreshment, refitting, exploration, and cross-cultural encounter. The first irresolute Islanders who were brave enough to canoe close by the ship tossed coconuts his way. Cook complained that others, though, when they came onboard "were for carrying off every thing they could lay their hands upon" including the rudder's rings, anchor buoys, and the ship's flag.[2] Acting tough, demonstrating British muscle, he ordered his crew to fire (over their heads, so he said) increasingly larger bore weaponry at retreating shiplifters, aiming to clear the bay of island canoes: first muskets, then a four-pounder cannon, and then musketoons. Afterward, Cook retired to his quarters to dine in peace.

And here, on 6 August 1774, is when Pavegen enters Pacific history, or perhaps he first appeared an hour or two earlier in the midst of Cook's shock-and-awe fusillade: "During these transactions a friendly old man in a small Canoe made several trips between us and the shore, bringing with him 2 or 3 Cocoa nutts or a yam each time and took in exchange whatever we gave him."[3] Pavegen continued to exchange presents with Cook and his crew during their visit, beginning again the following day when Cook ordered a watering party to fill casks from a freshwater pond near the bay's southern shore. A thousand Islanders gathered to watch the brash strangers, split into two groups, but blocking access to the watering hole. On one side of the beach, Cook presumed, stood people from the eastern fishtail and parts inland to the south. Those gathered on the other side had come down from an uplifted ridge on the western edge of the bay, a range of hills (Iankahi) that spreads west to Iasur volcano. Nineteenth-century disease later entirely de-populated these heights, and ridge land rights remain in contention today.

Pavegen represented the eastern party and Cook judged "from his conduct that his disposition was Pacifick."[4] The old man again canoed out to *Resolution* and Cook gave him another piece of cloth. This could have been a yard of the *tapa,* or barkcloth, that Cook had stockpiled in Tahiti. Cook made signs to the crowd surrounding the watering place, demanding that the boisterous throng set aside their thrusting clubs and waving spears so that his party could approach the pond. He acted out his demand by seizing Pavegen's weapons and chucking these into the bay. The astonished old man, it seems, took this calmly. The crowd on shore, however, was unmoved. Cook again displayed his firepower. Marines blasted away with small shot from muskets and musketoons at the occupants of a nearby canoe who had paddled off with a string of beads and some other trifles without surrendering their clubs in exchange.

Cook called more marines and sailors in three boats to the beach. These pulled up where Islanders had set down additional, if small, gifts of plantain, yam, and taro. Pavegen, too, had returned to shore and with two other elders, their weapons pointedly set aside, he stood alongside these offerings laid out in between the two opposed beach parties. Cook still was nervous. He ordered his men to fire again over the heads of the Islanders in the westerly crowd. This caused only momentary confusion and sparked a rude response. One man turned his naked ass to Cook and beat this "like a monkey." Ill-pleased, Cook called for *Resolution*'s booming cannon to fire four-pound shot over the crowd. After this ruckus, the crowd deemed it prudent to pull back from the beach; the *Resolution*'s boats landed safely and sailors roped off a sixty-yard stretch between pond and bay. Only old Pavegen stood his ground through all this, although "deserted by his two companions."[5] Eventually, people drifted back down to the beach and offered the landing party some freshly plucked coconuts. While fill-ing water casks, Cook also ordered his men to cut and stack firewood after, so he said, "obtaining leave" from Pavegen, his new island acquaintance.

Cook, the expedition's scientists, officers, crew, and Pavegen continued to hobnob during the following weeks. The day after the watering party landed,

Pavegen came again to the bay and gave Cook one small pig. The British were hungry for more, but Pavegen's pig would be the single porcine addition to *Resolution*'s larders. On 8 August, Pavegen returned an ax that a sailor woodcutter had left on shore. On 9 August, Cook renamed the entire island Tanna after Johann and Georg Forster shared results of their linguistic inquiries with bay inhabitants. The Forsters, earlier in the voyage, had picked up smatterings of several Polynesian languages, and many of the sightseers then massing at the newly named Port Resolution had sailed over from neighboring Futuna and perhaps Aniwa—two small islands where a Polynesian language is spoken today. Cook was pleased to mark another island name on his expanding charts.

On 10 August, Pavegen's family brought Cook even more bananas, a few yams, and some taro. On 12 August, Forster and a shore party wandered into Pavegen's village where they found most of the gifts that Cook had given the old man, including a hat with laces, hanging up on bushes. On 13 August, Cook invited Pavegen to dine onboard. Pavegen pretended disinterest as he reviewed the ship's alien marvels on display, although he did play with a box of sand (that Cook used to dry his inky journal entries) that somehow caught his eye. Cook, in turn, visited Pavegen's village on 15 August. Afterward, Pavegen walked Cook back to the harbor with more gifts of coconuts and a yam. The next day, Cook gave Pavegen additional tapa cloth and a dog. The Tannese, seeing canines for the first time, called them pigs. Cook particularly wanted Pavegen's permission to cut down a casuarina (she oak) tree that stood near the shore to replace *Resolution*'s sprung tiller and rudder head. The Tannese tended such trees (ironwood is another name) for club-making. Pavegen joined Cook onboard for dinner, a second time.

On 17 August, Cook again found Pavegen ashore, together with another old "chief" and his son; the two probably canoed over from neighboring Futuna Island to study the pale strangers. Voyage journalists variously named these visitors Geogy (Keoki), Yeoki, or Yogai (Iokai), his son Yatta (Iata), and a grandson Narep. Cook invited them onboard, too, for a meal. They made quick work of a banana pie, greens, and boiled yam but were not much impressed by British salt beef and pork.

On 19 August, things fell apart. The new tiller was carved and ready to install but Cook also wanted what remained of the felled casuarina tree, left onshore. He sent a landing party to fetch the remaining wood. William Wedgeborough, a marine sentry who guarded the landing party, suddenly shot and killed a man who was standing next to another who might have been putting arrow to bow. Cook was incensed and he cast Wedgeborough in irons, later writing that such display of bow and arrow had been constant among Tannese men who closely watched the intruders. After the musket blast, everyone up and scattered including the wounded man who didn't make it far. Cook called out for his ship's surgeon on *Resolution* who landed in time to watch the unlucky bystander expire, a bullet through his torso. That afternoon, only Pavegen and a few other men dared show themselves on the beach. Kindly Pavegen promised to bring Cook more food the following morning, but—the wind now in the southeast—Cook that evening seized the opportunity to make off. *Resolution* sailed out to sea from Port Resolution, clockwise south around Tanna, and then beat off to the north to round the island before turning south again. Cook was headed, eventually, home to London, to an escalating celebrity, and to his spectacular murder five years later on the Big Island of Hawai'i. Pavegen, rooted in his fishtail village, might have watched *Resolution* sail away from the newly renamed harbor and island. Cook vanished over the horizon, but he continues to haunt Tanna. As does Pavegen.

Chiefs

Cook appreciated hierarchy. British social inequalities thoroughly infused naval order. In *Resolution*'s small, floating domain, Cook was lord and captain. Making landfalls, he best preferred to consort with dignified island peers, but he had first to identify any such insular chiefs or kings. During his first venture on Tanna's shore, Cook attentively handed out cloth, dogs, souvenir medals, and other gewgaws to sundry older men, but he was disappointed that he could "distinguish no Chief." Summing up his island account, he concluded that Tanna chiefs "seemed to have very little authority over the rest of the people."[6] He was unimpressed by old Geogy/Iokai, unsure whether his stature rested on noble rank or mere old age. He recorded that people called Iokai, who probably sailed over from Futuna, *Areekee,* and *ariki* is Futunese for chief. If so, Cook was right to observe that Pavegen and other elders living around the harbor took little notice of him, a mere foreign dignitary.

When Cook invited Iokai to dine on board, others stepped forward also to assert their similar chiefly status hoping, perhaps, to be invited to dinner, too. Cook complained, "They all called themselves Kings or chiefs, but I did not believe any one of them had any pretentions to that title over the whole island."[7] Nonetheless, he kept an eye cocked for signs of proper hierarchy on the island. He was unimpressed when one putative chief had to climb a coconut palm himself after others asked refused to do so. Even "our friend Pavegen," who Cook judged to be "much respected in our neighborhood," proved not to be truly aristocratic. Cook "had many reasons to believe" that Pavegen had no more right to authority than any other.[8] Pavegen's political influence, such as it was, sprung mostly from his gray hair.

The British liked to find stratified social orders, though Tanna offered only a paltry one. Ship's artist William Hodges' etching *The Landing at Tanna one of the New Hebrides* offered a conventional hierarchical tableau (figure 2). Pavegen stands in the prestigious center of the scene with two fellow elders, arms raised to greet a king-size Cook who boats ashore, shaking a palm frond. Pavegen's two arms and his posture mirror Cook's. Weapons dropped on the ground, these three older men separate the two unruly mobs from the harbor's east and west sides. A few spare offerings of banana, yam, and taro lie at Pavegen's feet. The three venerable elders entreat spiritual protection, standing behind a line of four stalks of wild cane embedded in the sand. Everyone else on the beach shouts and twists and flourishes clubs. Cook orders his marines to fire muskets and then the ship's cannon. The roaring blasts will scatter the crowd. Only Pavegen stands his ground.

Cook was right to conclude that power on Tanna comes largely from age, not rank. There are, however, two sorts of leadership titles on the island, a version of Polynesian chiefly dualism. The Tannese position these titular chiefs within "canoes"—the canoe, and the house, their metaphors for local groups. Like Cook's *Resolution,* island social organization is one of boats and vessels. Some chiefs are *iani neteta* (spokesmen of the canoe); others are *ierumanu* (lords and rulers). Pavegen may well have laid claim to one of these titles but, as Cook noted, he would not have been the only one. Most every local group boasts at least one or another of these titles, if not both. Some of the interpersonal irresoluteness and lack of order that Cook and his crew remarked at Port Resolution stemmed from this dualism. On this island of many chiefs, people come and go largely as they like. No one need kowtow to a superior. No one need follow orders. No one climbs a coconut palm unless he chooses to do so himself.

Gray beards and hair, though, do afford some measure of authority. Old age brings wisdom. It also brings one closer to death. Family and neighbors must keep in mind that the elderly will transmute, one day soon, into ancestral spirits. And these spirits most hope never to have offended. Pavegen and his two fellow elders, as soon-to-be spirits, were culturally predetermined to step forward, between bay and watering hole, to deal with the untoward demands made by the possibly also spiritual Cook, his alien crew, and *Resolution*—that spooky oversized canoe.

FIGURE 2. Pavegen welcomes Cook's landing at Tanna. Selection from William
Hodge's engraving *The Landing at Tanna one of the New Hebrides, 1777.*

Names

Pavegen welcomed Cook ashore in 1774. Pavegen still inhabits his fishtail
today. Tanna local groups—those canoes—each possesses sets of men's personal
names that they reuse from one generation to the next. Names are bestowed
and re-bestowed on a group's children and grandchildren so that the island is
full of namesakes, often grandsons named after grandfathers. Groups with few
children of their own can name any likely candidate, and thus reconstitute and
sustain themselves from century to century by giving names to the sons of others. Local groups possess names for women, too, and for pigs. Only male names,
however, give titles to land, beach and reef, power stones, ritual prerogatives, and
other personal resources. Johann Forster, as he had elsewhere during the voyage,
thought to exchange his name with a new Tanna friend. No island man, though,
would give away his name that roots him to family and place. An outsider name
like "Johann," on Tanna, is not worth much.

  Island place names, too, endure through time. Some of the bayside villages
that Cook and his crew toured around Port Resolution, and also those up on
Iankahi Ridge, are today overgrown with coconut plantation or bush, but people
know where these places remain, in spirit. They clear these sites, repopulating
once ghostly locales whenever needed again. Just as a personal name may be

empty, unused for a generation or two until a new child comes along to bear it, places, too, may seem to vanish yet they survive in memory just beneath the surface of the landscape. Today's Pavegen, moreover, is also yesterday's. Not a reincarnation, rather each Pavegen is a replacement, an avatar of all previous persons who have carried that name and warmed that particular seat in the local canoe. The Pavegen who lives today, 250 years after Cook arrived, talks about when he met the intrepid explorer back in 1774, and he may use the first-person pronoun "I" to do so.

Tanna's landscape and its personages are changed, yet much unchanged, in the years since Cook visited. Local stocks of names, both personal and topographic, do occasionally expand. Just as Cook renamed Port Resolution, the Tannese took his name, Captain Cook, for a pointed fin of land that juts off the fishtail's eastern coast. This has eroded away, leaving behind a cluster of triangular rocky islets that rise from the sea. And Shark Bay cuts inland, just down the coast from the rocky Caption Cook. Increasing flows of tourists, nowadays, have replaced eighteenth-century explorers coming to Tanna. A scatter of entrepreneurial tourist "bungalows" pox the island, some built on land, and others up in the trees. Venturesome overseas tourists now find their way to Port Resolution. Some travel farther down the coast to Shark Bay to sleep a night or two under thatch, sometimes swimming with friendly ocean sharks that their island hosts know how to tempt toward shore. Keen tourist sharks from overseas meet and greet hungry island business sharks.

In August of 1774, Pavegen and Cook, too, were one shark receiving another. As Cook sailed from Pacific island to island, he appeared recurrently as a spirit or as a stranger-chief. Either way, Cook was a murderer, a spiritual man-eater—a shark that walks on land. He was dangerously unpredictable. He could be a killer. His marine sentry gunned down a man at Port Resolution's watering hole while Cook supervised the encounter. Other Islanders, adults and children, also must have felt the sting of musket pellets, although Cook would publish an excuse for the pounding gunfire: "I never learnt that any one of them was hurt by our Shott."[9] Still, the Tannese, hurt or not, have long known how to deal with sharks, and they are familiar with tricky and fickle spirits. Cook's apparition was remarkable but not extraordinary. Islanders knew how to deal with his uncanny, sharky kind.

Notes

1. J. C. Beaglehole, *The Journals of Captain Cook on His Voyages of Discovery,* vol. 2 (Cambridge: Cambridge University Press, 1955), 481.

2. Beaglehole, *Journals of Captain Cook,* 482.

3. Captain James King, *The Voyages of Captain James Cook Round the World, Printed Verbatim from the Original Editions by Captain James Cook,* vol. 4 (London: Sherwood, Neely & Jones, 1813), 48.

4. King, *Voyages of Captain James Cook,* 48.

5. King, *Voyages of Captain James Cook,* 51.

6. Beaglehole, *Journals of Captain Cook,* 507.

7. King, *Voyages of Captain James Cook,* 65–66.

8. Beaglehole, *Journals of Captain Cook,* 508.

9. Beaglehole, *Journals of Captain Cook,* 486.

Further Readings

Cook and Pavegen

Forster, George. *A Voyage Round the World.* Honolulu: University of Hawai'i Press, 1999.

Forster, Johann Reinhold. *Observations Made during a Voyage Round the World.* Honolulu: University of Hawai'i Press, 1996.

Jolly, Margaret. "Ill-natured Comparisons: Racism and Relativism in European Representations of ni-Vanuatu from Cook's Second Voyage." *History and Anthropology* 5, no. 3–4 (1992): 331–364.

———. "The Sediment of Voyages: Re-membering Quirós, Bougainville and Cook in Vanuatu." In *Oceanic Encounters: Exchange, Desire, Violence,* edited by Margaret Jolly, Serge Tcherkézoff, and Darrell Tryon, 57–111. Canberra: ANU E-Press, 2009.

Cook as Shark

Dening, Greg. "Sharks that Walk on the Land." *Meanjin* 41, no. 4 (December 1982): 427–437.

Tanna Chiefs

Lindstrom, Lamont. "Chiefs Today in Vanuatu." In *Chiefs Today: Traditional Pacific Leaders and the Post-colonial State,* edited by Geoffrey M. White and Lamont Lindstrom, 211–228. Stanford: Stanford University Press, 1997.

Tannese Personal and Place Names

Lindstrom, Lamont. "Naming and Memory on Tanna, Vanuatu." In *Changing Contexts—Shifting Meanings: Transformations of Cultural Traditions in Oceania,* edited by Elfriede Hermann, 141–156. Honolulu: University of Hawai'i Press, 2011.

CHAPTER 3

Mwatiktiki

A FEW MILES DOWN THE coast from Port Resolution, from Captain Cook and from Shark Bay, Mwatiktiki, hero and spirit, once stood to fish new islands out of the sea. These included Tanna's neighbors Erromango, Futuna, Aneityum, and Aniwa. And there still today is his telltale footprint, embedded in a lava rock on the surf-pounded shore. His pig and his club rest there too, petrified into stone. The road south is bad and few tourists trickle by. A local entrepreneur, with great expectations, threw up a billboard advertising the rocky relics. This is gone. It attracted more passing sea birds than it did tourists who were willing to pay the modest admission fee.

Mwatiktiki is a well-traveled Pacific spirit, an oceanic wanderer. He, along with the likewise peripatetic Tagarua (Tangaroa, Takaroa, or Kanaloa), the black-and-white striped sea snake, pop up on many islands. Tagarua lived, took a wife, died, and was buried on Tanna. His buried body generated both sea and coconuts that sprang from his hollow eye sockets. The ensuing flood caught up some people, washing them away from their island home. Those lost souls floated away over the horizon. They became the overseas ancestors of *Pitoga* who returned in strange canoes—white skinned wanderers commencing with Cook and his *Resolution* crew.

Mwatiktiki haunts southern Vanuatu and much of the Polynesian central and eastern Pacific, where people know him as Maui, or Maui Tikitiki. He fished up islands everywhere he went. He snared the sun in its path. He called up the several winds. He made fire and invented cookery. On Tanna, he fought and killed several ogres that had eaten almost everyone. He introduced kava. Around Port Resolution and down the southeast coast, each year people offer Mwatiktiki the first fruits of their yam crop. Some see Mwatiktiki in their dreams, and the occasional island *urumun,* or spirit medium (*kleva,* "clever" in Bislama), tunes him in during waking hours. Mwatiktiki is a shape shifter. Sometimes he passes as a caring grandfather, but he also comes as a small boy, although one with astonishing strength.

Vanuatu's leaders, achieving independence in 1980, hurried to invent national symbols: a new currency (the vatu), a flag, an anthem, even the new country's name. Expatriate Australian artist Rick Fisher, then living in Port Vila, designed a national coat of arms. This depicts a generic sort of traditional leader with northern island design elements. "We advance," so says the attached Bislama national motto, "with God." This emblematic chief stands proudly on Vanuatu's paper money as well as on sundry government documents. Down on Tanna, many presume that this pecuniary image must be Mwatiktiki. His powers have spilled from inspirited exchanges and annual gifts of first fruits in return for his bountiful fertility, to impel cash transactions in the marketplace.

Before Mwatiktiki inspired Vanuatu's currency (at least as some appreciate this), he killed the cannibal ogre Tramsumus who had devoured nearly everyone on Tanna, everyone save for a couple of children. Many versions of the story circulate. Tramsumus penned up Tanna's last few children to fatten them up for a feast, an island version of Hansel and Gretel's witch. Happily, Mwatiktiki appeared, sometimes as old, sometimes as young, and he led the children away to safety. In some versions, he hid them inside a breadfruit. Tramsumus happened to pluck this and threw in on the fire to cook. Mwatiktiki ordered the children to urinate to drown out the flames. So they did. They escaped, ran, and climbed up either a casuarina tree, or sometimes a cliff. Tramsumus, hungry still, was too clumsy to follow. Mwatiktiki pretended to help, lowering a long vine. Ravenous Tramsumus clambered up and up and just when he was about to grab the runaway children, Mwatiktiki cut the cord. Tramsumus smashed back down to earth. Ants and birds arrived to confirm that the cannibal ogre was positively dead. One small bird flew up his ass and exited his mouth, stained forevermore with ruddy head and breast. Mwatiktiki sliced open the fat corpse and all those once eaten escaped back into life. Tramsumus' body petrified into a mammoth, long rock, and there he rests today.

Mwatiktiki, too, still hangs about Tanna although in spirit rather than mineral form. Along the southeast coast, sometime during the month of March, people dedicate to him the first fruits of their annual yam gardens. Mwatiktiki sings up a cloud and he rides atop this back home to Tanna. He decorates himself with face paint and aromatic, long crinkly *nisei* (*Evodia hortensis*) leaves that celebrants there have laid out for him. He then eats that first harvested yam of the season, or at least consumes its smoky essence—something like Santa Claus' Christmas cookies and milk.

Yams are people's favorite dinner but kava (*Piper methysticum*) is equally appreciated. Mwatiktiki brought kava to Tanna as well. Two women, so goes the story, were down on the beach washing and peeling wild yams. They failed to notice that Mwatiktiki had hidden a kava root in a nearby tide pool. A kava shoot rose up and thrust into the vagina of one of the squatting women. She said to herself, "I feel something good, something sweet!" Kava continued to poke. She turned to her sister to ask, "What is pleasuring me?" They saw that it was kava. They took the satisfying shoot and planted it secretly in their garden. At the time, men only drank wild kava—not the real thing. When the sisters' kava plant had matured, they dug it up, prepared food, and brought the root to men gathered at a village clearing. "Drink this," they said, "and you will feel something good!" So the men did, and from then they forbid women to drink kava, monopolizing the drug for themselves. From that place, kava has reached every village on the island. Women discovered it, first finding and then enjoying Mwatiktiki's seaside gift. They continue to plant, weed, and harvest it; but only men may drink.

Kava is indeed pleasurable. Despite its earthy flavor and mouth-numbing side effect, chemically the plant is a muscle relaxant, a painkiller and a soporific. More alluring yet, it has the psychoactive property of smoothing out emotions, of offering a quick burst of calm peacefulness. Tannese include kava in all their ritual exchanges, especially those concerned with peace-making, with repairing broken relationships. The reconciling sides prepare and drink together their newly exchanged kava stumps and roots. Communal consumption symbolizes social harmony, just as kava goes to work to relax and delight the minds and bodies of the erstwhile antagonists.

But why not women? Should women drink kava, so say men, who would cook? Who would mind the children? Instead of imagining a kava plant's phallic shoots, men instead envisage kava stumps as feminine, dressed in a modest fringe of skirt-like side roots (figure 3). Masculine monopoly of rights to drink the island's premier and pleasurable elixir manifests male attempts to control access to spirits. Men prepare their daily kava in cemeteries, on top of the buried dead, in central clearings where mighty grandfathers have lain buried, some for three thousand years. They drink kava at dusk, the very time of the ancestors. Kava drinking infuses a welcomed altered state of consciousness in which one is likely to hear those hovering spirits speak.

Everyone agrees that sex prevents kava drunkenness, just as drunkenness impairs sex. Virgin boys, who are circumcised sometime between five and twelve years of age, chew mouthfuls of kava root for their fathers to drink. They mix and squeeze masticated kava cuds with their hands as cold water pours through, straining the infusion into coconut shell cups. As soon as a youth manages to pull

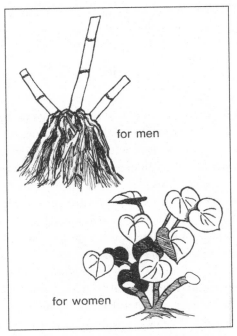

FIGURE 3. Kava as masculine and feminine.
Drawing by author.

a girlfriend into the bush, however, he blushingly declines to squeeze and infuse his father's chewed kava with his hand. Female sexual fluids counteract kava's powers to intoxicate. Mature drinkers without virgin boys within hailing distance have to make due with poking and mixing their own chewed and watered kava with short sticks. And women, some of them at least, back in the village complain behind men's backs that drinkers, returned home from the clearing, are good for nothing that evening except to swallow a bit of dinner and snore until morning.

Tanna's origin story of Mwatiktiki's kava recalls many other such myths, from Melanesia and beyond, in which women are first to find and use something valuable. But men step in to take control insofar as feckless and irresponsible females fail to use that thing properly. Women drinkers would abuse kava, and in more ways than one. But up in Port Vila, and even in Tanna's growing numbers of cash kava bars where people on salary come to buy and drink small (fifty vatu) and large (one hundred vatu) shells of the drink, a few brave women today also drink kava. They join the crowd at more cosmopolitan kava bars, or they take away the drink in empty plastic bottles to enjoy in private. Back in village clearings, however, although women plant, tend, and harvest kava, and cook most of the food that men eat after drinking, they do not indulge.

Spirits

Gardeners once a year dedicate first fruits of yam and kava to Mwatiktiki, but drinkers spit kava for dead ancestors at every evening's twilight. Fathers and grandfathers lie buried under men's feet in kava clearings. Grandmothers are interred instead in feminine spaces of village and hamlet. Draining the coconut shell cup, drinkers spit their last kava mouthful into the air. *Fwi tamafa!,* they say after an impressive spray. This is a libation, an offering of kava to ancestors whose bones lie buried below. After spitting, a drinker may utter a short prayer, a desire, or a demand for helpful ancestors to hear and perhaps allow or arrange. The ancestral dead, the *ieremha,* are Tanna's focal spirit beings. They haunt the island alongside the itinerant spirits Mwatiktiki and Tagarua, other island specters like Tramsumus, Karpwapen, and Karapenumun, and for the past century the Christian God, Jesus, and the Holy Ghost. One's own dead relatives are the spirit beings who can be the most helpful, or sometimes hurtful. Like parents, angry *ieremha* may punish their descendants, often with illness or even death. With good reason, people call ancestors older than the parents of their parents *kaha eraha* (bad grandparents). Regular kava spitting, though, induces ghostly benevolence.

The celebrated London Missionary Society martyr John Williams, on his mission ship *Camden,* anchored in Port Resolution in November 1839. Williams arrived to land three Samoan Bible teachers who would tutor and perhaps convert Tanna's heathen. The inventive London printer George Baxter, in 1841, sold a colored oil print of William's reception at Port Resolution. In this, we see William's secretary and fellow reverend, the top-hatted James Harris, sitting in the boat's stern. A *Camden* officer flourishes gifts of cloth and mirror. Williams came to Tanna fifty-five years after Cook, and growing numbers of sandalwood cutters and whaling ships had already found the harbor. Islanders, in these years, developed a keener desire for imported goods, including the fishhooks, cotton cloth, and scissors that Williams and his team bartered for island food.

Williams and Harris were wandering about Port Resolution's shores when a curious encounter occurred. Their shipmate J. Leary logged the scene: "I saw a very large native making signs for Mr. Harris to open his mouth; who acceded to the request, and the fellow immediately spat down this throat."[1] What heathen incivility! Worse would come the following day, on Erromango Island. Both

Williams and Harris were clubbed to death when they ventured ashore there at Dillons Bay. I had read and mulled over Leary's account before first coming to Tanna. Why did the unfortunate Harris open his mouth? An affable attempt at Christian fellowship, I figured. But why, then, did that very large man spit down his throat? This continued to puzzle until late one evening as I walked home with a party of friends from one of the all-night dance festivals that people organize during the harvest season. My companions burned one dry coconut frond after another, lighting up the shadowy trail. And they were spitting nonstop. I was sleepy and slow, but I finally asked, "Why are you all spitting?" How stupid was I? "It's to keep away the bad spirits, of course," they said. Metaphorically, this makes sense in that spitting externalizes the interior. It connects and unites two separate realms, be these the body and the world, or the dual spheres of the living and the dead.

Cook recorded no island spitting in 1774, but some Tannese who congregated at the harbor clearly guessed that *Resolution* had brought ashore a boatload of spirits. Cook complained that he procured no pigs apart from Pavegen's one smallish porker, and he found people annoyingly stingy in their paltry contributions of fruits and roots. Everyone knows, though, that the dead are satisfied with just a first fruit or two. Larger offerings to spirits are unnecessary. Islanders, instead, organize and exchange massive piles of food with living kin, their fellow humans. Pavegen and his two colleague elders wisely took spiritual precautions when Cook's boat rowed toward them. They sheltered behind that line of propitiatory shafts of wild cane stuck into the beach. Garden specialists who control kava fertility stones, and who tend the kava plants that will be offered to Mwatiktiki, mark these with similar spears of wild cane. Those gathered at Port Resolution were careful, too, not to touch Cook's iron nails, beads, and ribbons with their bare hands. They used leaves to pick up these spooky gifts. Cook, too, undertook his own ritual precautions at Port Resolution. He ordered his marines to stake and rope off an access path between bayside and watering pond. British rope and stake echoed Tanna wild cane. Islanders feared spirits while Cook distrusted natives. Both, certainly, may cause trouble.

Two weeks of fairly close observation at Port Resolution, however, improved each side's understanding of the other. Islanders soon figured that the visitors were fellow humans, not ghosts. When Johann Foster's assistant, carrying his plant collection bag, stepped into the bush to relieve himself, a few Tannese followed him to peek. Spying his male parts, they cried out, "a man, a man!" (*ierman*). William Wales recorded the word as "erramange" so perhaps those curious and astonished local investigators had shouted *ierman a!,* or "just a man!"

Islanders clearly were perplexed that the British party included no women, although they scrutinized some of the crew as possibly female. Ship's astronomer Wales recorded that a few island men endeavored "to entice certain of our People into the Woods for a purpose I need not mention," notably younger sailors and other beardless ones. But these two, they discovered, were men. Cook and Wales both journaled their relief that *Resolution,* as they put this, had not sailed into some land of sodomites. And, to be fair, the Tannese once offered up girls to entertain their guests. Georg Forster reported that the girls swiftly fled, frightened and shocked.

Fleshier sorts of intercourse, however, do not conclusively confirm that Islanders had mortalized the visitors. Sexual relations between humans and spirits are common fodder in island stories and dreams, and in the confessions of wayward village girls who disappear for a day or two, evading family surveillance. Those runaway, wailing girls might have been as much distressed by the prospect of sleeping with strange spirits as with *Pitoga,* alien pale men. Forster did notice, however, that people eventually stopped wrapping up weird British stuff in prophylactic leaves.

Stones

Slain ogre Tramsumus petrified into stone, and Captain Cook, too, is a rocky islet. Island spirits and their doings tend to mineralize into rock and stone. These formations, some large and others small, speckle the cultural landscape marking mythic beings, their lives and times. Mwatiktiki fished out of the sea the largest conceivable stone chunks—entire islands—and his footprint, captured in a seaside rock, proves that so he did. People's memory of names, both place and personal, permits the constant renewal, from one generation to the next, of island personages and the cultural landscape despite the entropic forces of death and natural decay. And stone, the hardest, most enduring of all things in this tropical realm, keeps memory alive. Important bits and pieces of island culture boast stone avatars. Most local groups, for example, claim loose allegiance to one of the moiety alliances, Numrukwen or Koiameta. These social constructs have materialized as two, now broken stones lying side by side in the east coast village of Ianamakel.

Men inherit, along with their names, control of a variety of power stones, or *nukwei nari* as people generally call these. Power stones come in various sizes, some of unusual shape and color, some looking like what they control. Possess a power stone with its associated uttered spells and deployment ritual, and one commands the world or at least one sliver of this. There are stones for the growth of island cultigens, kava, wild plants and nuts, for the fatness of pigs, the seven winds, a slew of illness and disease, earthquakes, Iasur's volcanic eruptions, and the calling of fish, sharks, and turtles. Rain stones remain especially popular in that, with these, one may keep dry one's own feasts and dances or drown those of a rival. *Nukwei nahak* are the most fearsome. These stones kill people. Few men today even hint of their possession. Holders are careful to keep secret the words and ritual of managing all their stones, and also the hiding places of even the most innocuous and helpful of these.

Christian conversion that increased in fervor after 1900 led many stone-keepers to offer these up to Jesus. Mission leaders cast power stones into the sea or cemented them into the foundations of newly built chapels and churches. Luckily, though, ancestors still speak in dreams. During the New Hebrides' final colonial decade, the 1970s, people busily revalued much of the *kastom* practice that their Christian grandparents had set aside. My neighbor Mak then was peeved. Although by his name he rightly controlled the power of calling sea turtles ashore, his ancestral namesake had lost, misplaced, or had given up the necessary *nukwei iaku* before Mak was born and named. But ancestor Mak came to him in a dream. In this, he pointed to where Mak should dig. Waking, Mak grabbed a spade, dug, and behold he found the power stone. Helpful ancestors likewise can remind dreaming namesakes of lost incantations and forgotten ritual procedures.

Soon after Vanuatu's independence, two more of Mwatiktiki's islands made the news. Matthew (Umaenupne) and Hunter (Umaeneag) islands, scruffy, uninhabited volcanic outcroppings in the far south of the archipelago, feature only a few trees although many seabirds. The two islands are close enough to New Caledonia (even though on Vanuatu's side of a major ocean trench) that the French also claim them with their surrounding waters. To counter noisome French contentions, Vanuatu's Ministry of Foreign Affairs documented pertinent traditional stories and other evidence of historical and cultural connections with the islets that they might use in international courts and tribunals. Proclaiming Vanuatu's sovereignty over Matthew and Hunter, the post office issued a set of stamps that featured the two islands and the new nation's expanded economic zone, with their original names recovered on Aneityum, the country's most southerly inhabited island.

I was back in Samaria in 1983, collecting linguistic data for a Nafe language dictionary. Recording stories is a fruitful way to discover words, and I was happy to tell friends that their government wanted to collect narratives of contact with mysterious southerly islands. Two men shared their stories. One of these featured another island-raising. Mwatiktiki's wife ran away from the evil female spirit Nihirapein (Shitstinks) who had deviously assumed her appearance and spousal identity. Escaping, Mwatiktiki's true wife swam out to sea. On her way, she commanded Futuna Island to surface above the waves so that she might find a place to rest. She next ordered Futuna to rise up even higher so she might look back from its raised lofty summit to her Tanna home. Eventually she sent two sons back to Tanna who denounced their mother's imposter. Mwatiktiki quickly made an earth oven and pushed Shitstinks onto its hot rocks, covering her with earth. The evil, roasting spirit exploded, leading to a happy family reunion (although Mwatiktiki's sleeping sons, reunited now with their father, accidentally urinated on him).

Mwatiktiki featured too, in a second story, one that the Ministry of Foreign Affairs better appreciated. An old man rapped on my door late one night. He asked to record his story without my neighbors knowing he was spilling any beans. There is not much of a public domain on Tanna. Even though stories are common knowledge, men inherit personal rights to tell them publicly given their personal names and home grounds. This story was, the elder assured me, his to tell and he gave me permission to share it. People, however, from time to time may dispute a person's right to his own name, and also the scope of his name-given rights, and he wanted to take no chances.

I turned up the wick of my kerosene lantern, and clicked on a cassette tape recorder. Storytelling began. Mwatiktiki confused a party of men canoeing from Tanna to Aneityum, and they came ashore instead on Imwainei, Mwatiktiki's private shadowy island that has the power to rise up and then fall back down beneath the sea. Mwatiktiki appeared to his visitors as a small boy, but he astounded everyone with feats of strength including chewing an entire kava root in a single mouthful. He revealed his wind power stone hidden inside his house, a house with seven windows each of which releases one of the seven winds. "When people on Tanna call up a wind," Mwatiktiki explained, "I open one window and close up all the others." Imwainei's trees also provide the driftwood that people, back on Tanna, burn to roast the first yam fruits for Mwatiktiki to eat. After some months on Imwainei, Mwatiktiki guided the visitors' canoe nearly home to Tanna. When close to shore, he hopped off and rode two coconuts, one under each foot, back to Imwainei blowing his panpipes as he floated off along his way. Today, one sometimes can glimpse Mwatiktiki's island, just visible within ocean mists when this rises up and out of the southern seas. And ghostly panpiping occasionally pierces the air.

Whether or not misty Imwainei is Matthew or perhaps Hunter Island, Mwatiktiki still comes and goes. He circulates from hand-to-hand on vatu bills throughout the land. He fertilizes yam and kava, island gift exchanges, and today's flows of cash. Should Vanuatu and France joust in an international tribunal, Mwatiktiki may travel even farther, as far as New York or Geneva. He travels with the winds, on the clouds and on floating coconuts. He sustains his abiding bonds, though, with his island home, an island anchored with power stones, dotted with the bodies of petrified spirits and ancestral bones. Everyone, spirit and human, cultivates this doubled appreciation of venturing abroad and returning home.

Note

1. George Baxter, *Two Specimens of Printing in Oil: One Representing the Reception of the Rev. John Williams at Tanna in the South Seas; the Other the Massacre of that Excellent Missionary on the Island of Erromanga when He and his Friend Mr. Harris Became the Proto-Martyrs of Christianity in the Australian Seas. With a Description by J. Leary, One of the Survivors of the Massacre* (London: George Baxter, 1841), 1.

Further Readings

Mwatiktiki

Humphreys, C. B. *The Southern New Hebrides*. Cambridge: Cambridge University Press, 1926.
Ray, S. H. "Stories from the Southern New Hebrides." *Journal of the Anthropological Institute of Great Britain and Ireland* 31 (1901): 147–153.

Majihjiki on Neighboring Futuna

Keller, Janet Dixon, and Takaronga Kuautonga. *Nokonofo Kitea: We Keep on Living This Way*. Adelaide: Crawford Publishing House, 2007.

Spitting

Lindstrom, Lamont. "Spitting on Tanna." *Oceania* 50, no. 3 (1980): 228–234.

Kava

Lebot, Vincent, Mark Merlin, and Lamont Lindstrom. *Kava: The Pacific Drug.* New Haven, CT: Yale University Press, 1992.

Lindstrom, Lamont. "Drunkenness and Gender on Tanna, Vanuatu," in *Drugs in Western Pacific Societies: Relations of Substance,* edited by Lamont Lindstrom, 99–119. Lanham, MD: University Press of America, 1987.

CHAPTER 4

Elau

C HINESE GHOSTS ARE HUNGRY for good smells and the living placate them with sandalwood smoke. Drug trafficking was the harbinger of today's global system and, in the 1830s, one small Vanuatu girl was swept into this international trade in heady substances. The British, who had become hooked on caffeinated tea, had to purchase this in China. But Chinese tea traders scorned tawdry British manufactures. Instead they demanded silver and gold coin or bullion, although they would accept sandalwood and, later, shipments of opium. Sandalwood loggers briskly chopped away at Pacific forests, stripping the wood from Hawai'i, and then Fiji for export to China. In 1825, one trader who called at Port Resolution noticed a man wearing a sandalwood ornament. When asked its origin, he pointed north toward Erromango Island. Traders during the late 1820s raced to the southern New Hebrides, seeking wood on Aneityum, Tanna, and especially Erromango. They ferried boatloads of Polynesians into the region to cut and carry the wood, paying them mostly in tobacco. This triangular trade of caffeine, nicotine, sandalwood and then opium swept four island children into its whirlwind. It dropped one, Elau, a six-year old girl, back down to earth in Plymouth, England.

In 1829, George Bennett, a twenty-five-year-old and freshly credentialed doctor and a new Fellow of the Royal College of Surgeons, embarked on the sailing ship *Sophia* heading to New South Wales. Bennett, who would later in Australia make a distinguished career as a physician and natural scientist, and the honorary secretary of Sydney's Australian Museum, was cagey when writing about that voyage. *Sophia,* in fact, was a convict transport. Beneath its decks the ship carried 192 Irish prisoners sentenced to penal transportation to Australia. *Sophia* with her convicts reached Sydney in the midst of the sandalwood rush. Sydney's waterfront buzzed with news that the southern New Hebrides boasted of virgin stands of the wood. Fortunes might be made if these could be exploited. Sydney trader Samuel Henry, born on Tahiti where his father William was a London Missionary Society preacher, chartered *Sophia* to find and load up sandalwood.

Convict transports were ideal in that Polynesian island woodcutters, hired on the cheap, could fill those emptied convict berths. Captain Thomas Elley and crew, including the ship's surgeon Bennett, set to sea heading for the aromatic forests of Tanna and Erromango.

Sandalwood trees grow to about ten meters tall, typically in mountainous regions. Aromatic oils are best in trees that are at least thirty years old. Harvesters like to dig these out whole instead of chopping them down, in that the marketable, long-lasting oils saturate roots as well as the trunks and branches. Prospectors had little luck trading for wood at Port Resolution, or down on Aneityum Island. On Erromango, however, they found thick sandalwood stands. Erromangans themselves, however, were hardly interested to climb mountains, uproot trees, and muscle wood down to the seashore. Standard offers of tobacco, knives, cloth, and other trade goods failed to induce them to work. Moreover, incoming flows of foreign goods, including guns, and raging epidemics of unfamiliar disease, had unsettled island political alliances and people hesitated to leave their home territories.

Sophia in search of cheap labor, sailed first to the east to load up crews of Polynesian loggers. These Islanders, already hooked on nicotine, would work for twists of tobacco soaked in molasses. In August 1829, *Sophia* landed ninety-five Tongan loggers on Erromango. The ship was loaded with a cargo of sandalwood already harvested by a previous party of woodcutters and headed north to Hawai'i to market the wood. Sailing south to the New Hebrides, *Sophia* raced against a small fleet of competitors. These included the ship of a company of British investors, and two ships belonging to high chief Boki, governor of O'ahu. Chief Boki, and his flagship *Kamehameha,* sank at sea along the way to Erromango. Hawaiian forests had already been denuded of the wood and, rapacious for cash, Boki sought to secure a new sandalwood source. He brought along his private militia, planning to conquer Erromango for the Kingdom of Hawai'i.

On the way back to Erromango, *Sophia* stopped again in Rotuma to load another 213 woodcutters. When the ship again reached Erromango in March 1830, the island was overrun with bickering logging crews, including 179 Hawaiians, 313 Rotumans, and 113 Tongans. Erromangans themselves were riled by this invasion although some hoped to convince the logging parties to help them smite inland rivals, or at least lend them a few guns. Many were sick, too. The foreign ships had brought ashore a raging dysentery that rapidly went epidemic. This sandalwooding turmoil, nine years later, would trigger missionaries Williams and Harris' fatal reception at Dillons Bay—first spit upon and then killed. Faced with island chaos, trader Henry and *Sophia*'s Captain Elley decided to cut their losses. They loaded up the crew of Polynesian loggers with whatever sandalwood was already gathered and sailed away to land at Rotuma and Tonga. *Sophia* then turned west back into the New Hebrides, calling at Port Resolution, before circumnavigating home to Britain via Manila and Singapore.

When *Sophia* sailed from Erromango with the woodcutters, four island children followed them onboard. A Tongan party, camped somewhere along the southern shore of Cook's Bay, south of Traitors Head, claimed to have rescued these three boys and one girl from their Erromangan neighbors. They were, so they said, convinced that the children were war captives, soon to be killed and eaten. This may be. Nineteenth-century missionaries, sandalwood traders, and even Polynesian woodcutters all firmly believed in New Hebrides cannibalism. As on Tanna, though, people lovingly nurture, foster, and freely adopt children. They don't eat them. Families may adopt a child to take the place of someone killed, in war or otherwise, and it is possible that people had this in mind. They, it seemed, were deeply anxious to retrieve the captured children, but the Tongans refused to give them back, not "even for the most valuable presents they could offer."

Bennett guessed that Elau, the girl, was about six years old. The three boys were around six, seven, and nine. Only one of the boys comes down to us named, as Mungo. This was a jokey nickname the British liked to give black men and boys, after a character in *The Padlock,* a popular, long-running 1768 London opera that featured white actors in blackface. Elau, though, was an Erromangan name. Bennett came to call her Sophia Elau after his convict transport and sandalwooding ship.

When *Sophia* offloaded its woodcutters at Rotuma, Captain Elley planned to dump the four Erromangan children on that island, too. The three boys went ashore but Elau lingered behind, playing with the ship's monkey, when a sudden brisk wind blew up. *Sophia* previously had to be winched off a Rotuman reef and Elley wanted no more problems. He briskly weighed anchor and away *Sophia* sailed with Elau still on board. *Sophia* first made land, however, back in the New Hebrides, at Port Resolution. Why didn't the ship detour the fifty miles north to Cook's Bay and bring Elau home? *Sophia* paused only at Port Resolution for several days to resupply. Tannese mothers, coming onboard, immediately took pity on Elau. They brought their own children to play with her, along with gift baskets of yam and sugarcane. One old woman took charge of Elau, staying by her side on the poop deck, feeding her until *Sophia* weighed anchor for Manila.

Young George Bennett, "under whose special care the child had been placed," was keen to make his name as a collector of exotic specimens. He already had pickled in a large jar a "pearly" nautilus, fished up along the western coast of Erromango. When *Sophia* reached Singapore, he purchased a gibbon that he named Ungka. Bennett also must have guessed that an exotic South Seas child could inflame the interest of London's natural scientists and, perhaps, even its high society. When *Sophia* blew away from Rotuma, thus, "arrangements were made with the commander to take [Elau] to England." Sailing out from Port Resolution, Elau could clearly see her Erromangan home receding on the northern horizon. She landed, instead, in Britain.

London offered popular stages where the exotic and the newly colonized could be exhibited. Elau joined a growing procession of world travelers who found a way to that city, willingly or not. James Cook, before landing on Tanna, invited Omai (Mai), a young Polynesian from Huahine, onto his expedition's second ship. Omai disembarked in London on *Adventure* to great acclaim. He met George III and Queen Charlotte. Joshua Reynolds painted his portrait. He inspired a stage play. He toured great houses with Joseph Banks, his scientific patron, demonstrating to sundry lords and ladies the Oceanic art of earth oven cookery. Other Islanders followed his lead, including Prince Lee Boo of Palau in 1784. Governor Boki and his wife Liliha, too, along with King Kamehameha II (Liholiho) and his half-sister Queen Kamāmalu, visited London in 1824, just a few years before Boki's botched invasion of sandalwooded Erromango. Cook would bring Omai home to Huahine on his third and final Pacific voyage. Liholiho, Kamāmalu, and Lee Boo were less lucky. All died of measles or smallpox after a few months breathing London's fetid atmosphere.

Elau, Bennett would have known, would be the first native visitor from Cook's New Hebrides. He promoted her arrival there as a scientific opportunity, just as he publicized his pearly nautilus and his gibbon. Elau wasn't Vanuatu's first trans-Pacific voyager, however. Two centuries earlier, in 1606, Portuguese navigator Pedro Fernandes de Queirós anchored in Espiritu Santo's Big Bay where he kidnapped three young boys. At least one of these, Queirós' expeditionary priests baptized him Pablo, came ashore in Acapulco. Pablo, who looked to be about eight years old, would die in Mexico six months later, in May 1607. Elau's travels, though, outdistanced Pablo's. She left the Pacific behind, sailed across the Indian Ocean, around the Cape of Good Hope, and up the coasts of Africa and Europe to London.

Bennett, as natural scientist and collector, recorded Elau's travels in a curious mix of paternalistic and scientific styles. He could be cool, even detached. While *Sophia* was still at sea, Bennett measured his child specimen. Elau was three feet, four inches tall; the length of her sternum was four-and-a-half inches; the length from the ensiform cartilage of the sternum to the crest of the pubis was ten-and-a-half inches; the breadth of the thorax was four-and-a-half inches; and so forth. But Bennett also could be affectionate, even fatherly, especially after he purchased Ungka the gibbon in Singapore whose bodily proportions, like Elau's, he also measured. Bennett was particularly amused by Elau's love of Ungka,

> the animal with his long arm round her neck, lovingly eating biscuit together. She would lead him about by his long arms, like an elder leading a younger child; and it was the height of the grotesque to witness him running round the capstan, pursued by, or pursuing the child. . . . Not unfrequently, a string being tied to his leg, the child would amuse herself by dragging the patient animal about the deck.[1]

Home in England in spring 1831, Bennett gave his pickled, pearly nautilus to the Royal College of Surgeons. The young Richard Owen, who later would become a celebrated natural scientist inventing the word "dinosaur," dissected this. He reported on the poor thing's guts in a surprisingly popular and well-received *Memoir on the Pearly Nautilus*. In these years just before Charles Darwin's celebrated voyage on the *Beagle,* the nautilus featured as one of the first living fossils, and Owen's nautilus dissection boosted Bennett's own fame as its collector.

Ungka regrettably died when *Sophia* was in sight of the English coast. Bennett, while still at sea, busily dissected the gibbon's corpse later giving its intestines and various innards to the Royal College. He saved the skin and skeleton, though, and had the animal "properly stuffed and preserved in its natural erect attitude." He donated the newly taxidermied Ungka "to one of the glass cases of the British Museum, where he was eventually deposited."[2] Ungka, too, attracted much attention, not as a living fossil but as another missing link in the early years of budding evolutionary imagination.

And Elau, was she a missing link, too? A young cannibal savage from the lowest rungs of human evolution? Bennett introduced the girl to scientific society at a *conversazione* convened at the Royal Institute. The gathered scholars peered and poked and "examined the child's head, which they pronounced remarkably well formed and the brain quite up to the average." Elau, Bennett wrote,

> although it was the first time that she had ever entered a large room splendidly lighted and filled with company, she did not for a moment manifest the slightest shyness or fear, but left me and mingled with the crowd, and permitted all of those who were attracted by her novel appearance to speak to her, was very affable with them, and would then walk about the room

inspecting the exhibits, some of which were from her native island. When placed on the table by Professor [Michael] Faraday for the inspection of the ethnologists who were present, she was also fearless, and appeared to be highly amused at the interest she excited.[3]

Bennett also showed Elau off at society parties hosted by writers, playwrights, actors, and artists. Several of these latter drew her portrait including Frederick Tatham, friend and eventual executor of the romantic poet and his fellow artist William Blake. Tatham published a lithograph of Elau's portrait "drawn from life," captioned "The Young Cannibal" (figure 4). This, dubiously, claimed that she wore a necklace of human teeth.

Bennett proposed further scientific experimentation with Elau. Could she, he wondered, be schooled? Might a savage be civilized? Elau, child of cannibals, "cannot fail of exciting much interest amongst those who engage in hypotheses in regard to the question whether savages are capable of mental improvement and civilisation." Elau "was like a new creation, upon which all were anxious to try the effects of civilisation and education."[4] These were no idle questions in the 1830s, in both Britain and America. Few children except from the wealthiest families received any elementary education at all, apart from occasional Sunday schooling, and there was grave doubt whether public money would be well-spent educating poor and working class youth. But Bennett had many Quaker friends, in Plymouth and in London, and he was influenced by their liberal proposals to establish a system of state-supported primary schools. If Elau could be civilized, then so might the young denizens of London's slums.

In pursuit of his project, Bennett brought Elau to Plymouth, his hometown, where he left her with his older sister Caroline. Caroline improved Elau's English. Already she had picked up Pacific Nautical Pidgin English, ancestor to Vanuatu's Bislama, from sandalwood cutters and from island sailors, the crew on the *Sophia*. Elau next learned to read. She entertained guests with her dancing. Caroline also taught Elau needlework and the Christian virtues. She also drew Elau's portrait. In this, doe-eyed and slightly smiling, Elau looks out into her new world.

Bennett, before Caroline's refining efforts might be fully proved, once again sailed away. Just about a year after leaving Elau in Plymouth, in May 1832, he disappeared again for New South Wales. Before departing, he promised Elau that one day he would take her home. Bennett wrote little of this paternal abandonment, although he praised Elau's affectionate disposition, her considerable intellectual powers, and her gentle patience. His Plymouth friend, the Quaker author Anna Marie Hall, who wrote up Elau's story for the *Juvenile Forget-Me-Not,* an

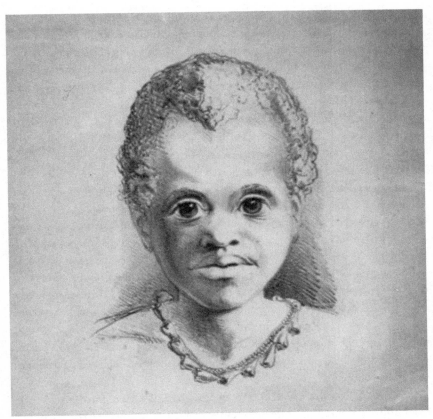

FIGURE 4. Elau, "The Young Cannibal." Engraving by Frederick Tatham, 1832.

early children's annual, revealed a bit more. Elau didn't want Bennett to leave her, and she didn't want to return to Erromango, either. She suffered "great grief" and regret when Bennett abandoned her.

School

Nowadays, of course, schooling is unavoidable, mandatory even, if children are to make a life within pitiless global systems. Young cannibals, so they be, are everywhere. We are far beyond Bennett's rudimentary experiment to turn savage into sophisticate. Children today absolutely must be schooled into adulthood. Elementary education systems spread in the 1840s, in Europe as in America. Missionaries, too, who arrived and stuck on Tanna in the late 1860s, established their own schools to teach reading, writing, and some arithmetic in amongst religious lessons. A century later, the Condominium colonial government also recognized the benefits, and accepted the duty, of educating at least some island children. The British administration fitfully supported many former mission schools, and the French by the 1970s were busy building their own system in hopes of cultivating young cadres of French speakers less committed to national independence or to English.

Most Tannese children make it through at least a few years of elementary education—attending junior and then senior primary schools. In the late 1970s, Samaria's weekdays were cleared of most of its children. The younger ones every morning wandered down the ridge trail to attend Iquaramanu Junior Primary School on the valley floor, in Nepraineteta, the "Body of the Canoe." A few walked the longer road to the free French school at Iamanuapen. Their older siblings disappeared Sundays evenings and only reappeared late Friday afternoons, boarding during the week at the English or French senior primary schools at White Sands, too far away for daily treks. Fathers, every dusk, gloomily contemplated their unprocessed kava roots, forced to chew and mix these themselves—their sons, helpful dogsbodies, far away at school. Most children, though, returned home for good after six years tutelage. There were in the 1970s no high schools on Tanna. Very few scholars, from Samaria or elsewhere, aced qualifying exams or had families who could scrape together the school fees required to pass into secondary school.

As did Elau, Tanna's school kids struggle with challenges of learning to speak, read, and write English or French, languages alien to most of their parents. Schools still offer the same smatterings of arithmetic, exercise and dance, and snippets of moral education as Caroline taught Elau. Children come to school knowing some Bislama, and they quickly soak up more of this during recesses from classwork, even though they, and their teachers, until recently were firmly commanded not to use Vanuatu's lingua franca. English or French workbooks, drawing, and much rote repetition fill dusty, thatched classrooms. Back home in Samaria, though, few children speak much English or French. Parents choose to hedge their educational bets. They send some children to English schools and some to French, so siblings speak Nafe with one another with occasional playful bouts of Bislama.

Independent Vanuatu's Ministry of Education has struggled to combine the colonial British and French systems. Students today may attend several new high schools on Tanna. Others go to church schools and seminaries. Some, like my friend Pita's youngest son Reuben, matriculated at the national Teachers College in Port Vila to become teachers themselves. Young village women earn a pittance as *kinda* (kindergarten) schoolmarms, offering a rudimentary preschool program. Peace Corps recruits and other youthful metropolitans volunteer their pedagogic services. But educational plans for suitable technological, agricultural, or hospitality/tourism training (Elau's needlework), for culturally appropriate pedagogy and curricula, even for teaching in the vernaculars, have come and gone. Mission and colonial roots still nourish much of today's educational substance and practice.

Like Bennett's pedagogic anticipations for Elau, island parents nonetheless are increasingly anxious that their children succeed in school. With the collapse of copra markets and the dilapidation of Tanna's coconut plantations, how is one anymore to make a living? New flows of tourists help and entrepreneurs by the score have thrown up bungalows, enticing visitor cash. Some of the very farsighted have purchased gallon containers of sandalwood cuttings hoping, in thirty or so more years, to harvest that fragrant wood for which the Chinese still pay big money. A good government job with a fortnightly paycheck, or one in a Port Vila bank, hotel, or store, offers another sort of future. But these jobs demand winning papers—qualifications and diplomas. Fewer than half of island children make it into high school. And fewer still study in regional universities. When they do, education at all levels costs money that many families do not have. Although the government has eliminated most tuition and school fee payments, parents constantly are on the hook for donations and subscriptions that underresourced schools desperately need. Schools, too, are sharks. Parents of secondary school students struggle exceedingly to scrape together regular tuition and room and board fees. Lucky that local group members and extended family are obligated to try to contribute. I chip in, too, when I can.

A generation ago, families with a smart and lucky child who was selected to attend secondary school sent one or two additional children up to Port Vila to scratch up any sort of job to help pay their sibling's school fees. In recent years, entire families migrate to Vila's fringe of urban settlements, seeking money and to enroll their children in urban schools. They hope these will provide a clearer road to success than do schools back home on the island.

Where Are You Going?

Elau's education in Plymouth comprised Christian ethics and courtesies. On Tanna, a century or so ago, mission schooling and travels abroad encouraged people to bend their customary greetings to fit a novel etiquette. They began to salute one another with wishes of "good morning," (*ramasan ianepnepen,* it is good, in morning), "good sunlight," and "good twilight." The traditional and still usual greeting is *ikuvaku?* (where are you going?). People on the move command endless interest. What's their project? Where's the hurry? All want to know the geoposition of everyone, always. Those who move in secret, in darkness, provoke deep suspicion; up to no good, they well may be. The polite response to "where are you going?" is to tell.

Should someone drop off the grid, nerves fray. My neighbor Natu once managed miraculously to disappear entirely for three days. No one knew where she had gone. Natu was in her late twenties, still unmarried, overworked, and a bit grumpy. I figured she needed some personal respite. Solitude, however, is hardly imaginable on Tanna, and the neighborhood instead feared the worse of her disappearance. People rushed to the grave of her grandmother, dead some few months earlier, and poked it full of holes. In these holes, they poured infusions of leaves while honking frantically on triton shell trumpets. Grandma's spirit, perhaps, was lonely on the other side, in the other world, and she might have returned to snatch up some younger company. No one, except me, was much surprised when Natu wandered back home to say that she had been pulled away by a spirit. She was up the mountain when the spirit figure took her by the arm and led her higher toward lofty Mount Meren. The Great Spirit Karupenumun, maybe, since this indeed is his mountain aerie. Natu titillated her audience, huddled closely about, admitting that she had even cooked dinner for him. Cook for a spirit, everyone knows, and one also has sex with him.

Where are you going? Travel is good so long as you can be tracked. Travel brings wisdom; it offers gravitas; and it boosts prestige. The Tannese are profoundly anchored to their home grounds by their personal names and by the bones of their ancestors, yet they much appreciate stepping out into the world when opportunity permits. In Elau's day, a few already had joined the crews of passing whaling and sandalwood ships. Beginning in the 1860s and throughout the rest of that century, thousands of men and numerous women left Tanna to work on sugarcane plantations and other colonial enterprises in Australia. Hundreds more shipped off to Fiji and Samoa. From 1942 to 1946, during the Pacific War, nearly every able-bodied man journeyed to Efate Island to labor there at freshly constructed US military bases.

Elau was the first of these world travelers and she went farther than most. Island travel today is largely circumscribed by Vanuatu's boundaries. My old research colleague James Gwero once catalogued the few roads that lead abroad: sports, the church, and education. Most Tannese only manage to travel as far as Port Vila's settlements. Unlike Samoa, Tonga, Cook Islands, or Micronesia, Vanuatu's colonial history left open few doors to go farther. A small number of ni-Vanuatu have migrated to Norway, France, Vermont, and Oregon, mostly by marrying Peace Corps volunteers or other overseas visitors. Only in recent years do Islanders once again travel abroad to New Zealand or Australia to take up temporary agricultural employment. "Apple," people call this, in that most are set to work picking New Zealand's annual apple, pear, and kiwi harvests, pruning grape vines, or working in fruit-packing houses. The experience abroad and the banked cash are worth it. Travelers return home with pockets of money that they invest in family projects. The host governments are careful, too, that no temp worker disappears or overstays. Should someone die, in Port Vila or abroad, friends and family strive to pool funds to airfreight the body back to Tanna. People happily may wander; not so their spirits who the island calls home.

Elau did not come home. She died of intestinal tuberculosis, ten years old, on 6 June 1834. Her spirit haunts Plymouth still. Bennett had recently returned, the month before, from his second trip to New South Wales. If he reunited with Elau before her final, deadly toil, he failed to note this. He did, however, quickly arrange for his surgeon friend Peter Bellamy to autopsy her cadaver. And, as with his likewise dead specimen Ungka the gibbon, he coolly reported the clinical results of this at the same time as he memorialized Elau's gentle, loving character. Plymouth newspapers published her obituary. A week after she died, Vicar John Mathew of Saint Andrew's Church conducted a funeral. Whether Bennett attended this, he never said.

In 1834, Saint Andrew's original burying ground was crowded and Elau was laid to rest in a subsidiary graveyard in nearby Westwell Street. This, too, was closed in 1879 and scraps of its disinterred bodies and retrievable headstones were moved to a larger cemetery away from Plymouth's city center. Tombstone inscriptions, those still readable, were recorded but none was found that honored Elau. In 1941, Nazi bombers blew Saint Andrews Church and Westwell Street into smithereens. After the war, the church was rebuilt and a new civic center was erected over the old cemetery grounds.

I traveled once myself, seeking remains of Bennett's specimens. London's Royal College of Surgeons is there, in Lincoln's Inn Fields. Richard Owen's dissection of the pearly nautilus left enough of its corpse, and the living fossil's pickled body is on display in the college's Hunterian Museum. Ungka the gibbon, possible missing link, no longer beguiles visitors to the British Museum. He has been demoted from glass display case to backroom shelving where his withered, moth-eaten and tattered skin sleeps in darkness. In coastal Plymouth, Saint

Andrews Church is rebuilt. But Caroline Bennett's house on Cobourg Street, where young cannibal Sophia Elau was schooled into an English childhood, has vanished, its site an empty lot. I walked around to the civic center building under which Elau once was buried. I spat on the sidewalk.

Notes

1. George Bennett, *An Account of Elau, A Malayan Papuan Child, Native of the Island of Erromango, One of the New Hebrides Group, Southern Pacific Ocean* (Sydney: privately printed, n.d.), 3.

2. George Bennett, *The Wanderings of a Naturalist in New South Wales, Batavia, Pedir Coast, Singapore and China: Being the Journal of a Naturalist in Those Countries during 1832, 1833, and 1834* (London: Richard Bentley, 1834), 143, 168.

3. Bennett, *Account of Elau*, 4.

4. George Bennett, "Elau, a Papuan Child," *Asiatic Journal* 7 (1832): 133.

Further Readings

Sandalwood Trade

Shineberg, Dorothy. *They Came for Sandalwood: A Study of the Sandalwood Trade in the South-West Pacific 1830–1865.* Melbourne: Melbourne University Press, 1967.

Boki of Hawai‘i

Daws, Gavin. "The High Chief Boki: A Biographical Study in Early Nineteenth Century Hawaiian History." *Journal of the Polynesian Society* 75, no. 1 (1966): 65–93.

Sophia Elau

Hall, Anna Marie. "Anecdotes of Elau, A Papuan Girl." In *Juvenile Forget-Me-Not: A Christmas and New Year's Gift, or Birth-day Present,* edited by Mrs. S. C. Hall, 216–230. London: Ackermann & Co., 1835.

Lindstrom, Lamont. "Sophia Elau, Ungka the Gibbon, and the Pearly Nautilus." *Journal of Pacific History* 33, no. 1 (1998): 5–27.

CHAPTER 5

Mary

E LAU SAILED OUT OF the Pacific. Other young women not many years later sailed into it. Elau traveled to Plymouth, England, to die of tuberculosis. Soon enough, missionaries and other visitors would bring the disease, and Bibles, direct to Elau's motherland. First to come were traveling Scots.

A century of highland land clearances and the great potato famine of the 1840s propelled thousands to emigrate to lowland cities, or to North America and Australasia. Mary Johnston, in 1837, was born into one such nomadic family that found refuge in Pictou, a lonely immigrant outpost on Nova Scotia. The Johnstons were dissenting Presbyterians. These Covenanters spurned the established Church of Scotland, partly in furious objection to the autocratic rights of rich landowners to appoint their ministers. The nineteenth century's several great awakenings stirred up new global commitments. Christian revivals propelled fervid evangelical crusades to save dissipated denizens of urban slums and the oblivious heathen of far-flung Pacific Islands. Impassioned young men and women journeyed forth from Scotland. Backwoods Pictou, too, celebrated its similar faith and devotion by contributing its own children to missionary enterprises.

Mary's uncle John Geddie, her mother's brother, was one of the first missionaries to settle anywhere in the New Hebrides. He set up shop on Aneityum in 1848. His wife, Mary's aunt Charlotte, was the first white woman in the New Hebrides. John Williams' and James Harris' notorious murders on Erromango attracted passionate Christian attention to the place. A stream of Presbyterian volunteers from Scotland, Nova Scotia, and New Zealand followed the Geddies to the islands, moving into mission outposts on Aneityum, Tanna, and Erromango Islands first established in the 1840s by the London Missionary Society's Polynesian teachers, or by Geddie's own Aneityum converts. New Hebrides mission reinforcements swelled from 1857 to 1859 with the arrival of Joseph Copeland, John Paton, John Matheson, Samuel Johnston, and George Gordon, all save Copeland with new wives tagging along. Presbyterian policy favored couples. Mission wives kept house, shared God's word with island women, and scrutinized husbandly dealings with these.

Newlywed Mary, after a voyage of seven months via Liverpool, Sydney, Tahiti, Cook Islands, and Samoa, in 1858 stood coughing on Aneityum's Anelgauhat beach with her tenderfoot, also coughing, missionary husband John Matheson (figure 5). The young couple had set forth from distant Pictou, Nova Scotia, itself optimistically called a "colonial Zion." One of seven siblings, Mary's parents put her to work at sixteen, teaching children in one of the new common schools then popping up in the colony. Her spinster years were blustery, at least in her imagination. Her unsettled emotions seesawed back and forth between ecstatic highs and depressive and guilty lows. Mary filled dozens of diary pages lamenting her levity and the number of her sins: "What anger, falsehood, and evil lusts are in me!" Lord, "I am filthy, and vilely degraded by sin; a child of Satan."[1] She promised to give up dancing, and yet she still wickedly danced. She promised devoted, co-dependent love with Lord Jesus if only he would save her from weakness and depravity. Her family and friends, rather, found her perceptive, sweet, cheerful, and petite.

After several years of teaching school, Mary took to her bed during the winter of 1857, debilitated by tuberculosis then endemic in British colonies. She wrote in her diary that the Lord in his great mercy had been pleased to afflict her— sooner dead, sooner transported to blessed heaven. Recovered instead by that spring, she married the also tubercular John Matheson who, with a new missionary license from the Presbyterian Foreign Mission Board, only needed to find a wife to be on his way to the mission field. The fatal bacilli probably found him at the Presbyterian Seminary where he had studied since 1850. Not very bright, it seems, John was at least steady, and possessed of "a true Scottish *dourness*." This bent him toward saving the heathen abroad. Nova Scotia's scattered, insignificant, immigrant communities didn't yet offer much in the way of the urbanely depraved. Despite a "hectic" flush on his cheek, "his heart was among the heathen."[2]

Mary and John married in October 1857. She was twenty and he was twenty-five. A month later, they boarded a steamer in Halifax heading for Liverpool and then the South Seas. Busy farewell meetings with family and friends bid them adieu. Doctors before and along the way warned the consumptive couple to hole up and rest, yet they kept on their beeline to the New Hebrides. Perhaps a warm, tropical climate might assuage their condition. They should have known that these islands already were much devastated by European diseases. John and Mary, two tuberculosis vectors, would contribute to the epidemic calamities.

FIGURE 5. Mary Johnston Matheson. From the Reverend George Patterson, *Memoirs of the Rev. S. J. Johnston, the Rev. J. W. Matheson, and Mrs. Mary Johnston Matheson. Missionaries on Tanna,* 1864.

Mary, immediately homesick, initiated a stream of letters she mailed to family and friends. On the way to Sydney, she reported that she was reading fellow Scottish Presbyterian David Livingstone's *Missionary Travels,* sewing, and tossing off heartfelt poems. One of these, "Emily, or 'Looking to Jesus,'" celebrated a young mother who watches her only daughter expire in blessed rapture. After a few months pause in Sydney, the Mathesons boarded the LMS' *John Williams,* which circled South Pacific Islands, dropping off missionaries along the way, before making land at Aneityum in July 1858. Mary reunited happily with Uncle John Geddie and Aunt Charlotte. She also met the Inglises, the other mission couple on Aneityum, whom she found "thoroughly Scotch." The natives, though, were "not such a fine race as on some of the other islands, but they seem manageable and affectionate."[3] She much admired local women's modest dress and, if island language sounded odd, it was pretty. Geddie, when he met his new nephew-in-law, wrote nervously about John's health. Mary kept up her diary: Oh God, "keep me from secret faults, and all presumptuous sins."[4] A favorite word "cumberer" marked many of her written prayers and contemplations. She must not be a hindrance, a burden.

Given grave worries about the Mathesons' condition and the expected arrival of additional missionaries Copeland, Paton, and Johnston, Geddie counseled John and Mary to delay throwing themselves into the work. Everyone boarded *John Williams* for a tour of mission outposts on Futuna, Aniwa, and Tanna where Geddie had placed trained Aneityumese converts, and Dillons Bay, Erromango, where fellow missionary George Gordon had already settled. The ship called at Port Resolution where the party purchased from "the chief" a land plot once occupied by LMS missionaries George Turner and Henry Nisbet from 1842 to 1843. Geddie preached, in Aneityumese, to a group of seventy or so of the curious.

In late October 1858, despite their colleagues' worried concerns, Mary and John sailed to Umairarekar passage near the southern tip of Tanna. John Paton and Samuel Johnston, when they arrived, would take over the Port Resolution station about fourteen miles to the north. In 1839, missionary John Williams, before his martyrdom on Erromango, had left three young Samoans, Lalolangi, Mose, and Salamea, behind at Port Resolution to begin Christian instruction at the harbor. The LMS would land another twenty of these teachers from Samoa, Raratonga, and the Cook Islands until the Presbyterians arrived in 1858. More than half of these Polynesian missionaries, some with wives and children, did not survive for long at Port Resolution, their lives cut short by raging epidemics or by angry Tannese who blamed them for bringing unfamiliar diseases to the island.

Islanders during the mission's first two decades learned Christian beliefs and practices from these Polynesian teachers, and later Presbyterian missionaries built on their work. They left behind one new hamlet place name—Isamoa—where their houses once stood. Subsequent European missionaries borrowed *Atua,* their Samoan word for "god," and also gendered seating arrangements during Christian services with men on one side and women and children on the other. In the south, where the Mathesons landed, teachers from Aneityum had likewise attempted to convert people living around Anuikaraka for several years, and John and Mary brought more Aneityumese converts with them, as servants, along with salt pork, chickens, goats, and lumber for a 15 x 40-foot three-room house. Local chief Kati agreed to host them. Living under his wing, the Christian party and its supplies boosted his prestige, particularly vis-à-vis his political rival Iaresi.

During the next six months at Umairareker, John built his house, then a church, and started a fitful Bible school while trying to learn the Nafe language. Writing to her brother, Mary showed off some new words: *baran (pran,* woman) and *lamar-sin (ramasan,* it is good). Concluding the letter, though, she reported that "three big Tannese" were watching her write, "jabbering among themselves." Nafe was still babble. She lent them scissors to trim their beards. John's beginning scholars learned the English alphabet although his outlandish schoolbooks made them uneasy. Mary, too, began teaching village girls and women to sew even though she was short of useable material. Young women popped in to see her once in a while to give her hugs. Too tired for much hard work, lucky she was "not required to do it." Those Christian Aneityum Island servants cleared and swept.

John reported that his church attracted about 150 Tannese who attended Sunday services, although these were mostly women and children. Curious, villagers checked out the missionaries and their novel rituals. At night, John fired up a magic lantern, projecting scenes from Bible stories, to astonish and captivate his new neighbors. The Mathesons' quick celebrity, however, began to wane. Finding Chief Kati increasingly unhelpful, John and Mary tried instead to cozy up with Iaresi, but he left them behind to cut sandalwood on Erromango.

During John and Mary's time on Tanna, widespread outbreaks of mysterious illnesses, new and nasty, baffled the Tannese. Sustained Western contact with the island began in the 1820s as sandalwooders, whalers, and then missionaries sailed into Port Resolution. Overseas vessels by then were common visitors. Every new ship carried alien microbes, and some of these escaped ashore to infect village after village where people lacked immunity to European scourges. People put two and two together. They connected the newly arrived missionaries with intensifying waves of illness and death sweeping their villages.

Local suspicion deepened when the missionaries themselves began to die. Mrs. Paton was the first to perish in early March 1859 after six months at Port Resolution. Her baby son expired two weeks later. Paton buried both and he stood sentry over their graves, guarding against sneaky cannibal body snatchers. Down south at Kwamera, John also was sick. Neighbor villagers, too, sank under a series of previously unknown ailments. The Mathesons retreated to Aneityum for rest and a cure. Mary lamented village suspicions: "After Mr. Matheson became ill, many of them left off attending church, and became very distant to us. They are very superstitious, and fancy when they are ill, that some person must have caused their sickness."[5] These fancies, of course, were entirely accurate.

On Aneityum, Mary and John recovered although slowly. John suffered more. "Large abscesses formed on the back of his head and neck, which for a time affected his brain. He lost his hearing and his memory to a great extent, and probably his other mental powers were affected."[6] Still, by August of that year, he was agitating to return to Tanna. His mission colleagues sensibly refused his demands and he "became alienated from his brethren." They sent him instead to a quiet Aneityum outstation where friendly converts could look after him and where "his sickness would not produce the unfavourable impression that it did among the Tannese."[7] Two young Tannese lived there, too, and John and Mary chased after them for more Nafe language instruction. Mary tended to John. She taught women more sewing. She spent time with her nineteen-year-old cousin Charlotte Geddie. And she wandered the wildly beautiful woods, gathering orchids beneath immense trees covered with creepers and lianas. All the while, she kept a written inventory of her manifold unworthiness, begging God's divine mercy on an undeserving rebel. Of herself, she did not think "so vile a creature walks the earth." Mary's occasional happiness was tinged always with undercurrents of sorrow. Sweet beauty, she wrote, lie beyond her grasp given the stubborn residue of filth, corruption, and vileness that blackened her heart.

In late 1859, most of the Geddie children left the Aneityum mission for a respite in Canada, and the Inglises sailed for England to arrange publication of the translated Bible in Aneityumese, taking along with them island pundit Williamu. With fewer caretakers available, Mary and John left, too, for Dillons Bay, Erromango. Here, they joined fellow Nova Scotians George and Ellen Gordon in their mission house, high on the hill above the harbor. From the Gordon's house, Mary could look across the island and spy the cloudy peak of Cook's volcanic Traitors Head, looming over Elau's native territory. In February, an obliging Erromangan brought in a fleshless skull that he identified as belonging to the unfortunate James Harris who, along with John Williams, had been bashed on the beach below two decades before. Mary didn't record what they did with this mortal relic. Instead, she fancied that puffy trade wind clouds floating above might carry her thoughts back home to Nova Scotia, to her mother, her dear Ma. She wondered if Pictou had yet experienced the global Christian revival then stirring Evangelicals. Mary prayed God to fill her, too, with the Holy Spirit. John, meanwhile, dosed himself with cod liver oil. He recovered enough energy to print some school manuals in English and Nafe on Gordon's hand press. Both Mathesons continued to cough.

Tubercular symptoms can come and go, and John felt healthy enough to agitate once more for a return to Tanna in April 1860. Back at Umairarekar, only a handful of Tannese resumed church going. Most remained hostile, telling Mary that they hated Jehovah and his worship. Their desire for trade goods grew, though. Many men had acquired steel axes. Some had traded pigs for muskets. Already they were addicted to tobacco. John and Mary traded fishhooks, beads, and red cloth for garden food. Men were fond of tying up their hair with strips of the cloth. The Mathesons returned in the middle of Tanna's yam harvest season, and the crop was abundant enough that year for people to circumcise their sons and arrange other exchange ceremonies. Then, as often today, these culminate in all-night dancing. Mary was no fan of the celebrations suspecting that they were another cause of rampant illness: "They spend a great part of their time in dancing and singing their heathen songs, &c., and many make themselves quite ill with dancing, shouting, &c."[8] Her village neighbors, nonetheless, honoring island hospitality invited her to come along to one of these fetes, "to see them feasting and dancing."

Even more villagers, though, died throughout late 1860 and 1861. One promising convert lost his wife (although he permitted her a Christian burial). Aneityumese teacher Nohoat, who had close kin connections to Kwamera, died. His namesake, young son of local chief Namaka, also died in August. Mary bemoaned the deaths of six other children with whom she had played and shared Jesus stories. A "promising young man" died of tuberculosis. Seeking a healthier prospect, John took apart their seaside house. He hired Islanders to drag the framing, roof, and walls up Imoa hill, and rebuilt it there.

Things went from bad to worse with the outbreak of a widespread measles epidemic in November 1860, affecting all the southern islands. Dead bodies became too numerous to bury. Missionaries estimated village death rates as high as 50 percent. The virus for some reason killed more adults in their prime than it did children or the elderly. "The mortality is so great in some places that many persons are left lying here and there on the earth unburied, or the door of the house is closed and the dead body left to decay with the house."[9] John blamed a trading ship for bringing measles to Kwamera. But he had volunteered Kapuku, his best pupil, when the traders had requested that he send some local chief onboard to receive the usual token gifts. When Kapuku, soon after this duty, broke out in spots on mission premises, people had even more cause for suspicion. Laid low with measles, a simultaneous upsurge of dysentery carried hundreds more over the edge of the grave. Few villagers had strength to work their farms. In January 1861, two powerful hurricanes swept through, ravaging the Mathesons' boathouse and church, and also their house, kitchen, and storehouse all now up on Imoa hill. The wind shifted to the north, blowing in Iasur's volcanic acidic ash that rained down burning away what tender garden shoots there were.

Mary gloomily admitted that people blamed her for the collected calamities, especially since neither John nor Mary then appeared sick: "They declared that I had smitten them with the measles, in order to be revenged on them for having recently stolen from us with such a high hand."[10] Devastated island survivors begged the Mathesons to leave, or at least to shut up about Christianity. They ceased trading food with them. When John visited other southern villages to preach, people drove him away by throwing stones and, when he wouldn't leave, ran off themselves or shouted, chopped, and banged clubs on trees or old logs to drown out his deadly preaching. Mary, understandably, wrote her brother: "Lately I have had such longing to soar away up amid the peaceful clouds, in other words, to enter that haven of rest." She wrote to a friend back in Pictou: "I trust that this people will learn that Jehovah is a God not to be trifled with."[11] In February 1861, Mary was pregnant. It's difficult to know if the concatenation of disasters had drawn her closer to John, or how Mary accounted for her condition. Was this God's gift? Or was it further proof of vileness and degradation? Mary, or some other, later destroyed her diary pages that bared too much.

Measles and dysentery cut through Port Resolution, too. Another Nova Scotian, Samuel Johnston with wife Bessie (Elisabeth), had arrived the previous February to reinforce the widower John Paton. The Johnstons soon fell ill and treated themselves with larger and larger doses of laudanum, tincture of opium. This only stupefied them, and Samuel began to babble in Nafe. He died and Paton buried him, too, in the small but expanding Christian graveyard near the harbor. That May, a party of Erromangans whom Mary once had taken to be friendly and docile, axed George and Ellen Gordon to death at Dillons Bay. At Kwamera, the Mathesons' coughing grew worse. Mary suffered attacks of asthma and bronchitis. Her belly swollen, she refused leave John alone on Tanna and retreat to Aneityum where her aunt might care for her in the last months of her pregnancy. She continued journaling her self-criticism: "Oh what a hardened wench am I!" She hated both her depressions and her passing delights. Little Minnie, probably a diminutive of Mary, was born on 21 November 1861.

Things boiled to an end in January 1862. This was the rainy season and John's and Mary's coughing worsened. Poor little Minnie died on the 17th. Mary's youthful poetic sensibilities about sweetly dying children may have cut a bit deeper. John buried the infant on Imoa hill. Kapuku, who had recovered from the measles, felt pity. He gave Matheson twenty of his power stones that controlled fortune in war, the winds, and safety at sea. Up at Port Resolution, people sought to rid themselves of both missionaries and diseases. Paton's remaining island friends warned him to leave, and on the 20th he fled south to Kwamera to join the Mathesons. But here, too, villagers were desperate and outraged. They burned down John's thatch-roofed church on Sunday night, 2 February. News of the turmoil reached Aneityum, and Geddie paid a sandalwooder then moored at Aneityum to remove the besieged missionaries and their property from Kwamera. Christian supporters Kapuku and wife Kaiou, along with Iaresi, Viavia, and their families, joined the exodus south to Aneityum. Safer there than to suffer blame for all that illness and death. John, at the last minute, refused to leave. He barricaded himself in his Imoa house. His fellow missionary John Paton, though, threatened to send a letter with the ship to accuse John of virtual murder if he was forced to remain behind on Tanna with the foolish Mathesons.

Mary, in hospice on Anietyum with her uncle and aunt, breathed only a few more weeks. She died on 11 March 1862. Back in Pictou, her mother too was ill. While dying, she refused to leave Mary any last words. Sweet Ma instead expected to find Mary in heaven. John, surprisingly, outlived Mary although not by much. On Aneityum, he continued to struggle with Nafe language with the help of Kapuku, Iaresi, and Viavia. That June, he decided to cut his losses. Seeking more salubrious climate, he sailed south to Mare in the Loyalty Islands. There, although he could barely talk, hardly swallow, and survived on boiled batter pudding, he continued translating Nafe psalms and wrote a school primer. He died in October 1862, a "frail and shattered tabernacle of clay."[12] Tuberculosis destroyed Mary and John as it had Elau. Unlike Elau, though, no one autopsied their bodies.

Sickness

Mary and John added tuberculosis to the parade of strange new diseases that marched onto Tanna: pneumonia, measles, whooping cough, influenza, dysentery, cholera, diphtheria, smallpox, gonorrhea, and more. Poky new church buildings (like modern airplanes) might especially have dispersed germs among coughing and sneezing congregants. Epidemics accelerated in the 1830s; but forgotten plagues also may have arrived earlier with Cook, or with several subsequent expeditions that visited Tanna. No one knows how many Tannese were alive when Cook landed in 1774. Expedition scientist Johann Forster then

estimated the island's population at twenty thousand, but he had to extrapo-
late from his Port Resolution experience and from what villages and plantations
could be seen from sea. Others, later, doubled his guess. By the 1920s, when
island depopulation leveled out, fewer than six thousand people lived on the island. Disease killed even more people on Erromango and Aneityum. By 1931, Erromangans numbered only 381, and by 1941 Aneityum's population had crashed
from a possible high of nine thousand to a sparse 186.

When the Mathesons visited the Gordons on Erromango in 1859, Mary noted
the scarcity of inhabitants around Dillons Bay. She walked two-and-a-half miles
to a hilltop, from which she could see Tanna, without meeting a single person.
She failed to ponder the cause of this depopulation, however, concluding merely
that the absence of natives was sometimes a trial, but sometimes a great relief.
When I was first on Tanna in the 1970s, parents then were still busy bestowing
unused personal names on their children who would thus gain the right to repopulate long-emptied villages and lands. Currently, more than thirty thousand
people live on Tanna. Some thousands of others have migrated to Port Vila's
settlements and other parts of Vanuatu. Even with this rebound, population
remains scanty in parts of the island.

LMS missionary George Turner, who lasted six months at Port Resolution
from 1842 to 1843, learned something about island disease theory. He reported:
"Coughs, influenza, dysentery, and some skin diseases, the Tannese attribute to
their intercourse with White men, and call them *foreign things.*" Missionaries
found this hard to swallow, although Turner went on:

> The opinion there was universal that they had tenfold more of disease
> and death since they had intercourse with ships than they had before.
> We thought at first it was prejudice and fault-finding, but the reply of the
> more honest and thoughtful of the natives invariably was: "It is quite true.
> Formerly people here never died till they were old, but nowadays there is
> no end to this influenza, and coughing, and death."[13]

Neither side yet understood germ theory. The Christians spun stories of God's
will, sinfulness, and uncleanliness to explain all the coughing. Sick Tannese,
who infuriated missionaries with their certain knowledge that some men work
power stones that cause illness, suspected either Christian maleficence or the
displeasure of their own ancestors.

Mission apologists argued that Tanna's disease-makers projected onto the
missionaries equivalent death-dealing powers in order to preserve their own
status. But, in His mysterious way, "it pleased Divine Providence again" to visit

Tanna with more sickness and death "which the natives were so apt to connect with Christianity." They did spot the puzzle: "It is certainly a singular dispensation of Divine Providence that while the natives of this island have such superstitious notions regarding Christianity as causing disease and death hitherto almost every attempt to introduce Christianity among them has been followed by severe epidemics."[14] God, indeed, works in mysterious ways.

The Patons and the Johnstons at Port Resolution, and Mary and John at Imoa, were shocked when their ailing island friends blamed them. Only God, they hastened to preach, commands power over life and death. The Tannese could accept this argument, although it did not make it easier to embrace Jehovah. Surely, could not the white missionaries manipulate their god just as they themselves knew how to direct island spiritual powers? The unwell vacillated. Some blamed the missionaries, others blamed neighboring and rival power stone workers who were unhappy and jealous that they hosted missionaries, controlling thus access to foreign largesse. And still others blamed their own neglected yet still watchful ancestors and spirits who were punishing apostasy.

The Mathesons rummaged through their medicine chest. Their mid-nineteenth century concoctions, tincture of opium, ground red deer horn, cod liver oil, vinegar, ammonia, emetics, and the like, were not much help. And only a few of the sick, John noted, "would receive medicine." Even friendly Uairau, Kapuku's wife, refused treatment. Mary wrote that they managed only to dose a few babies. Island parents, perhaps, were particularly desperate to revivify their expiring infants and willing to try anything, or maybe they figured better to experiment on children than on oneself. Those who make sickness on Tanna typically also can cure, but who could know if John's alien concoctions were antidote or some additional poison?

Mary and John were small-town Victorians and thus intimately familiar with death's domain. Disease and death were ordinary aspects of Nova Scotian life. Death, moreover, was instructive: a testimony to God's power and human weakness. Two of Mary's siblings died young. In 1859, she wrote her mother that she was not in the least surprised to learn of so many recent deaths back home in Pictou. Mission commentary sunnily interpreted Samuel Johnston's sad demise and burial at Port Resolution. This was the Heavenly Father showing the Tannese "how the Christian dies." There was cheerful anticipation that "his grave in that dark and distant land may speak in louder tones and yield more profitable lessons than even his living voice." Mary's own tombstone, when raised over her grave on Aneityum, offered sentiment as morbid as her personality: "For me to live in Christ and to die is gain." The Tannese accept that the dead indeed do speak, although they may have received their own sorts of messages from Mary and John's ghosts. They would likewise reject Christian fatalism. Death is not always gain. Cures exist or can be found.

Islanders have an established therapeutics that include an extensive pharmacopeia: concoctions of leaves, bark, and other materials curers use to treat a variety of conditions. They continue to be disposed to bloodletting. Certain experts set broken limb bones by cutting through flesh to expose the break, manipulating and realigning bones, and then wrapping the broken arm or leg back together in leaves with antibiotic properties. In earlier days, people also tried to identify which person, with which disease stone, might have conjured the disease. With the right payoff, a stone owner might be cajoled to reverse his hex. Everyone knows that those who conjure up a disease are best able to cure this.

Nowadays, passing yachts and two planeloads of tourists land on Tanna most days, eager to experience Iasur's fires. Some of these visitors, too, come with coughs and sniffles but these no longer lay low the locals. Islanders over the years have developed immunity to global scourges, augmenting their native resistance to endemic malaria and occasional leprosy. The Rockefeller Foundation funded a campaign in the 1920s and 1930s that eliminated yaws, an irksome skin disease. Today's epidemiologists instead worry about the spread of the modern maladies. To date, the worst of these, HIV/AIDS, has made only minor inroads into Vanuatu, and the coronavirus, as of mid-2020, had not reached the islands thanks to an interruption of international travel. Growing numbers, though, suffer the disorders of modernity including diabetes, hypertension, obesity, and heart disease. Men, almost all of whom avidly smoke homegrown or imported tobacco, suffer chronic asthma and other sorts of troublesome lung conditions.

Distressed and desperate, the Mathesons' neighbors connected the dots and blamed newcomer Scottish missionaries for making them sick. They sorted disease into two categories, a project that continues today. Some illnesses are *kastom*. Others stem from foreigners, the *Pitoga*. Missionary George Turner, at Port Resolution in 1842, recorded the early days of this distinction: "When a person was said to be ill, the next question was "What is the matter?" Is it nahak or a foreign thing?"[15] The Tannese continue to treat island conditions with local cures, and they swallow imported medications for foreign maladies. In years since Mary and John came and went, island men gave up their power stones that can sicken or kill. They repudiate sorcery and they police anyone who thinks to revive *nukwei nahak* stone practice. Ancestral spirits, not living sorcerers, today shoulder most blame for causing disease. Often, as did my friend Nakutan who was deeply worried about a sick young daughter, they first investigate possible ancestral displeasure. This potentially saves travel expense and hospital fees for the shallow-pocketed. *Kleva,* some of whom are women, who communicate with spirits in dreams and otherwise, can deduce a disease's cause and cure. One such seer advised Nakutan that his dead aunt was punishing him, by way of making his daughter sick, for failing to repay a pig he had borrowed years previously for his wedding celebration. He hastened to do so but, when the child was slow to recover, he found enough money to rent a truck to carry the girl across Tanna to the government hospital.

Most everyone knows how to concoct curative infusions. *Nui* (water), they call these, or "leaf medicine" in Bislama. I drank a lot of this in 1978 when I caught mononucleosis, although sometimes a healer instead spat a shower of medicine into my face. People specialize in treating particular conditions. My kindly neighbor Kusi once brought me a bottle of murky, green liquid to treat, without great success, my aching lower back. Her bad back medicine is locally famous. Divining disease, and curing this, is one way that women can make a name for themselves.

Women

Disregarding Cook's deceptive beardless boys whom the Tannese first took to be female, Mary was among the first white woman to come to Tanna. Women at Umairarekar examined her closely as she came ashore. Since "few had ever seen a White woman before" she was "an object of great curiosity." Mary wrote her mother: "I am considered a perfect wonder, as they have never seen a White female. Many of them are afraid to shake hands and some run away."[16] Along with their first white woman, the Tannese also saw their first European family. Scottish appreciation of clan and extended family had narrowed to focus on the tighter bonds linking husband, wife, and children. Mission propaganda imagery liked to portray illustrative nuclear families, Pacific versions of hardworking dad, loving mother, and dutiful child. Scottish missionaries, also, were house proud. A house symbolized and encompassed family and it gave women a proper place. The Mathesons, like snails, hauled their house frame along with them from Aneityum to Umairarekar to Imoa. Mission sketches of Tanna showcased reimagined island families and their rudimentary village homes.

Coming from farming or lower middle-class urban trade backgrounds that demanded hard work from men and women alike, missionaries serving abroad aspired to Victorian respectability, even on remotest Tanna. The deep pool of island domestics was one welcome aspect of mission life. These servants came much cheaper than they did back home in Scotland or Nova Scotia, and they spared missionary wives considerable domestic labor. Mission wives' time could be given over instead to sewing, embroidery, and other respectable ladylike endeavors. But spreading forth into the world, Presbyterians ran into hardworking women everywhere. The overworked, downtrodden, and abused heathen woman was a common theme in mission propaganda. Donated Sunday pennies would convert dark islands and also there clarify proper gender roles.

On Tanna, missionaries quickly grasped that women and children provide most everyday farm and garden labor in between clearing new fields and harvesting these, when men pitch in. They deeply disapproved of the heathen custom of "widow-strangling" on Aneityum Island, where wives of newly dead chiefs volunteered to join them in the spirit world, fearing that some on Tanna were also adopting the practice. The Tannese and the Scottish alike commended patriarchy as warranted by *kastom,* by the Bible, or both. Gender relations, however, failed always to simplify into chiefly husband and helpmate wife, or dominant men and submissive women. Missionary wives, for instance, soon found themselves ordering about island men. Whiteness on Tanna trumped masculinity, and Samuel Johnston noted his wife's novel clout at Port Resolution. Bessie, in an outburst, would sternly order visiting men out of her house, and "Men who have been accustomed to trample upon women scarcely know what to say to a woman usurping such authority. But still she generally manages them."[17]

During her truncated residence on Tanna, Bessie strummed the overworked woman theme in letters home to Nova Scotia: "If you were here to see the abuse of women, I know your heart would ache for them. They are just slaves to the men—do the hardest of the work, and if they happen to give the slightest offence to them are severely punished and often clubbed to death."[18] Before her, George Turner who had a better eye for the tenor of Port Resolution marital relations, wrote: "Upon the whole we thought the women better treated at Tanna than they often are among heathen tribes."[19] And Glaswegian Agnes Watt, who with her missionary husband William replaced the Mathesons at Kwamera in 1869, even applauded judicious husbandly chastisement given their wives' notably sharp tongues.

Missionary ideals of proper households led them to overlook or misread much of island family life. Houses, yes, but these are mostly for sleeping. People live outdoors in more expansive home grounds that encompass broadly male and female spaces. Men's lives center on kava-drinking clearings on which, in Mary's day, they built shelters. Women, girls, and yet uncircumcised boys inhabit villages and hamlets that encircle these kava clearings. Thanks to mission notions of proper family life, most men nowadays after drinking kava leave the clearing to rejoin their wives and children in family hamlet houses. Despite mission lament about browbeaten women and unfair gendered responsibilities, loving fathers and diligent brothers do a considerable amount of child minding. They prepare fires and cook when necessary. Gender separation continues, however, when wives menstruate. Inquisitive island neighbors may well have wondered at Mary and John's baffling propinquity. Women once retired to private, menstrual houses outside the village, where they usually also gave birth. Today, although husbands and wives sleep in one house, they distance themselves monthly, and menstruating women quit cooking for their men. Those overworked Tannese women, once a month at least, enjoyed greater domestic leisure than did some of their Scottish sisters.

When Samuel Johnston was dying at Port Resolution, his colleague John Paton sliced open his arms to bleed him. The Tannese would have approved of this Scottish bloodletting therapy. They themselves bleed the sick, but mostly sick men. They share with other Melanesians deep respect for the power of blood, especially menstrual blood. Women, here, are sturdier than men. Female bodies are open, proved by regular bloody menses. Men, rather, are closed, in danger of clogging. One must cut open sick men. Women naturally wash away body taints and pollutants. If they survive childbirth, many women reach ripe old age. Most of my old lady friends from the 1970s outlived their tobacco fiend, smoking husbands by three decades. Women are tough in other ways, too, as mission wife Agnes Watt remarked. If men monopolize the right to speak at public meetings, women who mutter along a meeting's edge can salt the air with reproach and backchat. Sharped tongued still, some find it most difficult to suffer fools. My strong young friend Sara, for one, married late. The boys in the neighborhood were terrified of her.

Along with kava, men like to monopolize the spirit world, too. But everyone dreams. Some women gain celebrity as seers, as *kleva*. Others are popular healers. Like Kusi, they inherit pharmacological recipes from mothers and grandmothers, or they discover these in dreams. Lispet of Sulphur Bay until her death was a famous spirit medium and curer. She possessed a direct conversational pipeline to John Frum and his spiritual sons. Leading men didn't know how to handle her. They tried but failed to marginalize her amplifying power and fame. Agnes Watt, in 1882, wrote of another old woman *kleva* who, by communicating with her dead husband, enticed the spirits to spill forth knives, tobacco pipes, cotton cloth, beads, and other newfangled goods. The skeptical Agnes and William Watt challenged the woman to extract, spiritually, some item from their Kwamera house but she refused. Her dead husband's ghost declined to risk Christian contact. Agnes' mistrust, here, was surprising as her own superior status, and that of Mary too, depended on her immediate connection and service to the supernatural.

The mission agenda, pushed by ambitious middle-class Victorians, aimed to substitute one island form of patriarchy for another. They imagined hard-working husbands supported by helpful wives who kept proper houses. This project never completely succeeded although gender relations have much transformed since the mid-nineteenth century. Although women, then and now, continue to work hard in their gardens and at other daily tasks, men and circumcised sons gradually abandoned their men's houses that once were located on kava-drinking grounds, moving to live with wives and children in the surrounding hamlets. Chiefly Christian converts also sloughed off second wives, although polygyny was never common. The missions instructed women in several useful skills, particularly sewing, which remains today a key source of feminine income. Over the years, women's educational opportunities have improved and several of the young village girls I met in the 1970s subsequently enjoyed successful teaching careers.

Men, though, still monopolize land, and they attempt to control access to the spirits be these Christian or island. Parents, when they can, continue to manage the marriages of both daughters and sons, and daughters suffer greater family pressure to acquiesce to a union. Men, through their names, are more firmly tied to their home ground. Women leave their parents and siblings behind to move to new husbands' places, sometimes distant. This female mobility, however, can offer opportunity. Men must remain committed to protecting their home ground for their children and grandchildren. Women, who typically leave home villages, thereby escape at least some male supervision. Joining the urban migration flows that amplified after 1980, some like Sivur have abandoned Tanna to find a more independent life in Blacksands, one of Port Vila's surrounding settlements.

Mary, too, left home for good although she maintained epistolary ties with her family in Pictou. In a letter home to her brother, Mary supposed that some of her sister mission wives could "feel interested in natives without becoming attached to them."[20] But she herself strove to cultivate deep friendships with island women. The next world, she was sure, would recognize no distinction of color or class. Back at Imoa in late 1860, though, she contemplated a gloomy island future: "Poor Tannese, I fear their days of independence are nearly over. As soon as this island has been opened up by the gospel, probably the White man will take possession, and the poor natives die out."[21] She and John, coughing away, contributed their part to this vision. Only Tannese struggle and hardiness, in the end, proved her prediction incorrect. It was Mary, and John, and little Minnie who died out.

Agnes hiked to the top of Imoa hill when the Watts first arrived at Kwamera in 1869. She was hunting for remnants of the Mathesons who had retreated just seven years before: "We searched in vain for the grave of their infant daughter. . . . They buried her near their house and put a fence round the grave, but already it is unknown. Poor little thing!"[22] Poor things all around. Minnie's grave vanished faster, even, than Elau's. The Presbyterians sent missionary reinforcements to replace their dead. Island women and men, too, found other ways to live on. They took up new opportunities. They sometimes accepted and sometimes rejected novel overseas messages. They expanded their traveling. Like Elau and Mary, many hit the road as did bold Soarum, looking down from his mountain village at the Port's comings and goings.

Notes

1. George Patterson, *Memoirs of the Rev. S. F. Johnston, the Rev. J. W. Matheson, and Mrs. Mary Johnston Matheson, Missionaries on Tanna* (Philadelphia: W. S. & A. Martien, 1864), 313, 320.

2. Patterson, *Memoirs*, 154.

3. Patterson, *Memoirs*, 350.

4. Patterson, *Memoirs*, 356.

5. Patterson, *Memoirs*, 396.

6. Patterson, *Memoirs*, 405.

7. Patterson, *Memoirs*, 406.

8. Patterson, *Memoirs*, 453.

9. Patterson, *Memoirs*, 275.

10. Patterson, *Memoirs*, 471.

11. Patterson, *Memoirs*, 477.

12. Patterson, *Memoirs*, 502.

13. George Turner, *Samoa a Hundred Years Ago and Long Before, Together with Notes on the Cults and Customs of Twenty-three Other Islands in the Pacific* (London: Macmillan, 1884), 322–323.

14. Patterson, *Memoirs*, 467.

15. Turner, *Samoa*, 322.

16. Patterson, *Memoirs*, 389.

17. Patterson, *Memoirs*, 257.

18. Patterson, *Memoirs*, 261.

19. Turner, *Samoa*, 317.

20. Patterson, *Memoirs*, 465.

21. Patterson, *Memoirs*, 465.

22. Agnes Watt, *Twenty-five Years Mission Life on Tanna, New Hebrides* (Paisley: J. and R. Parlane, 1896), 91.

Further Readings

Mary Matheson

Adams, Ron. *In the Land of Strangers: A Century of European Contact with Tanna, 1774–1874*. Pacific Research Monograph no. 9. Canberra: Australian National University, 1984.

Polynesian Teachers Stationed at Port Resolution

Latai, Latu. "Covenant Keepers: A History of Samoan (LMS) Missionary Wives in the Western Pacific from 1839 to 1979." PhD diss., Australian National University, 2016.

Missionaries and Disease

Douglas, Bronwen. "Autonomous and Controlled Spirits: Traditional Ritual and Early Interpretations of Christianity on Tanna, Aneityum, and the Isle of Pines in Comparative Perspective." *Journal of the Polynesian Society* 98, no. 1 (March 1989): 7–48.

Agnes Watt

Lindstrom, Lamont. "Agnes C. P. Watt and Melanesian Personhood." *Journal of Pacific History* 48, no. 3 (2013): 243–266.

CHAPTER 6

Soarum

SOARUM ASORI WAS INDEED a *kaha eraha,* a great and forbidding ancestor. His home, Iankwanemwi, is up the eastern flanks of Mount Meren, down the coast between Port Resolution and the Matheson's abandoned house at Imoa. After John and Mary fled in 1862, more dogged and persistent missionaries continued to come ashore. Thomas and Lucy (another Geddie daughter) Neilson revived the Presbyterian enterprise at Port Resolution in 1868. A few months later, in 1869, Agnes and William Watt moved into the Mathesons' old station, near Kwamera.

Entrenched up at Iankwanemwi, Soarum stood firm against creeping Christian incursion. Ancestors dishonored, power stones destroyed, kava drinking disrupted, dancing disapproved, polygyny disallowed, the missionaries aimed ambitiously to remake island *kastom* and the Tannese themselves. Soarum's descendants say that he was the Soarum Naias who chopped down John Paton's Port Resolution banana trees in 1862, although this may have been a previous namesake. Events, though, undercut Soarum's resistance. He held the line for tradition but he was in a tight spot. Christian teaching continued to make headway. The Neilsons and Watts wanted a safe road linking their two stations, saving them from sailing or rowing back and forth. They focused conversion efforts on intervening villages along the way, and Iakwanemwi sits smack on the road that links Port Resolution and Kwamera. Laid low by killer plagues, people blamed missionaries yet they also sought their cures, following the precept that those who cause an illness can also cure this. And increasing numbers of men and women were abandoning the disease-infested island. They jumped onto overseas labor-recruiting ships. The first of these arrived in 1863 to embark indentured Islanders for newly established plantations and other enterprises in colonial Queensland, New Caledonia, Fiji, Samoa, and elsewhere in the New Hebrides. More than four thousand men and women left for Queensland alone between 1863 and 1904. Many others left for work elsewhere abroad, and this from an island population base already much depleted.

Queensland labor contracts ran three years and when these expired, indentured workers could either reenlist or return to Tanna with a developed craving for store-bought goods. They lugged home trade boxes crammed with muskets, ammunition, axes, cloth, tobacco, and the like, although usually they gave much of this away to family and friends. While abroad, most men became tobacco fiends. Where to find more back home on Tanna? Sandalwood and whales, by the 1860s, were mostly wiped out and sandalwood and whaling ships had thus moved along. Missionaries, along with a few penurious traders dealing in coconuts, for some years would control the importation of tobacco to Tanna along with European manufactures. To acquire foreign goods, one could recruit to work in Queensland's sugarcane plantations; one could plant coconut palms for the copra trade; or one could convert.

Soarum, like most important men, had commandeered a musket. Many guns imported to Tanna were Snider-Enfield rifles that escaped from British Army sources. Workers returned home from employment overseas with cherished muskets and ammunition. Queensland authorities banned the export of weapons into the Pacific in 1884, but trade in firearms nonetheless continued. Many Islanders shifted to working in New Caledonia where they could still buy guns. Local disputes once pursued with clubs, spears, bows and arrows, and throwing stones became deadlier. For safety, Soarum slept in a cavity in one of the huge banyan trees shading the Iankwanemwi kava-drinking ground, his musket at hand. His brother Nousi wasn't as lucky. A kinsman Kwaniamuk shot and killed him one day as he walked down the mountain, heading to Port Resolution desperate to scrounge some tobacco. Soarum, in turn, gunned down Kwaniamuk.

Missionaries and their converts could call up even bigger guns to protect their backs. British and French naval frigates patrolled the archipelago with increased frequency to show the flag, demonstrate sporadic authority, and randomly punish. Three men-of-war bombarded Tannese villages in 1858, 1865, and 1894. HMS *Curaçoa*'s assault on Port Resolution in August 1865 was the most infamous of these attacks. Missionary John Paton, driven off Tanna along with the Mathesons in 1862, nursed a grudge. Paton helped convince Naval Captain William Wiseman to "inflict punishment on the Natives for murder and robbery of Traders and others." With fellow Presbyterian missionary George Gordon, he sailed on the Presbyterians' new mission ship *Dayspring*, shadowing the man-of-war. They joined the expedition, so the missionaries said, merely to interpret and mediate. Onboard *Curaçoa*, British traveler Julius Brenchley figured instead that "Both these gentlemen were bent on dangerous enterprises, in which they hoped to succeed by favour of her Majesty's guns, that were soon to be employed in punishing and terrifying the natives of Tanna and Eramanga for their misdeeds."[1]

Curaçoa blasted Port Resolution's villages with her artillery. Her cutter, alongside, fired rockets. Brenchley effused that "very soon our big guns loaded with shell began to carry very unpleasant messages to the culprits, while our cutter further enlightened them by discharging rockets among a great crowd of natives that clustered about the harbour."[2] After several hours of bombardment, Commander Dent led a landing party of 170 men ashore. These invaders busied themselves burning down houses, wasting food gardens, and chopping and holing canoes.

The Tannese managed to kill one of the landing party, a Mister Holland who had previously "served unhurt in the Indian Mutiny, the Crimean War, and in New Zealand." The British carried his body back onboard, fearful that the Tannese would eat him. For their part, the invaders shot dead Kwatangan who they took to be a chief. Brenchley and other observers reported only this one death although, later, a dud shell exploded and killed three more island men who poked at it. Paton, the next day, met with as many friendlies as could be rounded up. These, so Brenchley reported, counted higher casualties: "Many more are hurt, and we know not how many are shot and dead."[3]

Violent retribution didn't much help Christian efforts. Two years later, John Geddie tried to land his new son-in-law John Neilson and his daughter Lucy at Port Resolution to revive the mission. The first thing that met his eye was a large conical shell from the *Curaçoa*'s guns, standing in an upright position in the sand. When the Presbyterians offloaded timber for the Neilsons' house, local folk chucked this back into the sea. Geddie confessed that one old man spoke to him "in a very angry strain, saying that we had come to settle a new missionary already who had brought a man-of-war to kill them and destroy their property, and they would receive no more missionaries."[4] *Dayspring* retreated to Aneityum with the Neilsons still onboard, but they would slink back to Port Resolution the following year, in 1868.

Soarum as a young boy may have witnessed *Curaçoa*'s bombardment, dodging rockets and shells. Brenchley, who quizzed Paton for his knowledge of the enemy, recorded two "tribal names," the Naraimene of the bay's eastern peninsula and the Nasebine (i.e., Nasipmene), Soarum's own territorial group located upland from the harbor. If not Soarum, someone from Iankwanemwi was there because he carried away another unexploded artillery shell. This survived for the next 140 years, displayed in the center of the Iankwanemwi kava ground. The captured shell boasted and proclaimed *kastom*'s powers and people's firm resistance to outside meddling. Luckily, I once took its picture. A few years later, a *kleva* fingered the artillery shell as the cause of a spate of illnesses, and pulled it up and dumped it somewhere in the deep bush.

Even if daringly resisted, British naval muscle must have unsettled Soarum. Even worse for stubborn island traditionalists, most of those who departed for Queensland and farther afield were younger men and women, many of these ambitious. A flush of returnees came home from 1906 to 1908, including at least 104 in January 1907 alone. When the Australian colonies federated in 1901, the new Parliament passed white Australia legislation that mandated the deportation of most Melanesian workers. Back home on Tanna, many of these disrespected their stick-in-the-mud, traditionalist elders. Several self-made island preachers attracted missionary attention including Tommy Tanna, Nirua Monkey, and Johnny Pata. These were former Queensland canefield workers who returned to Tanna and shared the Christian gospel without missionary supervision. This turn to Christianity gave younger men a leg up in political status competitions and shielded them from oldsters rattling their power stones. Soarum's great-grandchildren say that he had secreted somewhere at least one of these, a war stone (*nukwei naruagenien*).

John Paton and the Mathesons certainly believed in spirits but they scorned island power stones, trusting instead in Christian prayer. Nonetheless, they confiscated these stones whenever they could from converts, like Kapuku at Imoa. They cemented them into new church foundations and entry thresholds so that Christian converts had to walk over them. Paton once volunteered himself as sorcery victim in a spiritual challenge that he thought would demonstrate Jehovah's higher powers. He took a few bites out of a *nekori* (dragon fruit) and passed along his leftovers to three "sacred men" sorcerers who controlled deadly *nukwei nahak* stones, challenging them to do their worst. The sorcerers worked their stones heating the half-eaten plum over a fire, aiming to toast the annoying missionary's innards. Things turned out well, for Paton at least. The week during which he was meant to expire came and went, and he happily acquired new material for subsequent sermons on island wickedness and folly: "This whole incident did, doubtless, shake the prejudices of many as to Sorcery; but few even of converted Natives ever get entirely clear of the dread of Nahak."[5] Even so, Soarum and other traditionalist elders faced more and more young converts and intensifying challenge to their chiefly and senior authority.

When Soarum's own son Kauke admitted that he wanted to learn more about *nafakiien* (Christian gospel and prayer), Soarum threatened to kill him. Instead, he banished him to Iankahar, a small associated kava-drinking ground a quarter mile away from Iankwanemwi. Iankahar had come to shelter the community's growing number of Christian converts, leaving Soarum and other resistors entrenched back at Iankwanemwi. Soarum's kinsman Iapwatu also worked in Queensland, and when he returned home to Tanna his son (a namesake Iapwatu) went on pilgrimage to the mission at Port Resolution to take Christian instruction. Kauke went along, as did Iau and his wife Nahi both of whom had moved up from the valley floor to escape their angry, traditionalist neighbors.

Today's Iapwatu recalls that his ancestral namesake joined Iau in a Christian Iankahi hamlet, on the western shore of Port Resolution, to investigate the alien religion. To bring Christianity to Iankahar, their home village, Iapwatu, Iau, and Kauke followed local practice. Given Tanna's scant public domain and the absence of a cultural commons, they assumed that Christian knowledge was private property owned first by Presbyterian missionaries and then by their initial converts. To access these stories and spirits, they must apprentice themselves and acknowledge the authority of Christian masters. Knowledge and all other sorts of island exchange goods flow along *suatuk* (roads), networks of relationships that conjoin places. In addition to recognizing the primacy of Christian sources down at Port Resolution, Iapwatu, Kauke, and Iau would also respect the secondary rights of other Christian converts living along the road that connected Port Resolution with Iankahar hamlet. Christianity, thus, traveled from Iankahi up the mountain west of the harbor to Iankahar as might the gift of a pig. It emerged from Port Resolution, and then jumped from place to place as it ascended the mountain from Iuea, to Iamanuapen, to Ikurupu, and then finally to Iankwanemwi/Iankahar.

By 1910, many more Christian converts from the surrounding area had moved to Iankahar. The village grew large enough to erect a church alongside the three banyans that shaded the kava-drinking ground. They built this church (with surrendered power stones at its foundation), and rechristened the village as Samaria, after the capitol of ancient Israel's northern kingdom, the year missionary William Watt and his family retired to Melbourne. Their descendants in 2019 funded and built a new cement block church where the original wooden chapel once stood. Some of Soarum's great-grandchildren, his *mwipwuni eraha,* remain committed Presbyterians. Others have joined a plethora of newfangled churches that crowded onto Tanna after Vanuatu's 1980 independence. Most living over at Iapiro, Soarum's old Iankwanemwi home, are active or lapsed supporters of the John Frum movement. The original religious schism between Iankwanemwi and Iankahar still endures, although it was remade in the 1930s with another, overlapping divide between John Frum supporters and remnant Presbyterians in the area.

Place and Road

Just as island personages endure across generations, so do places. When I first came to Tanna, friends pointed out the sites of phantom villages and invisible kava-drinking grounds. To me, these appeared only as lush forest and overgrown bush. Three decades later, many of these empty places are back in business, just as unused personal names/personages can lie dormant in memory until enough babies are born who need these. A topographic grid of used and unused named island places, linked by roads, lies just beneath the surface, under the visible landscape. Since the 1970s, more than ten thousand children have been born. Many of these have moved into unpeopled places where they belong by virtue of titular personal names. A post-1980 influx of new sects and missions, funded by the metropolitan televangelist boom, also scattered people about as fresh converts moved away to repopulate empty places. When they can, people prefer only to live with family with whom they share political-religious affiliations. Once vaporous places, like Iakwanemwi's neighbor Ikurupu, are again bustling hamlets.

Tanna's network of named roads, some seen, others unseen, connects kava ground to kava ground from one end of the island to the other. The longest of these roads, including Kwatarhen, Neivo, and Mwatakeiu, loop around the island. Perimeter sea roads also encircle the island, while others connect specific landings or passages on Tanna with neighboring islands, and with other places far over the horizon in north-central Vanuatu. Men, thanks to their personal names, gain titular rights to send messages and goods up and down the roads connecting with partners at the next kava-drinking ground along the way. These roadmen control what properly flows through the network. In Bislama, people call these mediators "gates." In Nafe, road partners call one another *napugi nen-imen* (pupil or eyehole). Looking down the road, they stare directly into one another's eyes, catching attention. At kava grounds where major roads meet and cross, *kout kasua* transduce information and goods from one system to another. These *kout kasua,* who belong to neither island moiety, once stood between the two opposed solidarities Numrukwen and Koiameta. In Soarum's day, restless with new weaponry, they could pass information between hostile camps. Today, people use the label disparagingly to criticize those who let down their side or betray their family.

The Tannese insist that the island's grid of place and road, like its sets of personal names, is eternal and never changing. But men's names have indeed adjusted, in historic times at least, as most have transformed into binyms. Soarum became Soarum Isaac. People also name or rename places to celebrate personal experiences. New place names that augment island toponymy also get stereotypically reproduced from one generation to the next. Taken away to Australia, Iapwatu signed a labor contract to work in Queensland's Pioneer Valley, upriver from the sugar town Mackay. He may have toiled three years at Homebush or at another one of the valley's cane plantations. European migrants settled the area in the 1860s, some planting cotton then scarce in global markets thanks to the American Civil War. After 1865, planters shifted to sugarcane and recruited Tannese and other Melanesian workers to cultivate, harvest, and process this.

Thirty miles southwest from Homebush, the eroded remains of Nebo Volcano rise at the edge of the Pioneer Valley. The small township of Nebo lies farther west beyond this, connected then by bush track with Mackay. Coming home to volcanic Tanna after his years in Queensland, Iapwatu commemorated his travels abroad. He named a small plateau and resting point on Iankahar's southerly road after Mount Nebo. Another labor recruit who worked at the Homebush plantation carried that name, too, home with him. Ombus today names an area on the southern flanks of Iankahi Ridge, where the valley road splits to go either north to Port Resolution, or south to Kwamera. Another overseas recruit named his garden Imwaisuka, "place of sugar," after his Queensland experience. And still another brought home the name Iantina, now a hamlet namesake of Yandina, a small river town located seventy miles north of Brisbane.

The island's new Christians, too, were no slouch at renaming places. Near Ianpinan, the site of Neilson's and then Watt's Port Resolution church, a hamlet once inhabited by London Missionary Society Polynesian teachers came to be called Isamoa, after Samoa. Christian converts ransacked the Bible for new place names to signpost their faith. Ikurupu became Jericho; Irumanga Jerusalem; Isaka Galilee; and Imreag Nazareth. Other Christian communities around the island renamed their villages Bethany, Bethel, Tarsis, Athens, Macedonia, and Antioch. And, more secularly, also Sydney and Melbourne. Iapwatu and Iau rechristened Iankahar as Samaria.

Missionaries and their Presbyterian converts also remade Tanna's network of roads. They focused on those they actually could see and traverse on foot or horse, not so much the invisible *suatuk* exchange nodes veiled beneath the land or seascape. The road between Port Resolution and Kwamera, although these places are only a dozen or so miles apart, climbs high to cross an eastern spur of Mount Meren that falls precipitously into the sea. The Mathesons and Patons, and then the Watts and Neilsons, much disliked sailing in choppy waters along the coast between the two mission stations. A linking land route became viable when sufficient numbers along the way converted, ensuring safe passage. They cleared and widened footpaths as part of their new Christian duties, and by the 1870s mission parties were hiking back and forth, or riding on horseback.

The road from Port Resolution south to Kwamera passes through Iamanuapen, Iatapwir, Ikurupu, and then Iankwanemwi before it crests the ridge to descend again to the sea. After Iankwanemwi, the trail follows a deep and narrow passage, eroded between earthen walls. Agnes Watt, who knew her book of Numbers and who walked this mountain path many times, liked to call this defile "Balaam's Pass." Rushing to confer with the Moabites, biblical Balaam encountered an angel of the Lord who stood in a vineyard trail, a wall being on one side and a wall also on the other. But only Balaam's ass noticed the angel who stood in a narrow place, where there was no way to turn. The donkey, respectfully, fell at the angel's feet. Hapless Balaam then whacked her with his staff. Miraculously and suddenly talkative, she roundly rebuked her oblivious master.

Although lacking asses or angels, the south road today still squeezes through the narrow defile near Iankwanemwi. When the Presbyterians established additional east coast stations at Weasisi, and then at White Sands, the road between these new outposts and Kwamera passed through Iankahar, through Balaam's Pass, and then down south. This footpath today carries considerable traffic as people travel back and forth between east and south Tanna. A more recent, very rutted, sometimes impassable truck road parallels this as the colonial government pushed along the original missionary project of road expansion and improvement. Chinese and Australian international aid supported cementing the muddier patches, and later concreted the road's steeper stretches.

Missionaries schemed to put Christian converts to work, upgrading island roads for horse traffic, and building houses along the way for sleepovers. The new roads spread across Tanna after 1900 when swelling numbers of islanders, boosted by returnees from Queensland, organized novel Christian polities governed by Presbyterian moral codes. This religious regime—local folks called it "Tanna Law"—lasted from the early 1900s to the late 1930s. During this period, church police nabbed, and church courts tried and punished, backsliders and miscreants. Traditionalists like Soarum were outraged. Tenacious heathen they might be, Christian police arrested them too on morals charges. Drinking kava, adultery, cursing, stealing—any of these new sins was likely to get a man sentenced to thirty lashes, to impromptu imprisonment, or to forced labor on those expanding Christian roads. Iapwatu recalls Sero's punishment. Christian leaders forced him to plant mangoes, coconuts, and orange trees along a new Christian road that cut through Iankahar. Many of these trees, especially now stately mangos, still stand today. These lines of mangos and oranges mark the course of the old Christian pathways most still in use. A few, though, are lost beneath tropical overgrowth, with isolated mango trees surviving in unexpected places.

Soarum Again

Soarum held firmly to island *kastom* despite the mounting waves of Christian conversion that soon isolated him and other stubborn traditionalists. It was a losing battle. By 1890, Ikurupu, the next village down the mountain road to Port Resolution was hosting Sempent, a Christian teacher from Erromango. Ikurupu villagers also built a house for the itinerating Watts to use. Sempent died, and the Watts replaced him in 1892 with an Aneityumese teacher couple, Kamil and his wife. Just up the road at Iankwanemwi, Soarum's old kinsman Nasueiu converted that year. Agnes Watt wrote that Nasueiu put on a shirt, truly upsetting his orthodox wife who drew back in terror when busybody Agnes tried to shake her hand. She "uttered an exclamation of horror when she saw her husband being dressed in a shirt as the outward sign that from henceforth he was going to attend church."[6] Agnes reported that one or two "wild-looking fellows," Soarum perhaps, stood sullenly by eyeing this *kastom* apostasy.

Soarum's great-grandchild and namesake followed his grandfather Kauke, Soarum's prodigal son whom he had exiled to Iankahar, now renamed Samaria village, into the Presbyterian church. At least he did until he married a granddaughter of Nouar. Noaur's family was one of the first to join a new sect, the Seventh-day Adventists, brought to Port Resolution by subsequent missionaries in the 1930s. The newcomers had ambiguous relations with the Presbyterians. The Nouar of 1860 was an early supporter of John Paton and the mission, although Paton thought he was "changeable and doubtful" (figure 6a).[7] In 1862, Nouar urged Paton to abandon Tanna for both their sakes. His subsequent namesake (figure 6b), along with most families in 1930s Port Resolution, jumped from the Presbyterians to the Seventh-day Adventists. They replaced their pigs with goats and looked for a quicker end of the world.

After Vanuatu's independence in 1980, Soarum was one of the first teenagers from Samaria to attend high school. Completing this, he returned to Tanna and then, in 1987, moved up to a Port Vila migrant settlement. He wasn't alone. Most Samaria families then had already decided to send their children north to seek work in Port Vila. By the 1970s, even traditionalists admitted that education was the road for the good life. Young men and women headed for Port Vila to access better schooling and to earn more money to pay vexing school tuition and fees for their children and their siblings. In the 1970s, Samaria families earned

OLD NOWAR OF TANNA.

FIGURE 6A. Nouar, C. 1860.
From Maggie Whitecross Paton,
Letters and Sketches from the New Hebrides, 1894.

FIGURE 6B. Nouar, 1985. Photo by author.

an annual cash income of not much more than US $500, and school fees could burn through at least half of this. In years since, primary schools (except for many subsidiary charges) are tuition free, but parents still struggle to support any lucky children enrolled in Vanuatu's secondary schools.

Soarum, in Vila, found a job working for Unelco, Vanuatu's monopoly electric company. He disconnected and reconnected electrical service in the town's cash-poor settlements when people failed to pay, or then found enough money to cover the bill. After several years of working this depressing job, he saved enough to buy a used taxi. International tourism surged in the 1990s, and a swarm of taxi entrepreneurs made a living waiting for fares at Bauerfield Airport or at Port Vila's cruise ship dock. For twenty years, Soarum followed a different kind of road, driving around Port Vila's potholed streets. His own children are now grown; one son has studied law at the University of the South Pacific's Port Vila campus.

The Melanesian Labor Trade, too, has returned although transformed. Beginning in 2007, New Zealand and then Australia permitted the recruitment of temporary agriculture workers from Vanuatu. Islanders once again travel abroad to pick apples, kiwis, and grapes, or to fill boxes in fruit-packing houses. More than a century after Iapwatu sailed for Mackay's sugarcane fields, Soarum several times has left Port Vila behind to work in New Zealand, as has Glenda, his wife. Between the two of them, they made enough money to swap the taxi for a four-wheel drive Mitsubishi pickup truck, a vehicle sturdy enough, they hope, to survive Tanna's rough roads. They left Port Vila for home in Samaria, although Soarum has temporarily returned to town to take up a job as a driver for his relative, a member of Parliament. Thanks to Iasur and Port Resolution, tourism is booming on Tanna. Soarum and Glenda figure to raise and sell chickens to the string of tourist bungalows that have popped up along the road under the volcano. Motor transport remains limited on Tanna and, in addition to visitors hungry for chicken dinners, Soarum's taxi truck will also attract tourist vatu.

Most urban migrants claim, someday, that they too will come back to Tanna. Soarum and Glenda are among the first to attempt a homecoming. They returned to the island with plans to cultivate cash crops and raise chickens for sale. Migrant strategy, though, almost always involves leaving one or more grown children back in Port Vila. The trans-island family is now the modern ideal. Economic calculation suggests keeping one foot in Samaria, the other in Port Vila. Back home in Samaria, Soarum again walked and drove the road that skirts the gravesite of his unbending ancestral namesake. In Port Vila, his son pursues a degree in real estate law. The last century and a half of peripatetic people, of roads rerouted, of places renamed, has unsettled the landscape and clouded personal and village claims to home grounds. People are lawyering up.

Notes

1. Julius L. Brenchley, *Jottings during the Cruise of H. M. S. Curaçoa among the South Sea Islands in 1865* (London: Longmans, Green, 1873), 194.

2. Brenchley, *Jottings*, 202.

3. Brenchley, *Jottings*, 204.

4. R. S. Miller, *Misi Gete: John Geddie Pioneer Missionary to the New Hebrides* (Launceston: The Presbyterian Church of Tasmania, 1975), 300.

5. John G. Paton, *John G. Paton, Missionary to the New Hebrides: An Autobiography* (London: Hodder and Staughton, 1890), 231.

6. Agnes C. P. Watt, *Twenty-five Years Mission Life on Tanna, New Hebrides* (Paisley: J. and R. Parlane, 1896), 343.

7. Paton, *John G. Paton,* 187.

Further Readings

Labor Recruitment in Queensland

Adams, Ron. "Experiencing Outside Worlds: Tannese Labour Recruitment in the Second Half of the Nineteenth Century." In *Common Worlds and Single Lives: Constituting Knowledge in Pacific Societies*, edited by Verena Keck, 231–250. London: Bloomsbury, 1998.

Moore, Clive. *Kanaka: A History of Melanesian Mackay*. Port Moresby: Institute of Papua New Guinea Studies and University of Papua New Guinea Press, 1985.

Weapons Trade and Work in New Caledonia

Shineberg, Dorothy. *The People Trade: Pacific Island Laborers and New Caledonia, 1865–1930*. Honolulu: University of Hawai'i Press, 1999.

Maps of Tanna's Network of Kastom Roads

Guiart, Jean. *Un siècle et demi de contacts culturels à Tanna, Nouvelles-Hébrides*. Paris: Musée de l'Homme, 1956.

CHAPTER 7

Manehevi

SOMETIME AFTER 1900, MAPMAKERS found an English name for Green Point, a grassy headland on Tanna's southwest coast. Southerly Tanna rises steeply up toward Mount Meren and Tukosmera, and jumbled creeks and ravines cut down to the coast. Nafe language, spoken in Kwamera and Port Resolution, shades away along the southwestern coast into Naha. Green Point is isolated. When William and Agnes Watt left Kwamera for Port Resolution in 1891, mission attention focused northward. In the 1930s, the nearest Presbyterian mission to Green Point was nine miles up the west coast in Lenakel, and many people drifted away. Some listened to rival Roman Catholic and Seventh-day Adventist missionaries. Others recovered customary spiritual ties to their ancestors, to Mwatiktiki, and particularly to Karapenumun, a mountain spirit who haunts Meren's cloudy peak.

Manehevi, one lapsed Presbyterian, was a young man born about 1912. He lived along Meren's lower slopes at Isiwan, a hamlet associated with Iankwaneniai kava ground. His family had been nominally Presbyterian but abandoned the mission around 1930. Manehevi's celebrity, so far as we know this, began a decade later in 1941. He appears in the historical record, arrested and imprisoned, as the first of many prophets of John Frum, Tanna's latter-day and illustrious spirit guide.

Manehevi's troubles began when he tangled with the British district agent James Nicol. Nicol, a onetime mechanic who married into the planter community and worked his way up the colonial hierarchy, had ruled Tanna since 1915 as the island's sole colonial authority. Based in Lenakel, he relied on select, local leaders whom the British called "assessors" to surveil their villages, report misconduct, and help judge and punish mischief-makers. Nokues, one of Nicol's assistant assessors, in November 1940 brought forward a complaint about eight missing goats. A lukewarm convert to Seventh-day Adventism, Nokues nonetheless built up his own herd of goats after SDA missionaries instructed the congregations to substitute goat meat for the island's prestigious pork. Although feted throughout the Pacific, the Hebrew texts that American SDA prophet Ellen White consulted declared pig meat and pig carcasses most unclean.

Nicol did not bother much about the missing goats although he interrogated two likely suspects, Kahu and Karaua. The goats, the two explained, had fed crowds recently gathered to greet a shadowy apparition who called himself John Frum. Nicol, on 3 January 1941, noted the name in a letter to his superiors in Port Vila, launching John Frum's subsequent global celebrity. The island's handful of missionaries and traders were increasingly uneasy. Something was brewing. Rumors proliferated. Folks acted up. Almost everyone stopped producing dried coconut, then Tanna's only cash crop. The copra market had evaporated in 1940 when France fell to Germany. Mission bans on dancing and kava, in place for a generation, collapsed. People organized nighttime dances that pulled neighboring villages together, reviving customary exchange relationships. Many once abstemious men resumed kava drinking, spitting out their final gulps to honor and call out ancestral spirits.

And now John Frum. The spirit appeared regularly, but only during the night at Green Point's Iamwatarkarek kava-drinking ground. Various stories circulated. John Frum wore a white robe with a white veil that covered his face; or he wore long white trousers, white shirt, and tie; or he wore a long coat with shiny gold buttons. He spoke Nafe language, or he spoke some mystical spiritual tongue. He spoke with a high squeaky voice, a voice later described as "like radar." He cured disease with jabs. He foretold that the island would turn over. High and low places would level out, and the land would connect with neighboring Erromango and Aneityum Islands. John Frum preached: People must unite and disputes should cease. Hard work is finished. Whites will leave Tanna along with their money. Islanders from elsewhere should likewise go home. He will provide new money, John Frum money, to support a comfortable life. John Frum wrote down requests for favors in a big heavy book. One man requested power to revive circle dancing (*nupu*), banned among Christian converts. Another from Bethel village wanted a truck. Johnson Abil begged for wisdom. People today are pleased to argue that John Frum fulfilled most of these requests. Many trucks today drive Tanna's potholed roads. Nearly everyone dances *nupu* at important occasions. Johnson Abil's grandson was elected president of Vanuatu. Only one request failed to be fulfilled. A man from north Tanna, the last in line, wanted to become a child again after he died. John Frum refused the appeal, saying it was too late.

Messengers (or ropes) traversed the island's roads to spread the message, and people from all corners arrived in pilgrimage at Green Point. John Frum's new acolytes lined up to shake his hand and feel his flesh, including Soarum's son Kauke and his grandson Iau. Sometimes, though, when one reached out to him he faded away. Or, John Frum disappeared inside his round house leaving Kahu or other middlemen outside to translate his squawky mumblings. Pilgrims heard anchor chains of invisible ships rattling off Green Point. Back in Samaria, Soarum's son Kauke and his grandsons chewed over John Frum's message. Most left the mission, avoiding Presbyterian services and schools. Samaria's old church house went dark. Iau and others planted a red cross atop Nukwaneinupum, one of Mount Meren's foothills that overshadows the village. Today, a mobile phone transmission tower rises in its place. Years later, however, Iau and other disaffected followers would grumble that crafty Manehevi and Kahi had concocted John Frum's appearances, scheming merely to boost their chances for twilight sexual encounters with girls.

District Agent Nicol finally took action after Sunday, 11 May 1941, when only a handful of Islanders attended church and his own agency staff disappeared. Islanders that month mobbed Lenakel's trade stores in a frenzy of spending that topped £1,000. They tossed onto store counters nineteenth-century gold sovereigns long removed from circulation. Nicol went down to Green Point where, so his agents reported, people had built a new village with a round house for John Frum. He found the village empty, as were shelters built around the kava clearing for the visiting crowds. Only a few women and children hung about. Nicol retreated to request police reinforcements from Port Vila. When two dozen colonial native police arrived, he again marched south to Iamwatarkarek and arrested Kahu, Karaua, and nine other suspects. The police torched John Frum's village. As they led prisoners back north to Isangel, angry family and neighbors followed behind, shouting out that everyone must hold firm to John and keep the faith. The situation escalated when the party reached the Isangel Agency, but Nicol and his police managed to secure their prisoners and disperse the hostile crowd.

Manehevi was among the arrested. He had painted his face, as Tanna men and women do at important occasions. Kahu fingered Manehevi when Nicol demanded to know who was pretending to be John Frum. Nicol presumed some devious charlatan was impersonating the furtive spirit to no good end. He interrogated Manehevi but couldn't get much out of him. *Mi pleple nomo,* "I was only kidding," Manehevi replied. He wouldn't say where he had hidden John Frum's costume and book (which may have been a medical text retrieved from an abandoned dispensary). Manehevi could neither read nor write, and if he had impersonated John Frum, making lists in that book, his scribbling too would have been unworldly. In disgust, Nicol ordered Manehevi tied to an orange tree for a day near the old British prison at Irifo, figuring to make an example of him. Island memory claims that Nicol's policemen lined up to pull and twist Manehevi's nose. John Frum though, so people say, appeared that night to break his chains. To appease Nicol, Green Point elders organized a donation of £100 to recompense the Condominium for its troubles arresting Manehevi and the other John Frum suspects.

When the police returned to Port Vila the following week, they brought Manehevi and the other prisoners with them. Sir Harry Luke, British high commissioner for the Western Pacific, visited the following July and snapped a photograph of Manehevi in a prison line-up. Luke, who in Fiji had struggled with another nativist movement led by the prophet Apolosi, also took Manehevi to be another trickster rebel. Like Nicol, he presumed that Islander ignorance accounted for political gullibility. He concluded that Manehevi "has been attempting, by imposing himself on the more ignorant of his fellow-Islanders as a sorcerer, to organize an anti-white movement in Tanna."[1]

The Condominium sentenced Manehevi, Kahu, and Karaua to three years imprisonment and banished them from Tanna for another five. Less than a year later, though, flotillas of American military forces arrived in Port Vila. The United States was desperate for native labor, and Condominium authorities emptied out the prisons to release manpower. They also permitted American military recruiters to draft Islanders into labor corps. Manehevi went to work at a US Army Air Force camp. After the war, he disappeared from the written record. He made his way back home to a quieter life on Tanna, but to a Tanna that ever since has been the island of John Frum. Manehevi settled in Ikahaka-hak, near Green Point, married Karaua's widow, and had two daughters. He died sometime in the 1970s. Kahu, if indeed he was the original movement mastermind, also died in the 1970s from a wasting disease. People say he fell sick when he married again against John Frum's orders.

James Nicol likewise departed Tanna, although more spectacularly. Hopping down to open a gate in December 1944, his runaway jeep (a bit of abandoned American military cargo) squashed him against the gate after he forgot to set the brake. Who wouldn't ponder the logic of this sudden, unexpected demise, John Frum devotee or not?

Manehevi wasn't the sole John Frum suspect or sucker scapegoat. Despite Manehevi's incarceration in Port Vila, John Frum kept popping up around Tanna. In years since, the spirit continued to speak through a series of island prophets. Fred Nase was among the more recent of these, reworking John Frum message's into the Unity movement to absorb, he hoped, all ideological island factions. Nase's prophetic fame rocketed when he predicted that Lake Siui, which nestled for centuries at the foot of Iasur Volcano, would drain away. In 2000, it did.

Back in July 1941, soon after John appeared at Green Hill, his spirit sons Isaac, Jacob, and Last One manifested themselves to several girls from Ipikil village on east Tanna's Sulphur Bay. Nicol arrested nine more suspects and exiled them to prison in Port Vila to join Manehevi and the other Green Point detainees. In 1943, John Frum appeared yet again to his prophet Neloiag at Green Hill, in far north Tanna. Nicol, this time, was rattled enough to call for an American reconnaissance team, the wartime New Hebrides Defence Force Troop, and more colonial police. The American officers reconnoitered and lectured gathered villagers that the USA had no need for the new airfield that Neloiag had encouraged his followers to clear with bush knives and axes. Defence Force soldiers demonstrated what their machine guns could do by shooting apart Neloiag's notice board. The police burned down Neloiag's house. *Echo,* a small American Army service boat, carried another forty-six John Frum prisoners north to Port Vila.

Colonial suspicion of Manehevi shifted when his arrest failed to stifle John Frum. No more a trickster sorcerer, he was framed instead as a foolish dupe. British authorities took him to be a sucker, probably Kahu and Karaua's pawn. He was, they concluded, a shiftless man of no great intelligence and no fixed abode. He wandered from place to place. He made no gardens. He sponged off others. But Jean Guiart, French anthropologist who surveyed Tanna in 1951 and 1952, pinpointed Manehevi's home ground at Isiwan. He recorded that Manehevi possessed the prestigious right to eat the heads of turtles exchanged along the island's ritual road system and to wear the shorter ceremonial feather headdress. Manehevi's mother, before she died, had been a celebrated *kleva.*

Why could Manehevi, when Nicol interrogated him, only answer "I was just kidding?" If wily Kahu and Karaua scapegoated him, Manehevi's innocence or idiocy alone does not tell the whole story. Younger Tanna men often offer to suffer punishments meted out to family and friends, as several teenagers did when Nicol's police rounded up their fathers and grandfathers along with Neloiag. Manehevi, a relative of Jack Kahu, had his own reasons for taking the rap.

Cargo Cults

Anthropologists and others soon tagged the John Frum movement with the catchy new label "cargo cult," even though John Frum appeared some years before the term did. No more mere anti-colonial obstinacy, John Frum was reframed as an exemplar, the classic case even, of widespread postwar Melanesian social movements. The label cargo cult first appeared in the November 1945 issue of the colonial news magazine *Pacific Islands Monthly*. That month, Norris Mervyn Bird, whom the editors identified as an old Territories resident, wrote to warn of postwar flare-ups among Islanders misled by ill-digested Christian teaching and increasingly liberal and dangerous colonial policies. Bird was particularly perturbed that the new Australian Labour government in Canberra might liberalize its native affairs policies, including maintaining wartime Islander militias into the postwar era. Cargo cult chatter quickly spread through Australian academia, and then into anthropological circles overseas as ethnographers and others borrowed the term to label almost any sort of organized village-based social movement that professed religious and political aspirations, movements that were increasingly on colonialist and academic radar throughout Melanesia.

Cargo cult, the label, has continued to spread far beyond dry ethnographic accounts into unexpected corners of popular culture. In the final scenes, for example, of the 1962 film *Mondo Cane,* Gualtiero Jacopetti's original "shockumentary," we watch yearning Papua New Guinea Islanders clustered around a huge, roughly made wooden model airplane. They are gathered high up in the mountains, sitting on a new homemade airstrip carved out of the forest (like Neloiag and his busy followers, on Tanna). Their eyes eagerly search the skies, so the narrator tells us, for airplanes full of wondrous cargo that they expect will soon arrive. But they will be disappointed. No cargo planes will land. These Islanders are misguided followers of a tragicomic cargo cult.

The war mortally undermined the colonial system although the final effects of this would not play out in the Pacific until the 1970s. Postwar anthropologists turned away from describing coherent cultural systems and explaining social order to more pressing problems of disorder and social change. Previous social theory digested with great difficulty the mad frenzies of cargo culting wherein people were liable to dump traditional marriage custom in favor of free love, or resist economic modernity by discarding hard-earned shillings and pounds into the sea. Protest, insurrection, insurgence, and upheaval were then in the air, even in the far Melanesian fringes of the colonial world. And, just over the horizon, were the 1960s. In much of the West, civil rights, women's rights, anti-war, and anti-authoritarian movements soon would shake established powers and norms. Trance, dance, free love, drugs, cult communitarianism, the New Man, and the New Age all impugned corrupt and immoral political systems. Bizarre cargo culting, in obscure Melanesia, echoed developments within the postwar capitalist mainlands.

Leading their movements, cult prophets commonly drew on Christian millenarianism, sometimes conflating the arrival of cargo with Christ's Second Coming and Judgment Day (often called the "Last Day"). The word cargo (or *kago* in Melanesian Pidgin English) was rich in meaning. It signified various sorts of manufactured goods (vehicles, packaged foods, refrigerators, guns, tools, and the like) along with European money. Or, cargo represented the struggle for a new political order, the assertion of local sovereignty, and the withdrawal of colonial rulers. Or again, cargo metaphorically stood for human salvation and a final transcendence of everyday reality. The defining motif of the cargo cult, though, was unrequited desire for cargo itself. Having observed transports of military supplies during the Pacific War, cultists took to scanning the horizon for cargo submarines, planes, and John Frum's invisible ships.

A common theme in cargo cult stories was that island ancestors were key players in the production of manufactured goods. Some spun stories of a technologically wise ancestor who long ago had sailed away to America, or Europe, or Australia and there taught the secrets of cargo, leaving behind his dimmer brother who was ancestral to less technologically advanced island communities. The Tannese knew a version of this story. The saltwater that flooded from the buried sea snake Tagarua's eye socket washed away Islanders who, like James Cook, would one day return to Tanna, transformed. Other cargo myth asserted that wily Europeans stole industrial knowledge from Pacific ancestors, or were filching cargo that ancestors beneficently shipped back to home islands.

Cultists invented new rituals to induce the ancestral dead to reroute cargo flows. The cultic task was to penetrate the secret knowledge that people presumed to support European technological and political prowess, and to acquire this knowledge and associated goods alike. The human task was to restore local dignity and establish egalitarian relations with troublesome white newcomers. Alexander Rentoul, who oversaw the British agency on Tanna when Nicol took a few months leave in 1943, modeled pervasive colonial inequalities. When island men reached out to shake his hand signifying that they would abandon John Frum, he could only reluctantly comply: "I had never been a man to shake natives' hands, but as their request appeared to be an opportune manifestation of their desire to return to a more regular life, I was happy to receive them." John Frum notched another small success. White men would now, sometimes, shake one's hand.

After the war, the American military in some places assumed the imagined role of cargo provider. Like the Tannese, many Islanders elsewhere in Melanesia had worked on Allied bases where they received slightly better pay and gained access to a welcome variety of new wartime goods and services. When the militaries withdrew from the southwest Pacific, money and goods became scarcer. On Tanna, John Frum supporters predicted the return of US military units along with the wartime cargo they had enjoyed as labor corps recruits. John Frum leaders also incorporated wartime experience of military routines and equipment into postwar cult ritual and liturgy, including drill-team marching, bamboo rifles, red crosses (from Army ambulances), numbered dog (identification) tags, and khaki uniforms. Movement leaders at Sulphur Bay over the years have raised several American flags when they could get these (figure 7).

Many Pacific movements, in addition to simple material goods, pursued various sorts of social transformation. This, too, reflected political conditions at the end of the Pacific War. The Japanese advance dislodged the Dutch and the Australians from much of New Guinea and the British from the Solomon Islands. Large American occupation forces destabilized colonial authority in the New Hebrides and, to a degree, in New Caledonia and Fiji. At the war's end, when the colonial powers moved to reestablish their authority, Islanders who had mainly governed themselves during the war years resisted the reassertion of European control. Some cult prophets, in response, predicted that ancestors, or returning Americans, would drive the colonial powers from the region. In these areas, as on Tanna, cargo cults laid the groundwork for the nationalist Melanesian independence movements of the 1970s.

Melanesian cargo cults may continue to erupt, or they may prove to have been a twentieth-century reaction to globalization, colonial inequality, and the disruptions of world war. The trajectory of most cargo cults was short. Followers abandoned a prophet and his movement when no cargo arrived and the world did not transform. Active culting melted back down into background, ordinary cargo desire. Some movements, however, successfully institutionalized themselves and remain active in different forms. John Frum today is managed by third-and fourth-generation leaders and has elected members to Vanuatu's national parliament. Other onetime cargo cults have likewise been institutionalized into political parties, or new religions, or both. Some, like John Frum, serve as minor attractions celebrated and promoted by touristic entrepreneurs.

Much of the desire and energy that once animated Melanesian social movements gush today into new Evangelical and Pentecostal Christian mission

FIGURE 7. John Frum followers raise the flag, 1979.
Photo by author.

enterprises. Beginning in the 1980s, fundamentalist Christian missions based
in Australia, New Zealand, and the United States notably strengthened their recruitment efforts throughout the Pacific. Influenced by this renewed Christian
millenarianism, many Islanders have joined Holy Spirit movements. Rather than
waiting for cargo ships, followers instead seek to be possessed by the Holy Ghost
in order to bring about sudden transformations of self, society, and world. Typically, Christian leaders undertake healing and anti-sorcery campaigns, cleansing
villages of hidden sorcery paraphernalia feared to cause illness, death, and disorder. New Christian prophets predict the Last Day, the return not of cargo but of
Christ, and the impending establishment of a new cosmos. As Pacific Islanders

are increasingly absorbed into the world's economic order where inequalities persist and grow more profound, resistance movements (Christian, cargoist, or otherwise) certainly will endure.

Whatever cargo cult's future in the Pacific, the label itself has come to be widely applied, and no longer just in Melanesia. Cargo culting today may be anything that some critic deprecates. The term reproves projects that demonstrate fervid desire (for wealth, or whatever); involve some group or collectivity of the desirous; and whose desires, or the recommended means to achieve these, can be discredited as irrational. Tragic cargo desire mistakes tawdry material goods or dubious political programs to be real solutions to life's problems. The Internet abounds with many scolding examples of global cargo cults, as a form of rebuke.

But cargoist desire can also be an honorable sentiment as it was, occasionally, in accounts of Melanesian cultists. Good cargo culting celebrates personal development, creativity, and individual freedom. Cargo cult is a parable of our peculiarly modern mode of desiring, desire that is always ultimately unrequited, unquenchable, and never ending. This theme sustains cargo story's enduring popularity. As cultural moderns, we take desire to be naturally unrequited. We rightly crave human perfectibility, freedom, and wealth but we would be astonished should we one day actually realize all this. Self-development is, and should be, a never-ending task. Should aching desire terminate, so would life. Tales of exotic Melanesian cargo culting, thus, capture our own understandings of human desire as a constant, essentially unrequited, and universal impetus. Doesn't everyone want cargo? Isn't desire always infinite?

Kastom

John Frum supporters deny firmly that they are involved in any sort of cargo cult. They are, rather, connoisseurs of telling stories and seekers of truth. His followers' core truth is that John Frum saved Tanna *kastom*. Had John not appeared at Green Point, and just in the nick of time, colonial and missionary meddling would have eradicated cherished traditions and proper Tanna social order. From Green Point onward, John Frum's prophets and followers have preached the recovery of island *kastom*. Into these cultural recuperations, they mix island conceptions of overseas goods and practices, including American flags, marching and drilling, and nowadays much talk of economic development.

John Frum, despite his several identities as John the Baptist Frum, or John from America, or John Clever, first appeared as an indigenous island spirit.

Kahu testified to District Agent Nicol that the figure he initially encountered climbing about Green Point's rocky shores wearing a white robe, or perhaps this was a long coat with gold buttons, was Karapenumun. The powerful mountain spirit had descended from Mount Meren and wanted a house to be built nearer the beach, at Iamwatarkarek. His new name, so he told Kahu, was John Frum. His message advocated revival of *kastom,* of the island's customary social order that worrisome and deepening contact with mission and colonial outsiders had greatly undermined.

People at Green Point today say that Karapenumun, now John, first appeared to them along with Nakwa, his evil twin spirit. The two island spirits struggled and wrestled until John vanquished Nakwa, who escaped, disappearing over the mountain. Some Green Pointers jealously suggest that the runaway Nakwa was the bogus, second John Frum who materialized later in 1941 to girls at Sulphur Bay. Still others, defenders of true *kastom*, castigate John Frum followers everywhere as seriously misled. If Karapenumun truly had come down to Green Point as John Frum, he would have sported a *kastom* penis wrapper and not wrapped himself in some white bedsheet or buttoned jacket.

John Frum demanded that meddlesome European administrators and missionaries must return home, but so should people from other islands then living on Tanna, and so should the Tannese themselves. Importation of rifles and shotguns from the 1860s and resultant bloodier feuds had shaken customary connections between personal names and places. People ran from their homes seeking refuge with distant kin and exchange partners. Many in the 1930s were living away from home grounds. Refugee children could take names from new places, but land issues increasingly simmered.

John Frum advocated a return to kava drinking. This revived the main means to contact ancestors, many of whose bodies lie buried under the island's kava clearings. That last mouthful of kava drinkers spit into the air sprinkles down on these graves, opening up a communication channel. Drinkers mutter prayers and entreaties, and ancestral replies come to them as they sit quietly listening to the kava. Missionaries condemned kava as an evil intoxicant, a heathen alcohol even. They feared kava drinking as a pre-Christian sacrament. John Frum at Green Point appeared first to men, since only men properly drink kava. His new devotees prepared and drank many cups. In this sudden revival of kava drinking, *kastom* changed. Drinkers in these years began straining their kava infusions into half coconut shell cups rather than the canoe-shaped wooden bowls or folded banana leaves that their fathers had used. Where, I asked Samaria friends, did people find enough kava to drink in 1941? Despite thirty years of Presbyterian abstention, they said, Nekahi and his family strategically had remained outside the church, cultivating both kava and village ancestors in case island hearts might adjust, in case the spirits bounced back.

John Frum urged people to dance again. Missionaries disdained dance almost as much as they did kava. Dances are all-night affairs and they distrusted opportunities for illicit sex that festivity might allow. John's revivification of dance also recuperated pre-Christian society. As people perform the island's common circle dance, *nupu,* they sing of ancestors and spirits. And the dances that accompany gift-giving among kin and neighbors sustain Tanna's reticulated exchange network. People in Samaria, so recorded anthropologist Guiart in the early 1950s, said that they were reluctant to return to church because they were ashamed of their John Frum dancing and their kava drinking. Shame, perhaps, but kava and dance make island life exciting and meaningful.

What of *kastom* sexuality? Nicol and the missionaries were appalled that John Frum's nocturnal meetings might climax in uproarious orgies. There is little evidence of this. The Tannese, thanks either to island *kastom* or to years of somber Calvinist training, are remarkably modest, even prim folk. John Frum followers did not recoup the once customary *pran vi,* or village "prostitute" (so missionaries tagged her), a young unmarried woman who once served men living on kava-drinking grounds. Christian converts had abandoned customary men's houses and also *pran vi* long before 1941. Man, wife, and children by then all lived together in newfangled boxy houses in surrounding hamlets. Nicol, nonetheless, complained that John Frum Prophet Neloiag had promised "prostitutes for his soldiers and as many wives as they wanted."

Like effective social movement leaders anywhere, John Frum prophets mainly concerned themselves with social unity, with defusing conflict among followers. On Tanna, they sensibly concentrated on troublesome issues of sex and sorcery as major risks to social unity. Movements that failed to cultivate internal harmony or innovate mechanisms of social control did not survive long. Cargo leaders across Melanesia commonly had much to say about sex, either declaring an end to customary rules and constraints on this, hoping that this might lessen conflict, or demanding sexual abstinence from all. Cult leaders, likewise, were wary of *kastom* sorcery practices. On Tanna, John's followers eagerly retrieved and put back in service as many power stones as they could but they avoided the *nukwei nahak* once used to sicken and to kill.

Whether cult or movement, whoever at Green Point took the initial steps to create a John Frum church also followed *kastom* practice. The Tannese are masters at devising complex divisions of ritual labor. Customarily, men possessed diverse *kastom* rights to make rain; others the management of pig and crop fertility; others to direct the winds; and so on. Christian converts likewise assumed several different leadership roles within the church as elders, deacons, teachers, and more. John Frum's new acolytes, too, took on complementary jobs. Some served as his ropes or messengers. Some, like Manehevi, acted as his police, keeping order among the gathered throngs. John Frum job titles proliferated: governors of wages, of light, of food, of hurricanes, and even lawyers. Seventy years later, the latter-day prophet Fred Nase replicated this system. His Unity movement divided into a rainbow of affiliates. The red company functioned as movement police; the black supervised *kastom* law; the green managed John Frum heritage and issues; the white sought out and destroyed sorcery stones and other miscellaneous evils; and the yellow specialized in curing the sick.

John Frum's message celebrated home ground and *kastom* but it also incorporated the alien and the new. Novel therapeutic techniques like *stik* (injections) addressed steady anxieties about health and healing. Money, too, had come to stay. John's followers ditched their British pounds and French francs to encourage whites to leave Tanna but in return John would provide a new currency. The £100 that Nicol received, presuming this was recompense for cultic bother, might have been payment for him to go home. If the Presbyterian and Catholic day of rest was Sunday, and the Seventh-day Adventists honored Saturday, John's day would be Friday. Friday remains the movement's holy day although the Prophet Fred later took Wednesday as his own. Like Christians, John Frum devotees conceived hymns and John Frum prayers. They erected John Frum crosses. They laid offerings of flowers at John Frum altars. Whether or not Manehevi could read and write, John Frum's other prophets have brandished various books, scribblings, and signboards, their own sacred texts.

And there is cargo. Islanders took the growing numbers of planes up in wartime skies to be John Frum's, as were those curious ships steaming north and south along the horizon. And what was *stil* (steal), marvelous technologies like radar with which one could see at great distances, or make the invisible visible? The world, and the war, were closing in. The Tannese, in 1940, were already where many of us find ourselves today, sinking deeper into economic regimes of unrequited desire, of unquenchable demand. They faced relentless questions of making sense of the outlandish, of resituating themselves within a changing world. What to make of messy and increasing global flows of people, of things, and ideas? What's with the new, the alien? What happens to the old, the familiar?

One response is to celebrate *kastom*: to become a cultural and religious fundamentalist and find comfort in local ideas, in home cooking, in mother tongues, and in faiths of fathers. Anthropologists have, with reason, explained cargo cults as social revitalization movements that preached fundamental themes of nativism, nationalism, cross-cultural accommodation and adjustment. More ni-Vanuatu again actively revaluated *kastom* in the 1970s, in the lead-up to the archipelago's independence. What would it mean to be ni-Vanuatu? What might glue the new nation together? National identity and unity, too, rooted themselves in honorable island *kastom*.

The world today is awash with comparable social movements that reflect and address present unhappiness and future worry, be these Tea Parties in the United States, Islamists in the Middle East, Hindu fundamentalists in India, or ultranationalist parties in Europe. John Frum's messages and prophesies likewise struggle with pressing questions, then as now. Manehevi, Kahu, Karaua, and Nicol are long gone from the island. John, though, remains as do the two elongated stones he left behind at Green Point to mark the promise of his second, third, and many more future comings.

In 1941, British and French colonials caught in the far Pacific suffered their own wartime anxieties. John Frum certainly echoed these. After the New Year of 1942, Presbyterian missionary doctor William Armstrong intercepted a letter that Joe Nalpin, in Port Vila, sent to his father Somo (Semu) in Lenakel, on Tanna. Nicol had arrested Nalpin, a traditional healer, for cheating his patients, jailing him in Port Vila. Nalpin wrote Somo that John appeared again to him, as he had for several years, asking for a house to be built in Sydney village, overlooking Lenakel. No one on Tanna any longer should fear arrest and colonial repression, for John "will send his son to America to bring the king." Here was another truthful John Frum prophecy. America arrived in force two months later.

Note

1. Harry Luke, *From a South Seas Diary* (London: Nicolson and Watson, 1945), 203–204.

Further Readings

Manehevi

Rice, Edward. *John Frum He Come: Cargo Cults and Cargo Messiahs in the South Pacific*. Garden City, NY: Doubleday, 1975.

John Frum

Barrow, G. L. "The Story of Jonfrum." *Corona* 3, no. 10 (1951): 379–382.

Guiart, Jean. *Un siècle et demi de contacts culturels à Tanna, Nouvelles-Hébrides*. Paris: Musée de l'Homme, 1956.

O'Reilly, Patrick. "Prophetisme aux Nouvelles-Hébrides: Le Mouvement Jonfrum à Tanna." *Le Monde Non-Chrétian* 10 (1949): 192–208.

John Frum and Fred Nase

Tabani, Marc. *John Frum: Histoires de Tanna*. Port Vila: Pacifique Dialogues—VKS Productions, 2014.

Cargo Cults

Lindstrom, Lamont. *Cargo Cult: Strange Stories of Desire from Melanesia and Beyond*. Honolulu: University of Hawai'i Press, 1993.

Kastom Politics in Vanuatu

Keesing, Roger and Robert Tonkinson, eds. "Reinventing Traditional Culture: The Politics of *Kastom* in Island Melanesia (special issue)." *Mankind* 13, no. 4 (1982).

CHAPTER 8

Nouar

RESIDENTS OF PORT VILA watched in panic as a fleet of dark ships appeared on the southern horizon on the morning of 4 May 1942. That same day, the Japanese invaded and captured Tulagi, the colonial capital of British Solomon Islands northwest of the New Hebrides. To the west, opposing naval forces fought the Battle of the Coral Sea blocking Japanese plans to occupy Port Moresby in Australian Papua. Those nervous watchers sheltering in Port Vila were relieved to spot American colors as the fleet approached. These ships, guarded by naval escorts, carried Task Force 9156's 6,500 men, comprised mostly of the old Buffalo Soldiers African American 24th Infantry Regiment and the 4th Field Artillery Battalion. The ships were crammed with cargo: trucks, jeeps, Quonset huts, seaplanes, bulldozers, hospital equipment, seacoast guns, radio stations, refrigerators, ammunition, a million dollars in US currency, and more.

Port Vila then boasted only rudimentary docks, and cargo laden on these ships and many more to come had to be winched onto smaller boats and lightered ashore. Those Buffalo Soldiers were onboard for good reason. African Americans offloaded and stored cargo, drove trucks, and worked other service jobs until, near the war's end, domestic pressure at home convinced political and military authorities to let them fight. But the regiment needed help, especially as military planners rushed to complete a nearby airfield, build roads, construct a large hospital, and set up water, electrical, and telephone systems. Working through Condominium authorities, the Americans recruited native labor corps, first rounding up men on Efate and then on the nearby Shepherd Islands. Needing still more hands, they soon swept up nearly all able-bodied men from Tanna and shipped them north to Efate's new wartime installations.

In August 1942, the military cargo ship *Cape Flattery* on her way north from New Caledonia moored off Lenakel to load up Tanna recruits. Islanders then called any sizeable ship like this a "mail boat." District Agent James Nicol ordered his assessors to round up island workers, appointing gang bosses from every corner of Tanna. John Frum already had prepared the way. Island men were ready to go. Assessor Nagia named Thomas Nouar and his nephew Nako Georgy as boss men over the Nepraineteta, the "body of the canoe," the valley that runs from Iasur Volcano east toward Port Resolution. Soarum's teenaged grandsons Rapi and Iau came down from Samaria to join the region's team of nearly one hundred men.

Nouar had some schooling and was young and ambitious. He was also a Seventh-day Adventist, or had been. After missionary William Watt and his family retired to Melbourne, Australia in 1910, island deacons and elders supervised Port Resolution's Presbyterian congregation. By the 1930s, however, distance from the main mission station at White Sands and economic disruptions of the global depression shredded Presbyterian enthusiasm. Taking advantage of this apathy, rival SDA missionaries found willing converts. People liked the different sabbath day, and pork taboos were perhaps no more onerous than Presbyterian bans on kava drinking. SDA converts learned American four-part harmonics, domestic cooking skills, and boosted their goat herds. Most of these disciples, including Nouar, would shortly forsake SDA affiliations a few years later in 1939 when John Frum materialized.

Called to gather in Lenakel, the Body of the Canoe work team prepared a farewell feast. Men roasted pigs, drank a last round of kava, and marched all night crossing the island. At daybreak, they sat on the beach, watching the horizon. SS *Cape Flattery* appeared at daybreak and anchored in Lenakel passage. American agents boated ashore, counted and medically examined the recruits, and recorded their names. They handed out dog tags. Nouar's number was 66. The beach filled with sobbing women and children. As men waited to board, American sailors called for them to "dance, dance." And while aboard *Cape Flattery,* too, the work teams continued to dance making the ship's steel decks ring.

Everyone embarked, the *Cape Flattery* sailed north at dusk arriving in Port Vila the next morning. Island recruits came ashore and were trucked to encampments scattered around the town. Nouar and his men found themselves sleeping in tents at Tebakor, near newly established American troop bivouacs. They went to work immediately, offloading cargo ships that steamed into Vila Harbor. They served ten-hour shifts, some working during the day, and some overnight, seven days a week, bringing cargo up from ships' holds and moving this from dock to trucks to newly constructed warehouses. They offloaded ammunition, fuel drums, and crates of food, unpacking ships' holds layer by layer. "Sometimes we came to work and carried out bombs," Nouar recalled. "We worked one ship each week. When this ship was finished, it left and another ship came. After we unloaded it, trucks carried away the food, the bombs, and the Marsden matting for the airport."[1] Nouar and his gang kept dancing. American sailors on the ships and soldiers on the docks called out dance requests. "If the night was cold, the Americans said, 'okay, dance, dance, dance!'"

Condominium authorities first insisted on managing Islander labor corps, only lending these to the US military. The colonials were edgy that the war could upend comfortable racial inequalities, and anxious that Americans not overpay workers causing future plantation wage inflation. After a month of colonial management, Nouar and other island workers complained bitterly about the food that Condominium authorities provided. "They gave us Fiji taro and rotten bananas, woody manioc, stinking salt meat. People nearly died the hunger was so bad." Nouar brought a plate of putrid food over to the American camp and spoke to a supervisor. Together, they went to consult a military officer based on Iririki Island:

> He took the food and led me, with police coming along with guns. We two went to find the bigmen in their office; one was white and one black. We went in and they discussed the problem and, that evening, the Americans had already sent us rice. And they gave us meat. And gave us different kinds of fruit, and all different foods. And they gave us clothes; they stacked up clothing in a huge pile. Trousers, coats, you passed by and if you saw your size you took it. And books, and hats, and shirts.

The US military had neither time nor patience for colonial decorum and none for colonial incompetence. After that first month, it assumed responsibility for housing, feeding, and supervising the labor corps. Colonel Steven D. Slaughter, general staff officer in charge of logistics, took command assisted by Major George Riser, helped by Sergeant Edward F. Power and Navy Boatswain Thomas Beatty (figure 8). Power and Beatty bunked in or near the workers' camp and memory of both endures on Tanna, today: Beatty as John Frum's American confident Tom Navy, and Power as a feisty amateur boxer who tutored young island workers in the sport.

Nouar recalled a continuous flow of hearty food and supplies: "America provided the food we ate; we ate until we were full then threw it away. They gave us food, gave us clothing, gave us shoes, boots, coats, long coats for the cold nights when we worked. Blankets, we slept in blankets. Pots, plates, forks, knives, everything." Pairs of men from the Nepraineteta gang rotated cooking responsibilities. American supervisors also loaded up Tanna workers with cigarettes,

FIGURE 8. Colonel Riser (center), Sergeant Power (right) with Tanna workers at Riserville and possibly Thomas Beatty, back right, 1942. Photo owned by author; courtesy of Colonel Steven D. Slaughter.

converting most into lifelong smokers with a particular penchant for unfiltered Camels that endures on the island.

After several months at Tagabe, Nouar and his work team moved to another camp near Bauerfield, the newly cleared landing strip where they built village-style housing. Riser (or his teasing friends) named the workers' camp Riserville. After military activity shifted north to extensive new installations on Espiritu Santo, cargo ship arrivals at Port Vila slowed. Nouar witnessed the beginnings of base installations on Santo. He caught a ride north on a US ship that also called at Malo and Malakula Islands. Back in Vila, the labor corps went to work building roads and spraying DDT on water sources to control malaria. They interacted with additional US servicemen besides their labor supervisors. Nouar befriended one officer who suffered from asthma. When not working the docks, he visited to fan him, keeping him cool. Nouar also met a black American soldier named Jesse and others named Thomas, Walter, and Captain West. Tanna workers were particularly impressed by African American soldiers. Nouar knew that the 24th Infantry Regiment had its own encampment, although he did not appreciate the depth of contemporary American racial segregation.

Instead, Tannese workers noted favorably that black men like themselves worked dock machinery, drove jeeps, trucks, and tractors, and managed the storage of military cargo.

The noise and constant hubbub of wartime Port Vila astonished island workers who until then were unfamiliar with trucks, electric lighting, aircraft carriers, airplanes circling and landing, anti-aircraft artillery, and a harbor full of cargo ships. Strange radar systems installed on towers and in trees and air raid klaxons particularly impressed them. They called both *stil* (steal) or *glas* (glass) and made ready comparisons with their own island power stones that also reveal and identify hidden forces.

Nouar and his team found time to watch American movies at a new outdoor military cinema built on Malapoa Point, or in a makeshift theater in Riserville. Some Islanders went into the curio business, making bark skirts and carvings to sell to servicemen. They occasionally drank beer secretly with Americans, or jungle juice, a home brew fermented with yeast and tinned fruit. They regularly disappointed Americans who were on the hunt for local women, telling them "we too have no women in Vila." American soldiers and sailors spoke no Bislama, but Tanna workers quickly learned pertinent military slang including *suk,* a term for sex that survives in Hawaiian Pidgin English. Nouar was thankful that women were scarce. He was suspicious of the condoms he came across during the war, and figured that if aroused soldiers had stumbled across some vulnerable girl, "she would have died!"

Nouar worked a year on Efate for the Americans. Some Islanders went home after three months, while others shipped north to take their place. Others served for several years. Wages were not great, 25 cents a day following colonial regulation, but many workers earned extra money laundering uniforms, climbing coconut trees, sweeping barracks, or even just dancing. Workers returned home to Tanna with caches of American coinage, clothing, blankets, dynamite, and other souvenirs, although Condominium authorities attempted to confiscate this. Nouar held onto his military dog tag, number 66, until it disappeared years later in one of his houses that decayed and collapsed.

Nouar and his fellow labor recruits were amazed by wartime sights and sounds, but not completely surprised. Nor were they frightened. John Frum, after all, had foretold what to expect. Nouar explained:

> John Frum had already told people that men would come. America. They would arrive and that when we meet America, don't be afraid. We knew that our brothers were coming. John Frum had already predicted this to us

so we weren't afraid of dying. He advised us that Americans would come. We were ignorant of planes and he was the first to say that planes would arrive. We were ignorant of lots of things but he said that trucks would arrive. Our trucks would come. Our planes would come. Our ships would come. Since then we have understood, and today black men have all these things. John Frum was the first to say the name of America. We know that he spoke truly in that we saw America arrive.

As the battle front moved northwest, operations at the US bases on Efate and Espiritu Santo peaked and then declined. The Americans, though, did not fully pullout until 1946. That year, mortuary teams arrived to exhume several hundred US burials at Port Vila's Freshwater Cemetery, shipping remains home mostly to Hawai'i's Punchbowl National Memorial Cemetery of the Pacific. War echoes linger, though, in Efate's road system and in Vanuatu's main international airport, Bauerfield, named after Marine fighter pilot Harold ("Joe") Bauer, shot down in action off Guadalcanal. Tourists who land on Bauerfield may find their way to a couple of local museums on Efate's north shore that curate all sorts of wartime detritus. And on Tanna, returning workers swiftly incorporated an array of military practices and symbols into John Frum ceremony. The movement smartly acquired drill teams, an army, red and black crosses, radio antennae, model airplanes, and more.

Home on Tanna, Nouar in the 1950s edged away from the John Frum movement and rejoined the Seventh-day Adventist mission. He took advantage of mission opportunities to travel widely, and he continued his leadership responsibilities, particularly after island converts assumed management of the Port Resolution SDA congregation. Most of his family has followed him into that church, including a granddaughter who married today's Soarum, from Samaria. Like John Frum, who celebrated his connections both with Tanna and with America, Nouar sought to deepen relationships with his American brothers. He appreciated the war's shared dangers and recalled its brotherly cooperation. If American servicemen gave much to Tanna workers, Islanders balanced accounts with their own solid support and hard work. Americans were young but good men, Nouar said, and "love was in them." But love was in the Tannese, too.

In 1989, I carried home to Tulsa, Oklahoma, a letter that Nouar had dictated and I delivered this to a neighborhood SDA pastor. Nouar, partly, was angling for a wristwatch that would remind him of his American wartime companions. One, he said, that would permit him "to see their faces again in it." Mostly, though, he just wondered, "Do they remember us, or have they forgotten?"

War

A century before American troop ships anchored in Port Vila's harbor, the Tannese studied their own wars. As had 1940s Nouar, so did Nouar's namesake of the 1840s and 1860s. Missionary chroniclers, especially the great Presbyterian propagandist John G. Paton, complained often of black-hearted Tanna assassins and bloody ambushes. Denigrations of dark Tanna justified Evangelical projects and the mission agenda of "winning cannibals" for Christ. This proved difficult. The series of pandemics that swept through the island beginning in the 1830s stoked intensifying intercommunal violence as survivors sought balance and revenge.

Islanders initiated an arms race, adding European muskets to their arsenals of clubs, slingshots, throwing stones, and spears. Flows of weaponry into Tanna increased significantly from the 1860s when many men and boys, and some women and girls, recruited to work on plantations in Queensland, Fiji, or Samoa, returned home with guns, powder, and bullets. People blamed missionaries, as well as one another, for the era's rampant death and disease. On Elau's Erromango Island, having dispatched John Williams and James Harris in 1839, Islanders two decades later would kill several other worrisome Presbyterian missionaries including, the Canadian missionary brothers George and James Gordon who set up stations on the island.

Missionary accounts of Nouar find him at Port Resolution, then on Aneityum, and later on Aniwa. Men then, as now, traveled around. In the 1850s, Nouar was living at Port Resolution, near the Fishtale's tip. Around 1855, he canoed to Aneityum to visit the Presbyterian establishment there, and he agreed to host two Aneityumese teachers, Abraham and Nimtiwan, who joined him back on Tanna. When Scottish missionaries John Paton and Joseph Copeland arrived at the Port in 1858, Nouar looked after them as well although this sparked a critical and sometimes violent response from his neighbors who blamed their ill health on the immigrant Europeans.

During Paton's three years at Port Resolution, Nouar supported the mission in regular community discussions and debates. More than once he rescued Paton from harm, for example warning him not to eat a poisonous fish. Paton wrote:

> The Chief Nowar Noukamara, usually known as Nowar, was my best and most-to-be-trusted friend. He was one of the nine or ten who were most favourable to the Mission work, attending the Worship pretty regularly, conducting it also in their own houses and villages, and making generally

a somewhat unstable profession of Christianity. One or more of them often accompanied me on Sabbath, when going to conduct the Worship at inland villages; and sometimes they protected me from personal injury.[2]

Paton hoped to deploy Nouar, whose influence he imagined extended eight to ten miles inland from Port Resolution, to spread the gospel. Nouar, however, was more concerned with defusing escalating island violence. He hosted a large feast and dispute-settlement meeting at which he declaimed "that all war and fighting be given up on Tanna, that no more people be killed by Nahak, for witchcraft and sorcery were lies."[3]

War (*naruagenien*) and violence, however, continued to spark. Himself targeted by sorcerers, Nouar begged to retreat with Paton to Aneityum Island, but Paton refused. Desperate, Nouar dropped his Christian shirt and lavalava for penis wrapper and face paint to keep his head a little lower. In January 1862, angry inland villagers met and decided to chase Paton and his Aneityumese teachers off the island and a regional war broke out. Again protecting Paton, Nouar took a spear in his right knee. His son-in-law Faimugo guided Paton's overland escape south to John and Mary Matheson's station at Kwamera, leaving Nouar behind to defend himself as best he could.

Paton grudgingly appreciated Nouar's patronage and his peace-making, but called him changeable, doubtful, wavering, unstable, cowardly, and of struggling faith. Mary Matheson was kinder. She met Nouar at Port Resolution in May 1860 when he helped paddle her ashore. She lent him her old brown hat which made him "a very comical looking figure head." Paton's second wife Maggie also appreciated Nouar's efforts to establish a new Christian peace. Paton and Maggie returned to the New Hebrides in 1866, but holed up on the small Polynesian-speaking islet Aniwa, off Tanna's east coast. In November 1867 she gushed, "Oh, how I loved and respected him!—this man that risked his life to save my husband. I had read of such devoted love, but have never seen another living specimen . . . he showed me the very scars on his body, where he had received the wounds intended for 'my Missi.'"[4]

Nouar met Paton again during a brief return to Port Resolution. There, he found Shark, or a Pavegen namesake, and charged him with Paton's keep, so Mrs. Paton wrote:

It seems that, when dear old Nowar found he could not have his old Missi [missionary] back again, he took Pavingin aside and told him that he now gave Missi Paton into his charge, and begged him earnestly to do everything

he could to make him comfortable, and to tell the people of Aniwa to be
strong to do the Worship of Jehovah. . . . then finished up by taking the
white shells from his own arm, binding them round Pavingin's, and telling
him to wear them, and every time he looked at them to remember his words
about being kind to Missi.[5]

Noaur along with a hundred other Tannese took refuge on Aniwa in 1875, escaping from the ongoing bloody violence and warfare that continued to unsettle
Port Resolution. Maggie might have welcomed her dear old Nouar, but Paton
refused to baptize him, always suspicious of his essential Christian convictions.

Nouar later returned home to Tanna, or a namesake took his place back
on the island. The Nouar of the 1930s and 1940s had moved inland, about a
mile south of the harbor. It was here that he encountered the Seventh-day Adventists and then the American military. His ancestral namesake had worked
persistently to restore peace to Tanna, building missionary alliances, hosting
regional debates and feasts, evoking new religious harmonies, lamenting wounds
and scars, and manipulating white shell armlets. Forty years of devastating illness, killings, and precipitous wars abated only toward the end of the century,
after many island men and women had left Tanna to work on Queensland's cane
plantations and cattle operations; after the arms race equalized and everyone
brandished Snider-Enfield breech-loading rifles; and after the island population
had crashed but then began to stabilize. People had enough of sickness, warfare,
and death. Multiplying Christian conversions after 1900 dampened Tanna's
communal violence for good.

Tanna today remains a reasonably peaceful place with few murders. Husbands and wives may get feisty and occasionally bash each other, but kin and
neighbors rush in quickly to soothe spiraling emotions. Neighbors argue about
rights to land and about pigs who steal from gardens. Men hold grudges quietly for years, but only occasionally flame into mad rages. Everyone watches
for violence, and hurries to appease and mollify antagonists before things get
out of hand. Social relationships sometimes can be raucous, but *namarinuien*
(peace) is the main goal. With no traditional central political authority, and a
distant government, Islanders are notably skilled at debating their problems,
settling disputes, or at least avoiding one another until tempers cool. Parents
indulge children, rarely striking them. Older children are schooled not to smack
younger siblings but rather let smaller ones cuff them instead. People have re-
claimed all sorts of the power stones that their forebears surrendered when admitted to church membership except for the *nukwei nahak,* the magic stones

of death. *Namarinuien,* that peace and calmness of the seas and skies, and in relations among neighbors and family, with foresight and effort ordinarily can be achieved.

Still, echoes of island violence and war redounded in the memories and life experiences of some elders when America arrived in 1942. John Frum prophecy stoked men's martial enthusiasm. They took the war as a new chance to paint their faces. They read the military's compound bureaucratic structure (army, army airforce, navy, marines, seabees, and Negro) in terms of Tanna's own moiety system that once shaped bellicose island allegiances. The stars and stripes, for the Tannese who combine lighter blue colors with green, and darker ones with black, was appropriately colored red, white, and black. Quonset huts reminded them of *kuvipehe,* the island's traditional house whose roof descends low to the ground. Islanders revised Tanna origin stories that narrate a mythic separation of the two original brothers Nuras and Patras, one staying on Tanna, the other lost away in America but now returned in force. The war celebrated their reunion. Magicians on Tanna withdrew to dense forests and shady caves, working their war power stones to ensure an American victory over Japan. American soldiers were their lost and found brothers-in-law from across the sea.

Dance and Song

Captain Cook, sailing away from Port Resolution at daybreak, 20 August 1774, caught a noise coming from the tip of the Fishtail "which was not unlike singing of Psalms." Ship naturalist Johann Forster, too, heard "a slow solemn song or dirge" coming from the point. Missionaries Mathesons, Johnston, and Paton likewise appreciated song. Good disciples of John Calvin who advocated hymning the psalms, they liked to join their voices in praise. On Tanna, they cast about for a Nafe word for hymn and found *nupu,* which can indeed mean song but also dance. They and their subsequent Christian converts translated more than 140 Presbyterian hymns into Nafe, and composed many new ones.

Whereas missionaries discriminated sacred song from mundane and possibly unholy dance, Tanna folk integrally connect voice and body. *Nupu* is the island's main circle dance which, like most southern hemispheric circle dances, rotates counterclockwise. Men dance together in a central cluster. Women form pairs to skip rapidly around this masculine nucleus. With no accompanying musical instruments, dancers create a rhythmic beat by clapping, stomping, humming, and singing. Islanders have other, choreographically more intricate dance styles, particularly those presented during regional pig-killing (*nakwiari*) festivals that incorporate clever miming performances. *Nupu,* though, is the usual village standard.

Celebrations of a boy's circumcision, his first shave, a marriage, or a death involve an exchange between principal families of raw and cooked garden produce, pigs, kava, plaited baskets and mats, women's bark skirts, blankets, and two-meter lengths of calico cloth. After eating, speech making, and kava drinking at dusk, celebrants begin *nupu* dancing on the village's kava clearing. Hosts lead off and then alternate dance sets with their guests. Dance continues throughout that night until daybreak, although some feast organizers in recent years have shortened dancing and moved this from night to day. People also dance *nupu* to mark other important occasions including Vanuatu's national day of independence, every 30 July, or the visits of politicians and other luminaries. Nowadays, entrepreneurial villagers arrange daytime *nupu* performances for passing tourists and charge them to watch and photograph.

Dancing on the decks of American cargo ships in Port Vila Harbor, Nouar and his World War II work gang jumped into *nupu* to entertain sailors and soldiers. Nouar recalled that they also performed other circle dance styles, including *nupu ikou* and *tarakini.* The stomping of dancers' feet on ships' steel decks produced a satisfying ringing thunder, reminiscent of the booming, volcanic soils back home on Tanna. Wartime dancing echoed island partnerships: Two sides united in some shared celebration of enterprise. Despite exhausting work unloading cargo, Nouar and his team nonetheless were pleased to dance. Goofy Americans sailors and soldiers joined in. "They called to us, 'dance, dance!' . . . when we danced some came to dance with us, to try to dance, too. They tried to dance like us. They swung their arms and stomped their feet."

Dance is also song. Feast organizers, properly to celebrate an occasion, commission songsmiths to find new songs. Customarily, these songsmiths receive gifts of kava and a white fowl. They retire to some secluded forest glade to listen for ancestral voices, eating chicken and drinking kava. Relying on inspiration, rather than personal creativity, expert island songsmiths tap into the world of buzzing spirits, eavesdropping on ancestral lyrics and melodies. A newly revealed *nupu,* once the songsmith reappears to teach this, often celebrates the festive occasion and the leading men and women involved. Villagers practice dancing the song, and then perform for their admiring guests. The *nupu* becomes part of a family's repertoire, although many *nupu* from times past have lost connection with particular families (or name-sets) and belong to everyone associated with a particular kava clearing.

Songs serve as an important historical archive. *Nupu* associated with this or that place chronicle past namesakes' achievements and remarkable local events. Every feast, every exchange brings these to mind as dancers tap into a thick repertoire of song. Island stories typically feature snatches of a song that ornament narrative myth, legend, or folktale. Orators and storytellers embellish truth claims by breaking into song, into some informative chant that asserts and reminds as an audience listens. Before he died, missionary Samuel Johnston described island orators working the crowd at one 1858 public meeting that he attended at Port Resolution:

> When these orators wish to show particular honour to the meeting and to interest the audience, they sing a portion of their address. The speaker walks the length of the ground occupied by him while speaking. While doing so, he sings a verse. He returns in silence, apparently composing another verse. After thus singing a number of spontaneous poetical effusions, he concludes his speech in prose.[6]

Only the poetical effusions that Johnston caught (but could not understand) were neither spontaneous nor composed on the spot. Orators, instead, would have sung familiar family lyrics to assert some specific point or claim.

The Pacific War inspired Tanna's labor corps recruits to come up with new songs to chronicle their wartime experiences. Entertaining American military personnel, Nouar and his work team sang island *nupu* as they danced. They also picked up American wartime standards including the Navy's *Anchors Away* and *You Are My Sunshine*. The war sparked a new musical genre based on the string band when Islanders acquired guitars and ukuleles. This style remains popular today, although augmented and renovated over the years with strong musical borrowings from global reggae and rap.

Tanna songsmiths went to work, singing their war experience as *nupu* and as string band tunes. A song from Nouar's gang (translated from Nafe) recalls the night march to Lenakel and transport to Port Vila on *Cape Flattery*:

> We were living well. Then heard the message the government sent first to people of White Sands;
> We got up and left to try to find out. The mail boat was coming. Our hearts were sad;
> Daylight broke. The soldier counted us. Hunger took us and our hearts remembered our homes;

Up the gangway, the soldier counting. Some went aft; some
went forward;
Looking landward we saw two airplanes coming; looking upward
we saw two stars on the wings;
Someone called out to us. We carried our portmanteaus, filled two
launches and arrived at Ballande's wharf;
The American bosses divided us and led us to Iariki plantation.

War songs, like this from the 1940s, continue to remind people of wartime
events just as earlier mission hymns circulated news of biblical personages and
God's grace, and as *nupu* celebrate ancestral lives. Every dance incarnates the
spirits. Every song reprises history. In song, Nouar of the 1840s and Nouar of
the 1940s are recollected and reanimated.

Notes

1. This and subsequent quotations derive from a recorded interview with Thomas
Nouar, 1983.

2. John G. Paton, *John G. Paton: Missionary to the New Hebrides, an Autobiography*
(London: Hodder and Stoughton, 1890), 214–215.

3. Paton, *John G. Paton*, 215.

4. Maggie Whitecross Paton, *Letters and Sketches from the New Hebrides* (London:
Hodder and Stoughton, 1895), 53.

5. Paton, *Letters and Sketches*, 51.

6. George Patterson, *Memoirs of the Rev. S. F. Johnston, the Rev. J. W. Matheson,
and Mrs. Mary Johnston Matheson, Missionaries on Tanna* (Philadephia: W. S. & A.
Martien, 1864), 252.

Further Readings

Wartime New Hebrides and Tannese Labor Corps

Garrison, Ritchie. *Task Force 9156 and III Island Command: A Story of a South Pacific
Advanced Base during World War II Efate, New Hebrides*. Privately published, 1983.
Lindstrom, Lamont. "Working Encounters: Oral Histories of World War II Labor
Corps from Tanna, Vanuatu," in *The Pacific Theater: Island Representations of World
War II*, edited by Geoffrey M. White and Lamont Lindstrom, 395–417. Honolulu:
University of Hawai'i Press, 1990.

———. *The American Occupation of the New Hebrides (Vanuatu)*. Macmillan Brown Working Paper no. 5, Christchurch: University of Canterbury, 1996.

Tanna Magic

Bonnemaison, Joël. *Tanna: Les Hommes Lieux*. Paris: Editions de l'Orstom, 1987.

Pacific War Songs

Lindstrom, Lamont and Geoffrey M. White. "Singing History: Island Songs from the Pacific War." In *Artistic Heritage in a Changing Pacific,* edited by Philip J. C. Dark and Roger G. Rose, 173–184. Honolulu: University of Hawai'i Press, 1993.

CHAPTER 9

Sivur

THE GIRL LUNGED AT Sivur and the two fell to the ground. Sivur had cursed her. Called her a name. Some boy was the problem. That boy pretended not to notice either of the girls but he knew that his parents were arranging a marriage with one of them. In 1965, or thereabouts, Sivur's parents agreed to marry their daughter to the boy, and the other girl wasn't happy. That girl, too, was sweet on the boy and she had great expectations of marrying him herself. A great-granddaughter of Soarum, the girl was tough and resourceful. Sivur's taunts and insults infuriated her.

Now Kahar, standing nearby, was enraged too. He called Sivur his "sister," his *katutu*. Island sisters and brothers are dismayed and ashamed if they chance to overhear one another talk about sex, about their bodies and persons, or about birthing and babies. Kahar strode in and whacked Sivur in the head. She dropped to the ground, twitching. He whacked her again. She fell terribly quiet. Her head was bloody. She wasn't breathing. Her wind (*nematagi*) was quiet. The verb *ouasi* means to strike, beat, knock unconscious, and sometimes to kill. Another word, *emha,* can mean both ill, unconscious, or dead. Was Sivur just unconscious, or dead altogether, *emha apune*? Others nearby heard the screams, curses, and struggle. They found Sivur sprawled senseless on the ground. Horrified, they carried her body back to her parents' village. Sisters rushed off to find experts in traditional medicine. Brothers spit on grandparental graves and called forth ancestral deliverance. But no use. Sivur was dead, *emha apune,* truly and most sincerely dead. Kahar ran.

The dead girl's mother's brothers arrived to dig a grave. Friends and neighbors approached, wailing groups of mourners paying their respects. They brought small gifts of cloth, blankets, and money for Sivur's parents and family who huddled, moaning, around her cloth and blanked-wrapped corpse. After hours of mourning, Sivur's mothers and aunts enfolded her body into a woven coconut frond basket. Their brothers carried her to the grave, the *tapu*. An elder led all in prayer as men buried the girl. Her parents calculated where to find the pigs and kava they would need to repay the gravediggers.

Word of the event eventually reached government headquarters at Isangel on the other side of the island. A couple of Condominium police in a rattletrap Land Rover arrived. Kahar's father hid him in the bush, so they arrested the rival girl instead. When they can, Tannese men like to shift blame from themselves onto women. The girl slept a week in the government lockup before the police let her go. Because of lax inclination or lack of resources, colonial authorities decided to let the families involved settle the crisis. Sivur's family sent word to the rival girl's people living on the next ridge, proposing to convene a *nagkiariian,* a dispute-settlement meeting, to deal with the murder.

The community gathered at the kava-drinking ground. Everyone was distraught, sorrowful, and apologetic too. Family representatives and leading men from the two villages discussed the tragedy throughout the day. The families resorted to customary restorative practice. Sivur's family had lost a daughter. A community consensus gelled. Yes, Kahar had hit and killed his sister, but the fundamental fault was Sivur's antagonist. She was the one who had started the fight, sparked by swearing and cursing, which led to the killing. The rival girl's family agreed to give her over to replace dead Sivur. One daughter takes the place of another, including her name. Satisfied that island ideals of restorative justice had been upheld, men prepared and drank kava, spitting *tamafa* on the ground to assure community harmony and reconciliation.

The Sivur's new family married her to Kahar's brother Nuvavo. Although Nuvavo and the replacement Sivur would have at least one son together, their marriage was not happy. Nuvavo, it seems, had favored another before Sivur, serendipitously if tragically, came into his family. Like many island boys, he left Tanna for a job in the French New Caledonian nickel mines and rarely returned home. His son eventually joined him there, in Nouméa the colony's capital city. Sivur, uncomfortable around her husband's family, remained with her parents in Samaria until the 1980s when she moved to find work in Port Vila. Here, she worked as a housegirl for several months, and then she planted peanuts on the farm of a local entrepreneur. Housegirls typically are poorly paid, overworked, and often abused by their employers, but this was about the only wage-paying job a young woman then could find. Her husband living abroad, and perhaps permanently, Sivur decided to remain in Port Vila. Helped by her children, she built a shanty in the Blacksands settlement just outside of town. An excellent seamstress, she found work in town sweatshops sewing island dresses and tourist

shirts. Her son living in Nouméa sent his own young daughter home for Sivur
to raise. In Port Vila, as have many other islanders, Sivur found refuge and an
opportunity to escape Tanna's knotted social fabric and constant personal scru-
tiny. Where are you going? Everyone demands to know.

Persons

Are humans always individuals? Or are there other ways to be a person? His-
torians have traced the birth of modern individuality to Christian dogma,
particularly Protestant insistence on the salvation of personally responsible,
indivisible, and inalienable souls. They also connect modern personhood with
the key significance, within capitalist systems, of private property, commodity
consumption, and wage labor. The individual becomes possible when he or she
is disembedded from kinship networks and home places. The modern individual
ideally is also disenchanted, having twisted free of supernatural fear, vanquished
by rational enlightenment.

Those, like Sivur and her rival who remain embedded in social networks,
firmly attached to their kin and their home grounds, might be different sorts
of persons: not individuals, but rather "dividuals." Anthropologists in Melanesia have explored different sorts of personhood by contrasting sociocentric (or
relational) dividuals with modern egocentric individuals. The individual is, or
should be, indivisible: A coherent, unique, unitary self who occupies only his
or her own body. The dividual, in counterpoint, is a self that is divided among
other persons. Parents, children, and other relatives claim parts of one another.
Children never separate cleanly from the parents who have born them, or from
the place whose food and ground has nurtured them. Those who trust in unique
individuality may find it strange that one person, like Sivur, can replace and even
assume the personhood of another. Dividuals, however, are less concerned to be
the one-and-only, a wonderful only me, and they more easily drop one personhood to embrace a different one.

Other signs of dividuality mark Tanna. Rapi, remember, called his sons
Soarum and Kauke "grandfather" and "father" because they carry parental and
grandparental names (along with some of their previous personhoods). The living speak of namesake ancestral actions as their own. Today's Shark, for example,
recalls the time "when *I* met Captain Cook," two centuries ago in 1774. When
Sivur's young cousin Sana fell ill with malaria and island medicines failed to cure
her, a *kleva* diagnosed the problem. Ancestors were displeased with Sana's father
Teman but poor young Sana suffered for her father's neglect. Years later, Teman's

namesake son, up in Port Vila, had an affair. His mother, back on Tanna, worrisomely fell ill. Closely related persons shoulder personal responsibility for the errors or crimes committed by one of their own, who own them in return. Kinfolk, thus, commonly contribute to fines assessed upon a relative, and they share in any goods he or she receives in return.

This, of course, is the law of the classic feud. You, personally, may have injured me but I am pleased to assault your brother or some other of your kin for payback if I cannot find you. Back in the 1940s, when colonial authorities arrested and deported early leaders of the John Frum movement, the sons and younger brothers of the accused begged to be sent to the calaboose ("prison" in Bislama) in place of their fathers or brothers. They were baffled when European authorities demanded only to punish specifically guilty individuals.

People's genealogies, and also island place names (like Captain Cook) that log memory, record several historical interpersonal replacements like Sivur's among village families. These, typically, were cases of accidental killings or manslaughters by some kin or neighbor. Murder by socially distant adversaries, in darker pre-Christian days, often sparked a feud leading to a second death as payback for the first. Violent feuds no longer occur, but people continue to move dividuals around to repair and patch, as much as they can, social tears and gaps that threaten island relationships.

In 2010, I attended a reconciliation ceremony in Port Vila's Freswota neighborhood. A young boy, one of Sivur's brother's sons, had poked down coconuts with a stalk of bamboo. He failed to notice that a baby girl was toddling nearby under the palm. He dislodged a nut that dropped and split open the head of the young child, killing her. Her family demanded a *tain,* a replacement, and Sivur's brother gave them his youngest daughter to take the place of the dead child. The dead child's grandmother, however, eventually agreed that her family would instead accept gifts of cloth, blankets, and money, and the young killer's sister returned back to her own family, resuming her original name and personhood.

Vanuatu's court judges, who tend to think in terms of individuals, have issued warnings that families must not follow *kastom* and make one person into another. The court zeroes down on those personally responsible, and worries about individual human rights, especially those of swapped children. Islanders, however, have different goals in mind. Sivur's story reveals the core significance of restitution as the main aim of village justice. People work for restitution, not punishment. Their objective is not to discipline, or not so much, but to repair the fabric of social relationships that some conflict or dispute has shredded.

Island notions of personhood allow one girl or boy to substitute, in a pinch, for another, taking the place of a lost one within the bosom of her mournful family.

Disputes

Tanna, ordinarily, is home to warm, generous, and peaceful people. But like any of us, they sometimes fall into dispute. On at least several mornings, I woke to anguished squabble and the growing buzz of public concern as people rushed to stop an angry woman from torching her house and fleeing in fury. Collapse of ordinary social harmony is a concern everywhere but particularly so in close-knit Pacific villages where people tend all to be related, one way or another, and where the ebb and flow of daily life rests on the long-standing, multiple, and overlapping claims they have upon one another.

Villagers are experts in settling disputes like the original Sivur's murder, and they do so without an apparatus of central authority, or even much hierarchy, and traditionally no police, prisons, prosecutors, courts, judges, or lawyers. When these adjudicatory processes appeared at the beginning of the twentieth century, imposed by Christian mission and colonial authority, people quickly took to these novel mechanisms too, but they almost always start the process with island dispute settlement methods before appealing to state police or courts for justice.

Adversaries deal with some issues, at least temporarily, by avoiding one other. Sivur, infuriated once with her original family for its lack of support, torched her house in a rage. The fire made the sharp point that she aimed to decamp from the village. Dramatic withdrawals from one's home ground signal hurt feelings and serious conflict with others in a community. Island *kastom* offers classic examples of what anthropologists have labeled "avoidance relationships." They work, so goes the theory, to smooth out areas of potential dispute between family members, say between a son-in-law and his wife's parents. On Tanna, the principal avoidance relationship is between brother and sister. Each is supposed not to speak of sexual or marital issues should the other be present. This is what provoked Kahar to lash out at his sister Sivur. I embarrassed myself once by asking a woman when her baby was due, not noticing that her brother Tio was sitting nearby. The boy leapt to his feet and ran out the door before she could blush. Avoidance practices reduce possibilities of conflict between people who might often have the occasion to argue. This certainly holds true on Tanna given the island's "sister-exchange" marriage system wherein the marriage chances of a brother hang directly on those of his sister, and vice versa.

Rapi, another of Sivur's uncles, came to blows with his sister's husband over use of garden land. This dispute was particularly shocking insofar as these two men, according to *kastom*, were joined together by a formal "joking relationship"—the opposite of an avoidance relationship. As brothers-in-law (*nieri*), their interaction should have been marked by lighthearted joking and easy camaraderie. As the two men fought, Rapi's elderly although still spry mother leapt in to slap and kick her oldest daughter, a dignified matron herself who was married to the *nieri*. Things went south from here and the brother-in-law and his family moved out that evening to a different ground, a half mile or so down in the valley where they built themselves new houses.

Relations between the two families remained poor for the next eighteen months as each side avoided the other. In the end, however, the dispute became impossible to sustain as shared social responsibilities demanded their eventual cooperation. Those caught in-between maneuvered to placate the irate men, bringing them back together, particularly women who were both mother and mother-in-law, and sister, daughter, and wife. Anthropologists call such overlapped relationships "cross-cutting ties." The two brothers-in-law soon found it necessary to rejoin forces to oppose a third party who threatened their joint claims to that disputed land.

Social duties and unanticipated events such as sudden illness, family exchange responsibilities, cross-cutting ties, and third-party threats can all reunite adversaries encouraging them to discuss their differences and to bury the hatchet. In particular, so long as one shares a home ground, one has the responsibility to settle whatever community disputes that might erupt. But withdrawal and avoidance do allow people, when they can escape co-presence and an affiliation with the same place, never to settle some differences.

When village problems must be faced, concerned parties convene a dispute-settlement meeting. These assemblies are called *nagkiariien*, which simply means "talk" or "talking." Legal anthropologists label them *moots* in that they are negotiation and dispute-settlement sessions that do not rely on judges or other third-party adjudicators. Instead, Tanna moots involve the two or more disputing sides and a mix of neighbors, uninvolved but friendly parties, and leading local figures who come to "witness" and to help guide a consensual settlement.

Missionary John Paton, who attended a number of moots during his several years at Port Resolution, wasn't much impressed: "The Tannese were instable as water and easily swayed one way or the other. They are born talkers, and can and will speechify on all occasions; but most of it means nothing, bears no fruit."[1] His Presbyterian colleague Samuel Johnston, writing home to Nova Scotia in October 1860, was a friendlier observer: "The ground on which these meetings are held is the marum, or dancing ground of the village. These generally occupy a lovely spot under the wide-spreading branches of the trees. After some time is spent in making general arrangements and conversation, the speaking commences. The speakers are chiefs or their counsellors."[2]

Island dispute-settlement meetings still take place at kava-drinking/dance grounds under those spreading banyan trees, which are central locations within Tanna's cultural landscape. Small moots might involve only the two disputants and a few family members from the same village. Bigger ones, which tackle thornier conflicts more difficult to resolve like Sivur's murder, may attract several hundred spectators and participants from throughout a region. Debates convene in the morning, the time depending on the distance participants must travel. In important cases, older and respected witnesses, uninvolved in the problem at hand, are summoned from neighboring villages. People attending a debate sit along the periphery of the circular kava clearing. Arcs of this periphery are connected with certain of the local groups involved, these situated near the point of egress of the trails, or *kastom* roads, that link kava ground to kava ground. Protagonists, consistent with island dualism, sit at opposite points facing one another across the clearing. Those who witness the debate mediate this opposition, positioning themselves along the sides. Women and younger men sit behind debate principals. To speak, as missionary Johnston noted, men stand and walk into the center of the clearing where they offer statements, advice, and songs before retreating to their seats.

Moots are remarkably effective in settling village disputes, and all in a single day as participants aim to reach consensus before dusk and the kava hour. If the cicadas are about to chirp in the trees, things rush hurriedly to a conclusion. But moots are only effective when both sides of a conflict appear to participate in negotiation. I attended numerous *nagkiariien* when only one side was present. Sometimes, in these situations, people call the meeting off. But sometimes they pretend that the other side is in fact represented by enough supporters and they go forth to find a consensus and head for the kava. Such settlements usually fail in that the absentee antagonists are not bound to respect whatever consensus might have been achieved.

Given pressure to find a resolution by the end of a day's talking, most disputants show up to negotiate only if, in fact, they are already disposed to settle a problem. It is always a good sign, therefore, when both sides come to a meeting, as chances are excellent (though not guaranteed) that they will resolve their conflict. Again, co-presence in the same place signals people's recognition of common interests and identity and their acceptance of shared social duty.

Village moots have no judges or anyone else with authority to weigh facts, determine responsibility, or impose a settlement, fine, or sentence. Accepted facts, distributed responsibility, and consensual settlements all originate in public discussions and debates. Moots are egalitarian, although only up to a point. Generally, only older, married, and established men feel comfortable taking the floor (coming into the center of the ground to speak). Younger men remain silent in the audience, although the more ambitious among these might dare to rise and offer a comment or two. The most experienced men with political clout tend to hold their council until the end of a meeting, maneuvering thereby to control the manner in which the outcome settlement becomes publicly enunciated. Women, on the other hand, have few rights to public speech and they speak through kinsmen. Although gender inequalities have eased somewhat, in previous years I often saw women, even those to whom direct questions were posed, whisper their responses to family spokesmen who stood to represent them.

Many island men command effective debating skills they deploy to deliberate and find workable consensuses. Effective stratagems are apparent in the language of debate and dispute settlement itself, as I discovered when I recorded some dozen such *nagkiariien* in the 1980s. Islanders recognize fine and critical discriminations among ways of speaking. As in Western courts, they pay close attention to language given that it is through language, *nagkiariian,* that they discover an issue's truth and assign shared responsibility to resolve this.

Settling disputes requires convincing talk and debate participants like to employ elaborate and florid ways of speaking, with occasional song. They *usapekin* (speak metaphorically). Whereas the major metaphorical scaffold that frames Western understandings of argument and debate is *war* (e.g., "your claims are indefensible"; "he shot down my argument"; or "our side lost"), Islanders approach debate in terms of a shared *journey.* Journey metaphors shape negotiation, aiming to mollify the anger of opponents (or fellow travelers, which better approximates the island point of view). Debaters leap, fly, tread into an argument. They descend into a story, or some defense, to make a point. Should two speakers disagree, one may note that their discussion is off-course: "we two are far out to sea." If a person refuses to respond to a point, he like the banded rail bird has vanished into the bush. Those who refuse to conclude an argumentative journey act like the sea in their pugnacious comings and goings. Should consensus prove difficult, "the rain beats down on all."

A consensus, like an island social group, metaphorically is a vehicle, a canoe, that speakers might unhappily capsize or toy with. If someone refuses to admit responsibility, explain in detail, or join a consensus, others object that he remains far away. Finally, when consensus at last is reached, disputants arrive at the summit. Debates, thus, are collective voyages during which competing claims are disentangled. All debate travelers must reach the same truth terminus, that mountain top. Metaphorically at least, consensus flows from the joint interaction and movement of moot participants as a group. It is not a balancing of personal interests or a compromising of wills. People arrive at consensus and resolve conflict when they together have straightened talk. Although speakers of English also metaphorically *arrive* at a consensus, and although Bislama speakers today will *win* their arguments, these journey metaphors are key in island understandings of negotiated dispute settlement.

Consensus, however mutually arrived at, often leaves unaddressed minor sticking points and side issues and these can always pop back into play in some future dispute. Dispute settlement, like the networks of regular gift exchanges that link family with family, is a never-ending process. There is no guarantee that any dispute, no matter a public consensus about this, is ultimately settled. People under new contentious conditions can always return to plow old ground and dig up past grievances and wrongs. Restored social equilibria inevitably create new imbalances. Village harmony demands constant and continuous dispute settlement, just as it requires ongoing and continuing gift-giving among families.

This disputative ethos jars with Western practices of justice wherein, even given appeal processes, courts have the power to determine a verdict once and for all. Although village dispute resolutions are sometimes temporary and fleeting, they bring people back into active engagement. Avoidance and hard feelings evaporate or are put aside, at least for some time being. An achieved consensus regularizes relations between the parties who may now again talk and drink kava together, which, ideally, they should do immediately after a moot concludes.

Dispute resolution parallels the sort of gift exchange that marks village marriages, celebrations of childbirth, the circumcision of sons and their first shave, and burials of family members in that this, too, consists of a ceremonial exchange of goods between families. Or, sometimes as with Sivur, the exchange of persons. One person replaces another. Organized island courts nowadays also impose cash and other fines, but these serve to make people whole again more than they do to discipline or penalize lawbreakers. The Malvatumauri, Vanuatu's National Council of Chiefs, has variously codified *kastom* policy. One of its regulations, notably, requires that fines "will be divided among the two sides that have agreed upon the custom peace ceremony."

Wariness of possible spiritual interference also encourages people to smooth away anger and hurt feeling. *Kastom* punishment of miscreants may flow down from God, the ancestors, or other spirits who serve as a sort of spiritual police force. Fear of ancestral retribution, a sudden unexpected illness or other misfortune, functions to dampen social dispute and to spur people and their families to settle their conflicts and to live up to consensual agreements. Keeping one eye on meddlesome spirits, people keep another open for suspect sorcery (*nakaemas, masing, su,* or *posen* in Bislama; or *nahak* on Tanna). Such attacks, so people suspect, are precipitated by bad men who are in cahoots with bad spirits. Anthropologists have documented notable increases in sorcery fear among many urban residents in onetime colonies around the world. This postcolonial, postmodern sorcery belies expectation that presumed irrational beliefs of the past will fade in the face of education and urban modernity. Instead, sorcery worries have increased alongside the hardships and everyday experience of rough life in townships and settlements, including those that encircle Port Vila.

Tanna's dividuated social personhood shapes the operation of its village moots. There is less concern in these to monitor if people are telling the truth: No vows, no hands on the Bible, no individualized promises to tell the truth, the whole truth, and nothing but the truth. The truth, rather, does not belong to some possessive individual but is collectively found, or arrived at, in cooperative journeys of public debate. People do not own their own truths. These instead belong to wider groups of concerned and interrelated persons. And debate, again, reflects island relations of inequality, particularly old versus young and men over women. Certain spokesmen fill in more of the discovered, collective truth than do others. As dividuals more than individuals, persons do not inalienably possess rights to speak in their own defense, or tell their own truths, especially if they are women or are otherwise inconsequential. Powerful figures instead represent and speak for them, and they are able to do so insofar as individual perspectives and rights are blurred, even rights to one's own words and experience.

As persons whose selves subsume facets of other persons, troublemakers like Sivur suffer more shame than guilt. Tanna's languages have strong words for embarrassment and shyness (*pus*), and shame (*auris*). Until John and Mary Matheson and other missionaries arrived on the island, they had no word for guilt. Only when one becomes a personally responsible individual does one much fret about inner guilt. Socially embedded persons instead worry more about shaming and embarrassing their families.

FIGURE 9. Breaking a branch off kava after a dispute, 1988.
Photo by author.

Dispute settlements, including moot-imposed exchanges and the fines that cap successful debates, aim to restore the status quo and to repair broken social relationships. People are less concerned to punish some guilty party or to set an example to deter future miscreants. The final act of successful debates is a quick exchange of kava and food between the newly reconciled disputants. Men immediately put these to good use, drinking the kava and eating the food, each taking *tamafa* in the island way spitting forth his last dregs of kava as a prayer to the buried ancestors underfoot that the newborn consensus holds and trouble be gone. One leaves a branch attached to the kava roots exchanged to cement a settlement (figure 9). The newly reconciled may take away and plant this branch and, if it sprouts, recall the settlement when they dig and enjoy that kava plant some years later. Even the most grievously injured party gives something to an offender, although the flow of exchange goods may be imbalanced according to the relative weighting of wrongs. Village moots always find at least a little fault on all sides. Antagonists reconcile by giving gifts to one another or, put another way, by sharing around the *kastom* fines each has been assessed.

Sometimes, the best gift is a child, a replacement person, who is swapped to repair some tragic rupture in the social fabric. Someone has disappeared but another is found to reanimate her personhood. Sivur, along with most of the village, has since been swept from Tanna to Port Vila in search of work, cash, and novel experiences. She remains, however, close to her mother who kept by her side since that sorry day. Elderly but spry, the old woman home on Tanna still does a bit of gardening. When Sivur can afford to, she sends her mother a little money, fried sweetened dough twists, and other gifts. Thanks to these endless gift exchanges, and traumatic personal replacements, island families endure.

Notes

1. John G. Paton, *John G. Paton: Missionary to the New Hebrides, an Autobiography* (London: Hodder and Stoughton, 1890), 216.

2. George Patterson, *Memoirs of the Rev. S. F. Johnston, the Rev. J. W. Matheson, and Mrs. Mary Johnston Matheson, Missionaries on Tanna* (Philadelphia: W. S. & A. Martien, 1864), 252.

Further Readings

Island Personhood

Lindstrom, Lamont. "Agnes C. P. Watt and Melanesian Personhood." *Journal of Pacific History* 48, no. 3 (2013): 243–266.
Strathern, Marilyn. *Gender of the Gift: Problems with Women and Problems with Society in Melanesia*. Berkeley: University of California Press, 1990.

House Girls

Rodman, Margaret, Daniela Kraemer, Lissant Bolton, and Jean Tarisese. *House-Girls Remember: Domestic Workers in Vanuatu*. Honolulu: University of Hawai'i Press, 2007.

Disputes and Debates on Tanna

Lindstrom, Lamont. "Straight Talk on Tanna." In *Disentangling: Conflict Discourse in Pacific Societies,* edited by Karen Ann Watson-Gegeo and Geoffrey M. White, 373–411. Stanford: Stanford University Press, 1990.

———. "Context Contests: Debatable Truth Statements on Tanna (Vanuatu)." In *Rethinking Context: Language as an Interactive Phenomenon,* edited by Alessandro Duranti and Charles Goodwin, 101–124. Cambridge: Cambridge University Press, 1992.

Debate Metaphors

Lakoff, George, and Mark Johnson. *Metaphors We Live By.* Chicago: University of Chicago Press, 1980.

Lindstrom, Lamont. "Metaphors of Debate on Tanna." *Naika: Journal of the Vanuatu Natural Science Society* 12 (1983): 6–9.

CHAPTER 10

Kusi

KUSI IS A DIGNIFIED grandmother, living in Port Vila. She was a wild child though. Willful and strongheaded, her parents called her. They greatly suffered her teenaged energy. Kusi's father died when she was a child but her mother remarried his brother Koke, her uncle. In the 1970s, Kusi's parents sent her to live with an older sister in Port Vila where, like Sivur before her, she found work as a housegirl with a Chinese trading family. Tanna parents then reluctantly let their daughters travel to Port Vila, and only if some family member could closely guard them. Kusi's sister did her best, but Kusi managed to evade sisterly surveillance. She found a boyfriend. Antoine, was raised in Ipikil village, John Frum headquarters on Sulphur Bay, and had also moved up to Port Vila. Like many Tanna boys in those years, he was enamored with boxing and, in Vila, he found a trainer who had opened a boxing club. Handsome and muscular, he was popular with many but Kusi especially captured his romantic attentions.

Island teenagers, in the pre-mobile phone era, used to flirt through third parties. Boys and girls found it difficult to speak directly with one another, at least publicly, although they might give one another sly, welcoming glances. A boy who liked a girl, or a girl a boy, entreated an intermediary to speak for them. Boys, hoping to charm, often sent along some love token: the gift of a handkerchief, or a packet of sweet biscuits, or some tinned fish. If Antoine gave Kusi a love token, it worked. The two found secret places and times to meet. Eventually, to escape critical surveillance, both returned to Tanna. One of Kusi's kinsmen in Port Vila paid her fare on the British administration's boat. (The captain was from Tanna.) Back home, Antoine returned to Sulphur Bay, and Kusi to Samaria, to ask their parents to arrange their marriage.

Antoine was the last male in his family and the last named heir to his abandoned kava-drinking ground. Down the mountain from Samaria, secondary forest had overgrown this historically significant site although banyan trees still towered over it. Antoine's father moved the family to Sulphur Bay during John Frum excitements of the 1940s, and he eventually died there. His mother remarried one of the younger leaders of the movement, and Antoine grew up participating in Friday night John Frum dances and marching and drilling in the Tanna Army.

Kusi's parents voiced several objections to the marriage although ultimately, they agreed. Antoine was a John Frum boy while Kusi was raised Presbyterian. Parents, however, scarcely consider religious disparities as they expect wives to convert to their husbands' religious affiliation. A newly married girl, who enthusiastically sang Presbyterian hymns one Sunday, will dance for John Frum the next Friday night. Kinship, though, was a more serious concern. Antoine also called Kusi's father "father" and, in island terms, Kusi was his sister. People deplore and certainly gossip about such awkward espousals. One of Kusi's uncles, however, figured that the kinship connection was distant enough to be overlooked. Islanders, in a pinch, skillfully readjust kin relationships to create exceptions to their cultural codes. My old friend Rapi, noting the regrettably changing times, commented that kids nowadays were marrying almost anyone at all, "just like white people." Antoine stopped calling Kusi's father *tata* (father) and began instead to address him as *kaka* (wife's father/mother's brother/father's sister's husband). Everyone else in the two families juggled revised kin terms as they could.

Kusi's parents embraced the opportunity to make the best of this awkward marriage. She had been a difficult daughter. The Tannese operate a complicated marriage system that anthropologists call "sister exchange." A boy cannot marry a girl without his family giving over one of its girls in exchange. This balances marriages between the two families. The return girl—the *tain*—should properly be one of the new husband's sisters, but marital debt often defaults to the next generation when a husband returns a daughter in exchange for his wife. Antoine had three sisters but all had already married and no *tain* for Kusi was immediately available.

The families convened a *nagkiariian*, a decision-making meeting, and invited interested parties to attend. At this, they devised a typically intricate marriage deal. One of Antoine's sisters had married a Sulphur Bay boy who had yet to return her *tain*. A third family (that had looked after this man's father and adopted one of his brothers) would provide Antoine's brother-in-law a girl whom he would then give to Antoine, in exchange for Antoine's sister. And Antoine next would give this girl to Kusi's family where eventually, everyone supposed, she would marry Kusi's brother Tio. But this convoluted scheme collapsed. Although the girl's mother and uncles were at the decision-making meeting, her father cannily avoided attending the meeting and he thus could refuse the deal, which he did. Antoine was left owing a girl to Kusi's family, and people contemplated the future arrival, someday, of one of his and Kusi's daughters.

The marriage, because of all this, was a low-key affair. Kusi and her mother merely brought along a basket of baked pig meat and a few of Kusi's dresses when she joined Antoine in Sulphur Bay. Parents in happier situations may arrange an elaborate series of ceremonial exchanges between the two intermarrying families. First comes the *nafukarua* (the doorway) when families who have concluded a marriage agreement exchange gifts of kava and food, either on the kava-drinking ground or in the village. Next comes the *tenarup* (the basket) when the bride's family transfers the girl, with her possessions, to the groom's (figure 10). And finally, ambitious families may arrange a *navegenien asori* (big feast) where more substantial gifts of pigs, kava, food, baskets, mats, dyed bark skirts, blankets, and cloth are exchanged, often after the birth of the couple's first child. The groom's family generally gives a little more than it receives, but all this balances out in the end, at the mirror marriage, when the groom's sister (or her replacement) marries one of the first bride's brothers, and gifts between the two intermarried families flow once more.

Families like to invite neighbors and friends to all-night *nupu* dances to celebrate marital exchanges. Fathers and other family leaders in attendance take the opportunity to speechify, reminding the new couple, and everyone, of the proper responsibilities of husbands and wives. The bride should prepare a *nufar*, a yam or taro pudding she has baked in an earth oven, that she shares with her new husband after they receive even more marital advice inside a house. During these lectures, boys, embarrassed, keep quiet. Girls, even more embarrassed, often cover their heads with calico cloth. The groom's family clubs a pig and lays its body across the house's threshold. Escaping with relief, the new bride steps over the pig—stepping over dead pigs being an island sign of cooperative harmony.

Afterward, the groom goes one way to hang out with his friends and brothers, and the shy bride goes another, sheltering with her new female affines and one or two of her sisters who keep her company for a few days. Men repair to the kava-drinking ground to prepare and drink kava and, when darkness falls, to dance. The groom's new father-in-law or his mother's brother (often the same person) prepares kava for him to drink. Officially, at least, this should be his first taste of the potion. Most boys, of course, drink kava as soon as they can get away with it. Particular leaves might be added to this supposed first intoxicating draught to sooth its effects, and to protect the just-married young man from the dangerous vaginal discharges of his new wife. Everyone spits *tamafa*, asking the

FIGURE 10. Bride handed over to groom's family with her "basket," Samaria 1985.
Photo by author.

ancestors buried there to safeguard the boy's health from baneful female secretions and, maybe, for his fruitful marriage.

Kusi and Antoine avoided all this ceremony and, perhaps because of this,
their marriage was not a happy one. Married women move to live with their
husbands' families. Teen boys build small bamboo and cane houses looking forward to their eventual marriages, and they tend to situate these next to parents'
dwellings. Some women do not travel far if they marry a boy from their home
village. Kusi, though, moved with Antoine to Sulphur Bay, a two-hour walk
away around the other side of the volcano. A man's mother and sisters can demand domestic assistance from his new bride, and Kusi once again was mostly
working as a housegirl. Island mothers-in-law can be critical, and she found Antoine's mother unkind.

Antoine's chronic flirting with other girls also angered Kusi. She discovered some photographs of girls that Antoine had brought home from Port
Vila. Enraged with jealousy, the two quarreled. Kusi called Antoine a lazy
good-for-nothing when he let some seed yams rot before planting them. Kusi
swore and cursed, and Antoine beat her. John Frum guards rushed in to separate
the two. She escaped, returning home to her family in Samaria. Marital swears
and curses evoke community concern, as do runaway wives. Kusi's father walked

down to Sulphur Bay to attempt to repair the marriage. Antoine's stepfather suggested that the boy was particularly troubled that Kusi wasn't yet pregnant. As the last man in his name-set, Antoine was determined not to "let his blood die." Kusi's father led her by the arm back down to Sulphur Bay. Antoine hid inside his house, refusing to come out to greet them.

Word was that, while working in Port Vila, Kusi had drunk *nui* (leaf medicine) to prevent pregnancies. This now became the main marital issue. The fathers sent word to a blind *urumun* (spirit medium) who lived up the mountain in Nazareth village. Keihaker had a secret recipe (which involved killing a tree by ringbarking and burning it) that reverses contraceptive potions. He demanded a pig and kava root to cure Kusi. The fathers sent him a chicken and smaller kava instead. Kusi drank the medicine and she did soon become pregnant, but bore a girl who Antoine named after his father's sister.

The two continued to bicker and Antoine left for a month or two to cut timber on Aneityum Island. When he returned, the couple quarreled again. They moved temporarily to Antoine's abandoned lands to collect, scoop, and dry coconut meat (copra) to sell. But then Kusi suddenly disappeared. This is difficult on Tanna where people ("where are you going?") closely track one another's movements. Her panicked family searched for her at Sulphur Bay, in Samaria, and parts in-between. Kusi turned up the next day, reporting that two spirits had appeared to lead her away into the bush. She only saw the backs of their heads, but she knew that they were her dead father and her grandmother. The spirits asked for food and she found something to feed them. Everyone accepted Kusi's story as indisputably true, knowing that ancestral spirits may indeed intrude if angered by discord among their descendants.

Spousal swears, curses, and beatings trouble families who hurry to mend a marriage, if they can. Spiritual kidnappings are even more worrisome. The two families convened several more community meetings to discover why Kusi and Antoine fought so much, and what to do about this. Family elders suggested that Antoine return for good to his original home ground, as geographic displacement can make trouble among the living, and with the dead. Home grounds demanding tending. Antoine eventually would do so, but with a different wife. Kusi's family instead gave up on the marriage as hopeless. Her father and uncles told Antoine that they could accept a divorce (no *tain* had yet been received), and they blamed Kusi (as men tend to do) for causing most of the trouble.

When the couple broke up, Kusi found her way back to Port Vila. Antoine wooed a second wife, Rachel, the daughter of one of Kusi's father's brothers (another girl whom he also should have called his "sister"). Kusi had more children,

including a muscular son who well could have been Antoine's. Officially father-
less, who would name the boy? Kusi's father Koke gave his grandson his own
name, having already bestowed this on one of Kusi's brothers. Samaria then had
three namesake Koke's all of whom shared the same named personhood. Kusi,
somehow managed to drop the baby on his head, and people since have blamed
this for the boy's deafness. Young Koke, hardworking and convivial, lives in Samaria where he looks after his grandmother. When she can, the now venerable
Kusi sends home small gifts for her mother and son in the village. Children may
cause worrisome turmoil, but families eventually absorb their wildness.

Families

Tanna is one huge family. Even with thirty thousand inhabitants, people know
and track one another. Should two strangers meet, if one can discover how
anyone in one family is related to anyone in the other, this immediately situ-
ates the two within the island's vast web of kinship. A person calls everyone
two generations older *kaha* (grandparent); and calls everyone two generations
younger *mwipuk* (my grandchild). Those who are one generation older are either
mother or father, or mother-in-law or father-in-law. Those in one's own generation are either brother or sister, or spouse or brother/sister-in-law. Everyone
one generation down is either son or daughter, or niece/son's wife or nephew/
daughter's husband.

This kin system corresponds neatly with island marriage patterns. One calls
all the children of one's father's brothers and of one's mother's sisters brother or
sister, and (despite the marriage of Antoine and Kusi) one should neither have sex
with nor marry them. Anthropologists call this sort of cousin a "parallel-cousin."
But the children of one's father's sisters or mother's brothers ("cross-cousins")
are attractive sex partners and marriage material, and the Tannese have been
marrying their first cousins for three thousand years. Island demands for marital
sister exchange shape families. In an ideal marriage exchange, two boys marry
each other's sisters. When this happens two generations in a row, a boy marries
a girl who is at once his father's sister's daughter and *also* his mother's brother's daughter.

With contemporary urban migration and increasing educational opportunities, children are even wilder than they used to be, but most island families continue to demand marital balance. People weigh marriages carefully. Debts must
one day be repaid and the exchange balance restored. When one girl leaves a
family, another must come. Sisters are not scarce. Even a boy from a daughter-less

family has many sisters. His father's brothers' and mother's sisters' daughters are his sisters; as are his father's father's brother's son's daughters; and so on. Island marriage arrangement, though, can be intricate and convoluted, as with Antoine and Kusi. A marriage between a boy from Family A and a girl from Family D may involve Family B (who has a marital debt with A) giving a girl to Family C, who gives one to Family D to balance the girl who is marrying into Family A. And a young man like Antoine, with no unmarried sister or other available girl to exchange, can promise to return a future daughter to his wife's family.

Traditional island marriage is both easy and hard on children. Easy, because parents undertake the work of finding their spouses. Maturing youth know the likely possibilities in the neighborhood, and they can nudge their parents toward one boy or girl or another. But sometimes parents abruptly announce a marriage arrangement to a surprised son or daughter. Fathers and mothers affirm that children have rights to refuse an arranged spouse, but complicated marriage deals and the hinging of one marriage on another make refusal difficult. Girls, in particular, come under much family pressure to accept the man whom their parents have found for them. Attempted suicide may be their only effective means of resistance. Koraku's family, for example, arranged her marriage with Johnny, an amiable, older man whom everyone liked. This marriage would balance that of a girl from Johnny's family who had married into Koraku's. But Johnny was deaf. Even though he was an excellent lip reader, and the community had invented an efficient sign language, he wasn't Koraku's husbandly ideal. Desperate, she climbed a banyan tree and jumped. She survived but she threatened to jump again if pushed to marry Johnny, and her family backed down.

The hinging of two marriages makes island divorce difficult and uncommon. Families pressure miserably unhappy women to stick with a marriage. Koke returned Kusi back to Antoine in Sulphur Bay several times. Dealing with a wayward runaway woman, men mutter that in the old days they could cut her hamstrings. Divorces, like Antoine and Kusi's, are easier if the *tain* has yet to be arranged. After both marriages are accomplished, however, the breakup of one undermines the other. Should a wife return home, her abandoned husband's family will demand a replacement (and Antoine's subsequent marriage to Kusi's sister Rachel is one example of this). Koraku's refusal of Johnny jeopardized a hinged marriage in this way. Exasperated by her refusal to marry Johnny, his family threatened to grab back the girl who had married into Koraku's family. Death also disrupts marriage exchanges. When possible, a widow (like Kusi's mother) marries a brother of her dead husband, thus keeping alive the marriage exchange that conjoins the two families.

Tanna families are difficult to escape. They provide children with names, identities, land, a home ground and other resources, and all the usual sorts of physical and emotional support. In return, children shoulder serious obligation to support their parents and siblings. Some, like Kusi, attempt to escape family surveillance by running off to Port Vila or beyond. But families today have members living abroad, too, and few island migrants manage to achieve urban anonymity, independence, or modernist freedom from their family demands and kin obligations.

Sex and Love

Love feelings bedevil systems of arranged marriage. Marriages are political agreements between families and name-sets. They establish alliances that last until the death of the last child born to a couple. When this death comes to pass, additional marriages between the families typically have already sustained that alliance. Diligent parents, who make these deals, can be dismissive of their children's immature romantic fancies and complaints. What's love got to do with it?

Island languages do not offer much by way of love words. The Nafe verb *okeikei,* which indeed means "love," also covers like, prefer, want, and need, as in "my truck *rokeikei* a new wheel" (this also can be *akeikei*). Presbyterian missionaries like the Mathesons and Watts brought new, alien understandings of love to the island, in tentative, fuzzy sermons that celebrated the love of God. A second Nafe verb, *api,* is sentimentally more profound. This means "cry" but also pity, sympathize or empathize with, or have feelings for. Women, especially, cry when a loved one leaves home or returns from abroad. Missionary William Watt put this word on his wife Agnes' headstone at Port Resolution, *IN RAPI NAKUR IPARE,* "she felt for the people of Ipare."

Island husbands and wives do indeed love and care for one another, but many couples find love after they marry, not before. Few, until recently, expect a spouse to be a best friend. Sometimes romance flares too fiercely, however, and lovesick youth like Kusi and Antoine elope and later beg their parents to make marital arrangements, cleaning things up, to satisfy burning desire. Parents, however, suspect that marriages that originate in love are bad bets, as they are suspicious of love feeling in general. Kusi and Antoine managed to convince their parents to make the best of it and arrange their tempestuous marriage, but family elders and also John Frum police and guards have chased down other eloping couples, separating these and dragging them home. When couples elope to Port Vila, parents sometimes contact related town policemen to arrest and ship them back to the island.

In addition to a modest love vocabulary, other island institutions work to dampen romance. Men's deepest emotional attachments typically focus on village age-mates, on other men, as do women's on other women. In addition to brother/sister avoidance, Tannese worry about cross-gender pollution, a concern common throughout Melanesia. Island etiquette maintains two gendered spheres, and gender also structures island topography. The masculine is centered, surrounded by a periphery of women. Hamlets of women and children encircle masculine kava-drinking grounds where, until missionaries boosted the nuclear family ideal, men and circumcised boys slept apart in men's houses.

Gender separation continues to structure a number of important everyday and ritual activities on the island. Farmers plant symbolically male yams in the center of their gardens, and surround these with female-associated taro and other cultigens. Men and women both join in *nupu,* the island's standard circle dance, but they remain in their own spaces, the men dancing together in the center surrounded by a periphery of pairs of bouncing women. *Nakwiari* festivals, large regional exchanges of pigs and kava, feature separate men's and women's dance teams. Male guards, protected by kava *tamafa,* monitor the space between women dancers and the assembled crowds, and only they safely may pick up any feathered hair sticks, odiferous leaves, scraps of bark skirt, or other paraphernalia that female dancers might drop. Most church meetings also are gender segregated, men seated on the left and women on the right.

Daily kava preparation notably enacts gender difference. Contact with female secretions pollute kava, making drinkers ill or at least spoiling the plant's psychoactive effect. As noted earlier, women thus must not drink kava. They must not see men drinking kava. No one should utter a woman's name as men prepare kava but rather use the euphemism, *nari ia rukwanu* "village thing." Only a circumcised boy may chew kava for his fathers and infuse this in water with his hand. After an initial sexual exploit, boys must no longer squeeze the cuds of chewed kava through their fingers but must instead, like mature men, use a short stick to poke and mix the kava and water as it strains into the drinking cup. Embarrassed teenaged boys, come one evening, whisper to their fathers to explain why they may no longer touch chewed kava.

After the yam harvest each year, families organize *tamarua* exchanges to celebrate a boy's circumcision. Island boys typically are circumcised between six and twelve years of age. Local experts once undertook the operation with sharp bamboo knives, but fathers now prefer to take their sons to one of the island's clinics. They also like to circumcise several boys at the same time, so these will have company during the six-to-eight week period when they are secluded in a *nimwa urur,* a circumcision house constructed on an out-of-the way kava-drinking ground or other place distant from female gaze. Twice daily, circumcised boys make their way to a water source or the sea to bathe. Their attendants blare triton shell trumpets to warn of their passing. No woman may look upon them.

During this period of seclusion, while circumcision wounds heal, fathers (or name-givers) gather the usual sorts of exchange goods (pigs, kava, cooked and raw tubers, mats, baskets, bark skirts, lengths of cloth, blankets) that they will present to their wife's brother (the boy's mother's brother), or some other man in that family. This uncle, or his representative, is responsible for feeding the secluded boy. A typical rite of passage, Tanna's boy initiates revert to the status of helpless baby. Men make boys into men, transforming their feminine wetness into masculine aridity, coldness into heat, and softness into hardness. In the past, a circumcised boy no longer could wander about naked but must put on the *ninhum,* the leafy penis wrapper, to conceal his newly exposed glans penis.

When everything is ready, fathers invite the community to attend the circumcision exchange and also to dance *nupu.* Uncles lead healed, face-painted boys onto the kava-drinking ground and around the heap of exchange goods piled up in the center. Mothers greet their sons for the first time since fathers snatched them away from the village. They burst into tears and offer them a snack of mother-prepared tuber or banana pudding. "What a man you have become!" The newly circumcised are now *tamarua,* handsome youths eligible to marry (even if still six years old) and to chew their fathers' kava. No longer are they puerile *kapiesi,* a rude term that refers to an uncircumcised penis.

Tannese parents assiduously circumcise all their boys, and *kastom* demands an exchange of significant goods between father's and mother's families. This exchange will be balanced when that boy's uncle, in future, circumcises his own son that his brother-in-law will look after, the flows of gifts reversed. An uncircumcised boy is never fully adult and remains unmarriageable. Families have the option of organizing a lesser exchange (*o napuei te nipran,* "arrange a coconut for women") to celebrate a daughter's first menses. This also involves an exchange of pig and kava between husband's and wife's families. Many skip this opportunity, however, unless they need to balance a previous first menses exchange.

Menstruating women no longer retire as once they did to a *nimwa opwei,* a secluded menstrual hut, but while blood is flowing they should neither cook for their husbands and children nor garden. They can still feed the family's pigs. Because they bleed, women are open. Men, in counterpoint, are closed, and curers often bleed sick men, unsealing them to let contaminated blood escape their plugged bodies by slicing open their foreheads. Couples ideally should avoid sex during a wife's pregnancies and during the subsequent two or three years when she nurses her child, lest unsafe sex contaminate and sicken the husband and child alike.

Men warn their sons that overindulgence in sex, which drains a boy's semen supply, will render him ugly and dry and wrinkle his skin. Islanders deplore adultery, and community moots assign fines to two-timing husbands and wives. If a man is particularly sickly, people may accuse his wife of an illicit affair. Men attribute contemporary decline in their masculine prowess to sloppy sexual precautions. In the old days, when men were tougher and more virile, after some sexual encounter they would disinfect themselves with a potion of coconut oil and medicinal leaves (including aromatic *Evodia hortensis*) to wash away *nipeki pran,* the "smell of woman." Today, men worry, is soap enough? Wet dreams are particularly troubling. People blame these on a malevolent spirit, *Nakwa,* who comes for sex in a dream, often disguised as a loved one, to steal men's semen. Wet dreamers suffer body fatigue and muscle stiffness, the typical effects of over-ejaculation.

Female connection, moreover, spoils male accomplishment. Men's dance teams, and their football and sports teams, gather the night before an event to ensure its success. They convene at a kava-drinking ground to drink kava, but also to monitor that none sneaks away for sex, as female affairs, here too, can undermine communal masculine perfection. Kieri's dance mates presumed his fling with Rigi explained his sorry, lackadaisical dancing and they fined him a kava plant.

In homosocial societies, one finds customs of men sharing the same female sexual partner. Before significant Christian conversion, Tannese men, too, cultivated manly relationships with mutual carnal relations with a *preinhap* or *pran vi* (new woman). Local groups of men exchanged girls and installed these in a hut on their kava-drinking grounds. Circumcised boys enjoyed their first sexual experience with a *preinhap* (although those six-year-olds might have to wait a few years). The girl also served married men, which could anger their wives. That period of customary sexual abstinence running from pregnancy through the end of a child's breastfeeding, however, was a lengthy one. Men at one kava-drinking ground without a *pran vi* could borrow one from elsewhere, with the return gift of a pig.

Presbyterian missionaries deprecated these arrangements and they insisted that their Christian converts abandon the girls. Anthropologist Clarence Humphreys, who visited Tanna in the early 1920s and enjoyed missionary hospitality, labeled them "prostitutes." After a circumcision *tamarua,* he reported, a *pran vi* arrived "to initiate the young men who have reached man's estate into the mysteries of sexual intercourse," but "when she is absent a period of abstinence prevails, and very little indulgence in sexual intercourse takes place."[1] Miscellaneous island prophets, dreamers, and would-be chiefs over the years have attempted to revive *pran vi*, but none have succeeded for long. That *kastom*, along with sorcery power stones, endures only in the amber memory of past times.

A century later, risky sex continues to cause worry and unease, and love increasingly troubles marital arrangements. Tanna today is flooded with powerful discourses of romantic love. String boy bands strumming guitars, ukuleles, and gut buckets became popular after the Pacific War, and novel love songs crept into island repertoires. Many youth who have migrated to Port Vila enjoy easy access to romantic movies, songs, and suggestive international advertisement. Those back home have smart phones that connect to global social media. Urban migration has loosened sexuality. Kusi and Antoine thereby escaped family surveillance, and young people in town continue to find private places to meet. They pursue boyfriends and girlfriends, and demand more say in spousal choice. Tannese parents have had to hone their negotiation skills when a child wants to marry someone from one of Vanuatu's central or northern islands, where families demand bride price gifts from boy's family to girl's, rather than some exchanged sister, and these interisland romances are increasingly common

On Tanna, beady-eyed neighbors are deeply suspicious should they find a boy and girl alone together. Girls and women travel in groups, and they avoid catching the eyes of unrelated men. A pigheaded Australian woman I once hosted refused cultural advice and she strode off alone down the road, eyeing men along the way. She returned bedraggled after repelling a lustful local boy. The night of a *nakwiari* festival, when teams of women dance until dawn, offers Tanna's main carnivalesque occasion when boys and girls might meet up in darkness. Town life multiplies these opportunities. Mediated gifts of handkerchiefs or candy have waned. Mobile smart phones are increasingly common, and youth today flirt through texting and sexting. Their phones also tap into the world of global pornography that offers frank images of alien sexual practices. Connoisseurs complain about the production values of locally produced material. Tannese men always firmly deny any homosexual dalliance on *their* island, although on Malakula and other islands in the north boys' initiation ritual included same-sex intercourse. But today, Port Vila shelters a number of homosexual boys and men who have latched onto global gay discourses to identify themselves.

In 2016, *Tanna* played on movie screens worldwide. This Australian-made film (*Two Tribes, One Love*), which featured amateur island actors, won several prizes and was a Foreign Language Academy Award nominee in 2017. Romeo and Juliet in the South Pacific, the film is a romantic pastorale that celebrates love, native virtue, and Tanna's brilliant green forests. The filmmakers relentlessly eradicated all signs of modernity from their sets: no mobile phones, no trucks, no wristwatches, no solar panels, and barely an aluminum cooking pot. Dain and Wawa, in traditional penis wrapper and bark skirt, fall in love. Their parents shatter the romance by arranging instead for Wawa to marry into an enemy village, hoping to make peace. The two lovers escape to the rim of Iasur's volcanic caldera where they commit suicide by eating poisoned mushrooms (which do not exist on Tanna). The sorry parents remorsefully decide to yield to their children's future romantic desires.

The film screened in Port Vila's only movie theater and Tannese people loved it. But the theater rang with hoots and laughter. Dain and Wawa hold hands. They even kiss! Island boys should only hold hands with other boys, and girls only with other girls. Everyone knows. Kusi in Port Vila, now genteel and gray-haired, deplores such modern licentiousness.

Note

1. C. B. Humphreys, *The Southern New Hebrides* (Cambridge: Cambridge University Press, 1926), 46.

Further Readings

Tanna Kinship

Classen, R. W. and R. J. Gregory. "Kinship in Tanna, Southern New Hebrides: Marriage Rules and Equivalence Rules." *Anthropological Linguistics* 18, no. 4 (1976): 168–182.

Island Gender and Sex Relations

Allen, Michael. "Ritualized Homosexuality, Male Power and Political Organization in North Vanuatu: A Comparative Analysis." In *Ritualized Homosexuality in Melanesia*, edited by Gilbert H. Herdt, 83–127. Berkeley: University of California Press, 1984.
Lindstrom, Lamont. "Tanna." *Encyclopedia of Sex and Gender: Men and Women in the World's Cultures*, vol. 1 (2004): 868–876.

Tanna the Movie

Jolly, Margaret. "Tanna: romancer la kastom, éluder l'exotisme? / Tanna: Romancing Kastom, Eluding Exoticism?" *Journal de la Société des Océanistes* 148 (2019): 97–112.

CHAPTER II

Kwatia

K WATIA, KUSI'S OLDEST BROTHER, despite occasional trips to Port
Vila has made his life on Tanna. Born about 1950, he was the oldest boy
of his generation living in the village. His widowed mother looked after
her family as best she could until she married her dead husband's brother. Kwatia
was in his mid-twenties when I first met him. Already he had ambitions to lead.
Age confers authority on Tanna and Kwatia was well placed to be a future chief.
Most young men are reticent to speak up during dispute-settlement meetings
until, when middle-aged, they have established families and solid exchange networks with others. Kwatia, however, although still young and then the father of
just one child, never hesitated to contribute to village discussions even though
his elders might sniff at this impertinence. At one meeting, I was unsettled when
he jumped to his feet to admonish us participants that "we *old men* need to
take charge of things!" I was nearly Kwatia's age, but hardly ready to embrace
my old man status. Power comes with age variously. Americans scheme to stay
young. Tannese men strive to become elders as quickly as they can. When the
Condominium government organized a census in preparation for upcoming
national elections in 1979, Kwatia took the opportunity to add a few years to
his official age.

Kwatia pursued as much schooling as he could, though he completed only five
years of primary education. The few island schools in the 1960s were staffed by
the Presbyterian and other missions, and children typically walked several hours
daily to attend these, or boarded on school grounds. Kwatia, like most children,
was not admitted to one of the colony's few mission-run secondary schools. In
his teens, however, he traveled north to enroll in several technical training programs, including plumbing, carpentry, and bookkeeping. Back home in 1969, he
found a job with one of Tanna's agricultural cooperative societies at Isangel, the
island's government station. The British and French each had established separate economic cooperative societies as an initial step toward the archipelago's
eventual self-governance.

In his twenties, Kwatia pursued Nancy, the daughter of Nase who lived a few villages south around the mountain ridge. Nase held the job of assessor. The British and the French appointed two dozen of these assessors to serve as local experts, advising the district agents during island court cases and transmitting orders back to their communities. Nase noted Kwatia's nerve. Instead of following traditional roads and asking help from intervening men to arrange his marriage, Kwatia handled marital negotiations on his own. He convinced Nancy to elope although he had no sister in hand to return to Nase in exchange for her. Instead, as do many men, he promised a future daughter. Family in Samaria helped with contributions of four pigs and the usual cooked and uncooked taro and yams, kava, bark skirts, baskets and mats, and fathom lengths of cotton cloth and blankets that Kwatia presented to Nase in celebration of their marriage and in return for Nancy's "basket."

Kwatia and Nancy's first child was a son, a boy Kwatia named after himself. Three years later, Nancy bore a daughter, and old Nase named her Maui after his own daughter Maui who would soon move to Pango village, near Port Vila, in exchange for a girl her brother had found there to marry. Maui, still a baby, would live with her parents but belong to her grandfather, her namer. Nase arranged a feast to balance the one he had received from Kwatia several years before. During this, Kwatia's family complained that Nase returned only three pigs (one already dead and eaten) while they had given him four. Kwatia employed his bookkeeping skills to keep careful counts of who had provided what during the first exchange, and he redistributed the food, kava, bark skirts, mats and baskets, cloth, and blankets that Nase provided so that everyone received, roughly, what they had given three years before. Grandfather Nase helped support Maui's education, and she successfully completed secondary school and then nursing college in Fiji and found work as head nurse at the main government hospital on Espiritu Santo.

The cooperative agricultural and marketing societies rarely functioned well and, by the late 1970s, Kwatia was back home busying himself in a variety of local affairs. Tanna's last Presbyterian missionary was then advocating technological training, cognizant of the island's pitiful educational opportunities and, for those few who were selected to attend secondary school, the problematic local value of a Western-style education. He worked diligently to find funding for a variety of projects, distributing these across his congregation. He established one endeavor down on the valley floor, below Samaria. This was a small and simple soap factory with improvised equipment to press and boil coconut oil to be mixed with lye to produce a rough soap. International funders, then, could be arm-twisted into supporting import substitutions. Hahakwi (They Scrub) Soap never made much product despite the persistent efforts of a young Scottish Voluntary Service Overseas advisor. Kwatia hurried to join the enterprise, but he became disillusioned with the broken press, wasted dried coconut, ongoing delays, and the volunteer who had various other duties elsewhere. Kwatia threatened to instruct Samaria's soap workers to abandon the enterprise, and indeed they would, he insisted, since all followed his lead.

Rambo and Kung Fu movies were then exceedingly popular, and Kwatia next leant on his connections with the British Education Office at the government center to arrange an evening film showing at the soap factory, but then shifted this to the local primary school. This festivity, though, would require both a generator and a projector as east Tanna, then as now, has no electric grid. Despite much arranging, many promises, and an audience eagerly gathered, the films, projector, and generator all never arrived.

Kwatia's next proposal to establish a *kastom* school also failed to attract much local interest. An offshoot John Frum group in Iounhanan village, west Tanna, had already founded one of these to much acclaim. (This is the community that would, years later, feature romantically in *Tanna,* the movie.) Despite declaring a special relationship with Prince Philip of Great Britain (secretly, a Tannese brother), the prince's followers celebrated their strong *kastom* knowledge and practice, and they refused to send their children to mission or government schools. The children instead, in *kastom* school, were instructed in traditional and island practicalities, not useless European knowledge. Men and boys also took up wearing penis wrappers, and women bark skirts, but usually only when visitors came around as the neighborhood rapidly turned into a tourist attraction. Back in Samaria, however, most people figured that while *kastom* should be cherished, government schools provided their children at least a possibly better future.

Kwatia had better luck, however, with island politicking. In the late 1970s, the New Hebrides moved bumpily along toward its eventual independence on 30 July 1980 from France and Great Britain. New resources, political organizers, and all sorts of campaign hoopla and puffery poured onto Tanna as colonial advisors and involved island leaders called meetings, ran trainings, and built political party structures, jockeying to win upcoming elections that would establish, first, the National Assembly, and eventually the National Parliament.

Kwatia also busied himself in ceaseless disputes and discussions involving Iasur Volcano that intensified during this burst of national politicking. Iasur, from the 1960s when an Australian trader organized a rudimentary air service to

Port Vila, attracted increasing numbers of tourists. But who owned the volcano? How much should tourists pay to climb it? And who would get the money? Disputing community members regularly found opportunity to club one another, block island roads, and interdict tourist visits. But visitor money was attractive and disputants also convened frequent meetings and discussions, setting up a series of not very effective joint committees to manage Iasur, seeking some sort of compromise that would release the tourist money.

Kwatia took part in these volcano discussions, and he found a larger stage with associated party politics. Years of Anglo-French rivalry in the colony spilled into emerging national politics, as each power looked toward an independent Vanuatu. Would this lean toward France (and maintain French as a national language?), or toward Britain (and Australia, New Zealand, and English)? A tiny elite group of English educated Islanders, many of whom were former seminarians, established what would become the Vanua'aku Party. This, supportive of early independence and suspicious of France, attracted mostly Presbyterian and Anglican adherents throughout the archipelago, including everyone in Samaria. In response, France helped establish a cluster of opposition parties, including John Frum and Kapiel (stone, for *kastom* adherents) on Tanna. These parties, which took independence to be a lengthy process only to arrive in some distant future, attracted the support of many in the Roman Catholic community, among others. They would, by 1978, coalesce with much French choreography behind the scenes as "The Moderates."

After an initial Representative Assembly collapsed, the two colonial powers scheduled a nationwide election for November 1977. The Vanua'aku Party, which objected to the composition of this, boycotted the poll and instead proclaimed the People's Provisional Government, at least in those regions of its greatest support. I was at the Australian National University at the time, waiting for official permission to start field research on Tanna. Administrative worry about growing political agitation throughout the archipelago sidetracked my request, although the Condominium finally allowed me to come as far as Port Vila in February 1978, and I managed to slip down to Tanna that April.

There, political party representatives were busy making connections and firming up support. The Vanua'aku Party appointed various *komisa* (commissars), "subcommittees" (committee chairmen), and secretaries across the island. Iolu Apel, a young organizer and future candidate for Parliament who had worked previously for the British Cooperative system, established the Nikoletan (Canoe/group of the land) as an island council of chiefs that would look after both *kastom* and local governance. Only leading men from Vanua'aku Party supporting villages, however, agreed to participate in this. In February 1979, John Frum and other French supporters marched on the Nikoletan house at Lenakel, burned it to the ground, seized the People's Provisional Government flag, and furthermore uprooted its flagpole. The Vanua'aku Party continued to convene various meetings, however, and Kwatia and Rapi, his father's brother, attended several of these where Kwatia was often appointed clerk to take notes.

Later that year, both sides agreed to participate in a new nationwide poll to elect a new National Assembly and also island government councils. Kwatia tackled the job of teaching women and younger folk how to vote, and how to vote correctly. He also counted up potential voters in the region, reporting these numbers upward. The parties held community meetings and posted election posters. Summoned to attend too many, and too frequent, of these meetings, Samaria families convened yet another to distribute responsibilities. Rapi and Iau would attend to *kastom* concerns; their brothers Koke and Nakutan would look after the church and school; and their son Kwatia would do politics. He participated in candidate selection meetings for the new assembly and for Tanna's island council, although Vanua'aku Party leaders already had made many promises here. When Kwatia returned home to Samaria to report meeting decisions, he often code-shifted into Bislama rather than using Nafe language, signaling his command of the new and still confusing field of national politicking.

Kwatia soon angled to run on the Vanua'aku Party (VP) ticket for the new Island Council, partly by contributing a little money to candidates on the national ballot. He had to pay a 5,000 francs Nouvelles Hébrides (about US$50.00) filing fee and I contributed 1,000 fnh of this. The two sides (Vanua'aku Party and the Moderates) each nominated fifteen candidates whose election to the council would depend on the breakdown of island votes. Kwatia was placed tenth on the Vanua'aku Party list, but only the first eight were elected as Tanna's voters reproduced the island's essential dualism: 2,784 votes for the VP versus 2,718 for the Moderates.

Kwatia's budding political career, however, was not much derailed by his loss. The Island Council never functioned well as only its Vanua'aku Party members would agree to meet, although Kwatia was later appointed council secretary. The New Hebrides became Vanuatu on 30 July 1980, but this was an unsettled independence. A rebellion on Tanna and a more serious one on Espiritu Santo, led by Jimmy Stephens and his Nagriamel movement, disrupted once rosy visions of national unity. On Tanna, John Frum and other French supporters proclaimed an independent Tafea Nation (an acronym of the archipelago's five southern islands Tanna, Aneityum, Futuna, Erromango, and Aniwa) and, on 26

May 1980, kidnapped several government officers. British forces retrieved these and arrested rebel ringleaders. On 10 June, the John Frum army marched across the island and attacked the government station at Isangel, and also the British prison, aiming to free their compatriots. There, they encountered an opposing force of Vanua'aku Party supporters. Rebel leaders, including Alexis Youlu (cousin of Iolu Apel, and likewise a newly elected National Assembly member who had received the most popular votes), attempted to negotiate a truce. Just before dawn, however, wild shooting started, the prisoners made a run for it, tear gas grenades exploded, twelve men were wounded, and Youlu was shot and clubbed dead. Although several inquiries looked into the fracas, no one was charged with his killing.

In subsequent years, Tanna's council of chiefs reformed and resumed its old Nikoletan name, although it has never attracted island-wide support. A new Nikoletan house opened in 2017. Political rivals established competing chiefs' councils that assert their own, purer *kastom* authority including the Council of the Twelve Nakamals. Kwatia joined the Nikoletan, serving first as its treasurer, then chair of the island court system, and eventually as Nikoletan chairman. He also advanced into another religious arena of leadership becoming a church pastor.

In the 1970s, the US Congress, the Federal Communication Commission, and television manufacturers all worked to expand the number of Ultra High Frequency broadcast stations. Miscellaneous pastors and ministers from across the land, including my fellow townsmen, Tulsa's Oral Roberts, Billy James Hargis, T. L. Osborne, and Kenneth Hagen, jumped into the medium if they weren't already broadcasting, becoming televangelists. On the air, they raised considerable funds from the fervid faithful, and some of this money sloshed into the mission fields, including Vanuatu. Jimmy Swaggart opened an outpost in Port Vila, as did Oklahoma's Rhema Bible Training College. A steady flow of missionaries from a variety of new churches, many from Australia or New Zealand, wandered about Tanna seeking converts even though most island families had been one sort of Christian or another since the turn of the twentieth century.

One of the several Apostolic missions, already active on Ambae Island in the 1970s, sent island missionaries south to Tanna. In 1978, two of these visited Samaria's environs, conducting faith healings. In Pentecostalist tradition, the Apostolics favor altar calls, laying-on-of-hands, speaking in tongues, and hymns accompanied with the guitar. Such flamboyant ritual astonished Tanna's staid Presbyterians. Kwatia's father-in-law Nase invited the messengers to attempt their faith cures, including treating Kwatia's brother Tio's painful shoulder.

Kwatia, when he married, moved out of Samaria. He cleared a small hamlet up the slope at Mount Nebo, and lived there with his wife Nancy. These geographic moves are strategic. Everyone living together in one home ground, like Samaria, has an obligation to support village leaders in community political and religious endeavors. Kwatia, though, was eager to escape the oversight of his elders, his father's generation. His new separate residence freed him to go his own way. He had also decided, when younger, not to drink kava, which also allowed a certain independence from daily exchange duties.

Captivated with the Apostolic message, Kwatia decided to leave the Presbyterian denomination much to his family's dismay and his uncles' fury, and so did Nase, his father-in-law. The upstart Apostolic mission then offered several tangible benefits, including three pickup trucks that its members could use, although these soon broke down. One of Kwatia's brothers, and several cousins, followed him into the new church although his half-brother Simeon was then training to become a Presbyterian pastor.

Grandfather Nase built a small Apostolic chapel in his village, but his son and Apostolic Pastor Harrison, a man from Tonga who was sent to lead the new church, disputed church responsibilities and the pastor fled, moving his family in with Kwatia at Mount Nebo. Kwatia offered to clear a parcel of his land on the valley floor and he raised funds to build a sheet iron church house. After some quick study, he next declared himself, or was declared, to be an Apostolic elder and then a pastor himself. When Pastor Harrison moved to Middle Bush to lead newly converted families there, Kwatia assumed his pastoral duties, moving down to the new valley church house, dubbed the Manse. Kwatia subsequently served as chairman of the Tafea District Council of Churches, adding to his various Council of Chiefs responsibilities.

What was left of the Manse blew away during the cyclone of 2015, and Kwatia subsequently has dossed down inside the Nikoletan house, rebuilt at Lenakel, Tanna's emerging urban center that people have renamed Blackman Town. Here, he is well placed to keep his eye on ongoing island political and religious concerns and percolating chiefly schemes.

Brokers

The Tannese are eager importers. As did Kwatia, they seek out interesting material they can broker among themselves: The two dogs that Cook left at Port Resolution in 1774, new cultigens and flowers, foreign place and personal names, novel spirits and rituals, modern political practices, and more. People are likewise quick to invent all sorts of homegrown novelties—John Frum among the most successful of these—although these command greater public attention if presented as a momentous spiritual inspiration rather than some humdrum personal idea or thoughtful proposal. On Tanna, individual creativity doesn't spark. It's boring. Brokers, who import appealing news from the outside world, thereby distinguish themselves. People admire, and sometimes need, their inspiring connections and they will usually give some inspired broker at least an initial hearing.

Kwatia, along these lines, built a winning career on brokering outside knowledge. He moved along from learning the secrets of plumbing, carpentry, and bookkeeping, to helping organize Vanuatu's pre-independence political campaign and elections. Other young men in those years also quickly made themselves into indispensable clerks, subcommitteemen, and secretaries. They admitted the authority of their elders, those chiefs, but they knew that their schooling and their national connections provided new bases of status and political influence. Someone had to take notes, to count heads, and to teach others how to use the electoral system where voters chose paper slips with candidate names, photographs, and symbols, placed these into envelopes, and then into ballot boxes.

Rival island brokers pushed other sorts of alien wisdom, whose inward flows increased as the colonial New Hebrides transformed. Some then, to give one example, advocated membership in a mysterious outland organization, the Red Cross. Pay up 60 cents for a "chair" and one could win money after every forthcoming island disaster or unfortunate house fire. Alongside politics and religion, Kwatia developed a reputation as a *kastom* expert although, given his father's early death, he relied on his uncles and on his active participation in dispute-settlement meetings to build this knowledge. He drew on this in his capacity of island court judge.

Kwatia was not alone in leaving the established island churches after 1980. The older mission churches lost members to glitzier brands of Christianity. Eager missionaries and new resource flows attracted many to join incoming Baptist, Latter-day Saints, Baha'i, Four Corners, Holiness Fellowship, Assembly of God, Living Waters, and many more congregations, most of which proclaimed gospels of health and wealth. Several Tanna families decided that Islam is the true *kastom*. Sulphur Bay's John Frum movement, in 2000, also broke up into three parts, one of these the Unity movement that followed the inspirations of the Prophet Fred.

Kwatia's Apostolic mission has roots in American Pentecostalism. In Vanuatu, it introduced novel liturgical ritual including altar calls (sinners come forward to be saved), immersive baptism, faith healing through prayer and touch, speaking in tongues and, where electricity is available, electric guitar performances. Nase's Apostolic chapel featured a cross inscribed with Acts 2:42: "And they continued steadfastly in the apostles' doctrine and fellowship, and in breaking of bread, and in prayers." I attended the ribbon-cutting of this chapel, joining the celebration. Collected area pastors wore white shirts, ties, and sunglasses. New converts shyly joined in with call-and-response antiphony and sinner altar calls. I can say, based on my Oklahoma experience, the attempted glossalia and clumsy faith healings were pitiful. People did their awkward best with all this. No Islander I knew in the 1970s could fall into an ecstatic trance. Tutored by sober Presbyterians, Christian ritual (apart from enthusiastic singing) was then very composed and mostly dull. Even those brokering novel information from ancestors and spirits merely went to sleep and dreamed, or sometimes secluded themselves inside a house or some forest glade. In years since, the Apostolics and other Pentecostal converts have honed Islanders' rapturous skills. The Prophet Fred who, after many years' employment on Korean fishing boats, returned to Tanna in 2000 with a new message of island unity and a distinctive connection to Fetukwai, the spirit of the morning star, likewise incorporated trance into his weekly Wednesday services. Women followers, who Fred dubbed *glas* (glass; mirror), somehow learned to trance, and in these trances they jerkily danced as they discerned through the Holy Spirit those in the congregation who had committed sin.

When I left Tanna for the first time at the end of 1979, I found myself caught between Kwatia and his uncle Rapi as I was preparing for a going-home feast. Both asked for my heavy black shortwave radio. This was a clunky piece of Soviet Union technology I bought in Australia, but it efficiently picked up broadcasts from across the world. I promised this to Rapi but Kwatia dearly wanted it, and he listed off all the various assistance he had offered me during the previous months. He threatened to bash Rapi, and alarmed family members jumped in to separate the two. I hedged by appealing to Rapi, who agreed that the radio might belong to everyone in Samaria although Kwatia would look after it. I promised to buy Rapi a new radio on my way home through Port Vila. The row continued, though, and Rapi yelled that he would rip the *kaio* (plumed hair stick, signifying chiefly status) from Kwatia's head; that he would never become a leader.

Rapi's prediction has come true, but only for Samaria itself since Kwatia has instead excelled in broader political arenas. That shortwave radio, that voice transmitting alien news, was then a broker's prized tool. Like ancestral dreams, it could inspire. Nowadays, however, outland voices stream into Tanna from many sources and devices and from many directions. Island knowledge brokers have likewise proliferated.

Respect

Brokers, with luck behind them, gather audiences who want to listen and learn. Tanna's diffuse systems of authority, however, along with its numerous and sundry chiefs, can undercut a particular broker's message, his popularity eventually draining away. It is difficult for chiefs and leaders to smother the competition. Yes, men do deny women and their juniors the right to drink kava and, thus, to be inspired while intoxicated. But anyone can dream up ancestral wisdom or connect otherwise to inspiring figures. Movement leaders for years, for example, sought to prevent Elizabeth, daughter of John Frum boss Nampas at Sulphur Bay, from contacting John Frum to diagnose, cure, and to prophesy. But to no avail. She simply accepted gifts of flowers from her followers, disappeared into her house, and emerged with novel, desired information. Travel, access to education, even radios, and today's tourists all offer brokering possibilities.

On Tanna, "the kingdom of the individual" as anthropologist Jean Guiart called the place, most anyone can achieve distinction even if this distinction is temporary as people move along to attend the next marvel, the next outlandish wonder. Brokers must be vigilant. Gusts of incoming novelty can unsettle carefully constructed island hierarchies, turning aside people's interests. Where brokers are attentive and messages effective, however, island hierarchies remain strong as was the Presbyterian Tanna Law of the early twentieth century, and the John Frum movement up through 2000. People willingly give support to wise leaders and to their projects. In November 1979, I worked the polling station at Iamanuapen School, finding voter names on the parliamentary electoral roll and handing out ballots. Privately, I ticked off the candidate I guessed a voter would support, based on that voter's home village. When we counted up the 220 ballots, I was off only by eleven votes. Nearly everyone had followed their village leaders' instruction about whom they must choose. In the 1970s, politicking was fierce and allegiances strong, and brokers could count on their supporters.

With intensifying global flows, political and religious alliances have increasingly splintered. An assortment of incoming overseas information and resources present richer brokering opportunities. Samaria itself, home of seven families in the 1970s, has fractured. By 2000, the village housed only two extended families as onetime residents staked out their own new hamlets along the ridge from valley floor to Mount Nebo, and as they enlisted in diverse new religious and political associations.

Chiefs, today, have many worries. They fixate on respect, or rather lack of respect. Respect, for dividual Islanders, is the converse of shame. While elders everywhere might grumble that younger generations ignore their hard-won wisdom, on Tanna these complaints are particularly rife. The *New Bislama Dictionary*'s definition of *respek* provides just one exemplar sentence: *Ol yangfala long taon samtaem oli no gat respek blong ol jif,* "Young people in town sometimes don't have respect for the chiefs."[1] Respect, when a chief command this, guarantees that people esteem his advice, admire his leadership, and contribute to his community projects. Lack of respect signals that people's ears have turned elsewhere. When missionary William Watt translated the New Testament, he mainly used the Nafe verb *isiai* to mean "honor," as in the fifth commandment, *Tikisiai remam rihnam,* "Honor your father [and] your mother." Its meaning has slid now toward respect. When trouble or community conflict occurs, frustrated talk turns to the need for, and the sad lack of, *nisiaiien* or *respek*.

In 2010, I recorded Kwatia's recollections of his career. He ended the story with a typical chiefly respect gripe: "Before, life on Tanna was good. But today young people are watching too many videos, learning how people in those videos and in Port Vila behave, and they adopt those behaviors and no longer respect their chiefs." Respect worries notably have increased in conjunction with Vanuatu's substantial urban migration flows, in that wayward migrants can partly dodge chiefly surveillance. In town, moreover, although they live with kin, migrants are surrounded by strangers from other islands who, lacking proper respect and honor, may be up to no good.

Respect worries color Vanuatu's national political discourse as well. Many continue to quote Father Walter Lini, the country's first prime minister who, combining respect with honor, wrote: "We believe that small is beautiful, peace is powerful, respect is honourable, and community is both wise and practical for the people of Vanuatu."[2] Focused adamantly on respect, few acknowledge Lini's associated appreciation of smallness, peace, or a wise and practical community. Iolu Abbil (Apel) from Tanna, who served as country's sixth president, reminded members of Parliament "about the importance of instilling youth with the value of loyalty and respect."[3] Government agencies likewise evoke respect. Vanuatu's Department of Correctional Service's motto is *Sefti, digniti, rispek mo gud fasin blong evriwan,* "Safety, dignity, respect and good manners for all."

Respect serves as a marker, a canary in the urban coalmine, of the strength and viability of hierarchical relationships that conjoin parents and children, husbands and wives, people and chiefs, and even prisoners and their keepers. *Respek* talk sustains these inequalities, or at least tries to. It signals ideals of cooperation that alien ideas and urban experience threaten and corrode. *Respek* is the antidote, so people hope, to novelty, to creeping individuality, and to troublesome urban freedoms. Kwatia, reflecting on his career, compared town and island and, like nearly everyone, deprecated life in Port Vila despite its occasional charms and excitements. Life, he said, is better on the island. In Port Vila, one must have money to eat, drink, and even to sleep. On Tanna, everything is free, at least for those with a family, pigs, and gardens. On the island, moreover, a man is his own boss, although elders like Kwatia enjoy such personal independence largely because they command younger dependents.

Making himself through the years into a chief, Kwatia subsumed politics, religion, and also *kastom*. As an island court judge, land concerns him greatly. Not just disputes over land, which are incessant, but worry that Islanders might sell their home grounds to outlanders, as has happened in Port Vila and around Efate Island where much land has been alienated. Tannese migrants themselves have purchased some of this. In 2012, Kwatia shared his chiefly wisdom with people gathered in Blacksands settlement, outside Port Vila, for the naming ceremony of his great-nephew: "Without our land we will starve. We are adrift at sea, but we must cling to *kastom*." Kwatia has clung to Tanna, and done well, but many other family members have sought a living in Port Vila's settlements. Samaria, since 1980, has emptied out. Or rather, village families now stretch across islands.

Notes

1. Terry Crowley, *A New Bislama Dictionary* (Suva: Institute of Pacific Studies, University of the South Pacific; Vila: Pacific Languages Unit, 1995), 200.

2. Walter Hadye Lini, "The Future," in *Vanuatu: Twenti Wan Tingting long Team blong Independens,* edited by Barry Weightman and Hilda Lini (Suva: Institute of Pacific Studies, University of the South Pacific, 1980), 290.

3. Anonymous, "President: Teach Youth Value of Respect and Loyalty," *Daily Post,* May 30, 2014.

Further Readings

Vanuatu Independence

Beasant, John. *The Santo Rebellion: An Imperial Reckoning.* Honolulu: University of Hawai'i Press, 1984.
Bonnemaison, Joël. *The Tree and the Canoe: History and Ethnogeography of Tanna.* Honolulu: University of Hawai'i Press, 1994.

Howard, Van Trease, ed. *Melanesian Politics: Stael blong Vanuatu.* Suva: University of the South Pacific, 1995.

Anglo-French in the New Hebrides and Vanuatu

Miles, William F. S. *Bridging Mental Boundaries in a Postcolonial Microcosm: Identity and Development in Vanuatu.* Honolulu: University of Hawai'i Press, 1998.

Chief Councils on Tanna

Tabani, Marc. "Tannese Chiefs, State Structures, and Global Connections in Vanuatu." *The Contemporary Pacific* 31, no. 1 (2019): 65–103

Prophet Fred's Unity Movement

Tabani, Marc. "Dreams of Unity, Traditions of Division: John Frum, '*kastom*' and Inter-Manipulation Strategies as Cultural Heritage on Tanna (Vanuatu)." *Paideuma* 55 (2009): 27–47.

Respect Concerns

Lindstrom, Lamont. "*Respek* et autres mots-clés du Port-Vila urbain." *Journal de la Société des Océanistes* 144/145 (2017): 23–36.

CHAPTER 12

Tio and Natis

H ENRI OHLEN'S PARENTS BROUGHT him from New Caledonia to the New Hebrides in 1913 when he was fifteen. In 1926, he purchased 250 hectares of land just north of Port Vila where he planted coconut palms and ran cattle. He later bought a larger plantation at Devil's Point, but his heirs held on to those original hectares. After Vanuatu's independence, urban migrants including many from Tanna, found room on Ohlen's former plantation to build shacks and plant gardens. Ohlen became one of Port Vila's main migrant settlements. Vanuatu's constitution declared that all land (except that within town boundaries) reverted at independence to *kastom* owners. Ifira Islanders moved to assert land claims outside the town as well as undeveloped land within, including much of Ohlen's plantation. Located at the entrance to Vila harbor, Ifira along with three other peri-urban villages managed to endure throughout the colonial period, in large part by providing labor for European settlers and traders. To advance Ifira's land claims and also to cultivate his political clientele, a member of Parliament invited urban newcomers to settle on Ohlen's former cattle paddocks, underneath the failing coconut palms.

Throughout Melanesia's colonial era, urban migration patterns tended to be circular. Men, and a few village women like Kusi, came to town seeking a few months' work and then returned to their island homes. These jobs paid low wages, but young men appreciated travel away from home as they did Port Vila's urban amusements. Most then went home to Tanna to build a house, enlarge their food gardens, marry, and start families.

After 1980, many new island migrants left Tanna for Port Vila, including Tio, Kwatia's younger brother. Finished with primary school on Tanna, Tio found his way to Port Vila several times, buying passage on interisland cargo ships. Employed on various Efate Island plantations, he tended pigs, built cattle fences, milked dairy cows, and learned to ride stock horses. Home on Tanna, he also learned to drive at the Presbyterian Technology Institute, and this skill would later support his family in town. Tio was in his early twenties, handsome,

unmarried, and living in Samaria when I arrived in 1978. He moved out of a wild
cane-walled, sugar cane-thatched house he recently had built so I could move in,
and he generously helped teach me Nafe language. Tio also would later fearlessly
sample wine that I fermented from local oranges and the beer I brewed from
manioc root, products of my second year on the island when I could not find
anything more useful to do.

Tio, when I met him, was not yet Tio but was rather named Nasu. Tio, then,
was a man in his fifties who had never married. Old bachelors are exceedingly
rare on an island of arranged marriages where every person offers a valuable opportunity to cement or augment a family's exchange relationships with other
families. Marriage plans for the old Tio, however, over the years had flopped
several times, and he lived alone although surrounded by relatives. He had his
eye, however, on Natis, a young girl owed him for the marriage of his sister. In
a year or so, he might at last find a wife. The last of his name-set, Tio managed
several tracts of land along with associated personal names. With no children of
his own, he adopted Kwatia's father and he gave a name, Nasu, to Kwatia's baby
brother, who would be his nominated heir.

A year after I arrived, old Tio fell gravely ill. He was unable to speak and could
barely move. Villagers worried. They consulted *kleva* spirit mediums seeking
a diagnosis. Several local healers appeared to treat Tio with *kastom* medicine.
They rubbed his feet with hot leaves. They sprayed masticated leaves on his
face. Nothing worked. The village then hired a truck that carried Tio off to
the French clinic at White Sands where the doctor ordered intravenous feeding. As is proper and loving, Tio's relatives slept next to him in his sick room
as no one ever should be left alone. They urged him to eat food from his home
ground to retrieve his strength. When Tio's health declined further, a second
truck was hired to cart him over the mountain to the British hospital on Tanna's
western coast.

Much anxious talk took place as villagers sought the cause of Tio's illness.
Was it ancestral displeasure at a recent fight between two brothers-in-law that
led one family to abandon Samaria for the valley floor? Tio's adopted kin sent
down a kava and a fowl, asking that the departed brother-in-law spit kava for
Tio's health. Or were ancestral spirits angry at young Natis' obvious reluctance
to marry an elder spouse? Or upset that two men who managed the power stones
that ensure a good harvest of Tahitian chestnuts had failed to organize a proper
First Fruits ceremony for these? Men from several neighboring villages gathered
together daily for kava. Fowls were sacrificed, one killed and thrown over the

ridge in hopes of placating those demanding ancestors. Nothing worked. The doctor diagnosed tuberculous meningitis, but Tio died unexpectedly of a stroke.

I woke to sharp keening in the middle of the night. A truck had returned late with Tio's body. The village filled with wails and sobbing. Death launches the final exchange in three generations of family dealings. Men from the deceased's mother's family must dig the grave and be compensated for their efforts. Samaria sent messages up the roads, and by mid-morning groups of mourners began to arrive. One could hear them approach, chatting and murmuring. They stopped to compose themselves at the village boundary, and then came through with gifts of cloth, blankets, and mats, everyone wailing vigorously. Women squeezed into Tio's small hut to hug and tug at his body. Men gathered outside for solemn talk and shared tobacco.

Islanders are caring and kind to their elders, having in mind that these will soon transmute into possibly unruly ancestral spirits. They are even more considerate of the newly dead whose unleashed souls lurk close by. Stand-ins for Tio's mother's people (who had yet to appear) dug his grave. Tanna graves feature a side niche at the bottom, an alcove that shelters the body from falling filler earth. This, too, comforts the deceased, as do the *tamafa* kava libations and prayers that gathered men uttered that evening: "We have buried Tio in love. No one be angry." Tio's family carried his body, wrapped in cloth, blankets, mats, and woven coconut fronds, to the grave. Two Christian elders offered prayers. As grave diggers lowered him into the ground, people restrained his female relatives who fought to jump in after him, to join him in the other side, the afterworld (figure 11).

Men, including the gravediggers who returned from a ritual cleansing at a nearby spring, congregated at the kava-drinking ground to prepare kava and to cook one of the two pigs that family members provided. The gravediggers would take away the second. Along the way, Nakutan spied a peregrine falcon flying overhead. A sign, he told me, that an *Ierumanu* chief had passed. That day, men in Tio's adopted family stopped shaving. They would let their beards grow for at least a year and celebrate shaving these off with another small feast of kava libation and family memories. The following week, they razed Tio's house, uprooted a few decorative and medicinal bushes he had planted, and cut down several of his coconut palms. In years past, people destroyed the gardens and all the palms of a dead man, but these had become too valuable as cash crops. A month later, men from Tio's mother's family returned to Samaria to clean the grave and to receive another gift of five pigs, giving several in return. During a

FIGURE 11. Tio's funeral, 1979. Photo by author.

final round of kava drinking, everyone spat respectful kava libations praying Tio to rest in peace.

Also about a month later, Tio's adopted heirs summoned important men from the neighborhood to a name change feast. My friend Nasu would take dead Tio's name, and his three-year old nephew who Nasu, while still a teenager, had himself named and adopted, would assume the newly available Nasu name. "My grandchild," I called out to him the next day, "what's your name?" "Why, I'm Nasu," he told me smoothly. The neighborhood luminaries drank and spit kava, announcing the two name changes to all, dead and alive. This was, I presumed, a strategic move on the part of Tio's adopted heirs. By quickly asserting their rights to the Tio name and its associated lands, they forestalled competing claims from other related name-sets.

Tio's family turned to the problem of young Natis. Natis, about fourteen, had come to Samaria after a typically complicated series of exchanges beginning with the marriage of her grandmother and then that of Tio's sister. Balancing out these previous marriages, she moved to Samaria where she cooked for old Tio. One day, perhaps, she might marry him. But before Tio died, she once eloped with a teenaged boy from her mother's village, one ridge west of Samaria. This precipitated a dispute-settlement meeting that ended horribly in a bloody fight. Various participants were irritated with Natis, but also much annoyed due to many other previous disagreements among families in the two villages. I tapped my bandage and alcohol supply to bind up wounded heads. The principal antagonists were elderly *nieri,* brothers-in-law. The fight thus embarrassed and shamed everyone as *nieri* should interact together easily, with banter and jokes. Everyone expects brothers-in-law interaction to be friendly, cheery, and teasing. Clubbing heads and drawing blood was seriously shocking.

The clash did end Natis' romance, the boy's family ordering him to behave, but she took refuge on the valley floor with her grandmother. Samaria demanded her back, and her uncle eventually led her up the ridge to the village with a rope tied around her neck. Men typically opt for restoring working relationships among themselves over any inconvenient woman's desires. The new Tio attempted another getaway to Port Vila, but his brother Kwatia blocked him before he could embark on an interisland cargo boat. Resigned to family designs, he began building a new house that he would need should he marry, since I was living in his original one. He walled this with sheet aluminum, provided by one of his brothers-in-law, this the first village house of many to come constructed of aluminum sheets and cement bricks. My field notes recorded my grumbles about ugly modernity.

Natis' father was long dead, so her grandmother's second husband and her uncle came up to Samaria to negotiate her marriage with the new Tio. Tio's father killed three pigs, kava was found, and food cooked in earth ovens. At the kava ground, Natis' uncle chewed root for Tio, and Tio as a newly married man took a few sips of his first sanctioned drink. His father, however, helped drain the oversized coconut shell as Tio, like his brother Kwatia, chooses not to imbibe. Men from both families spit their last mouthfuls of kava for marital success: "No sickness, no trouble." We all returned to the village to eat more pork and baked tuber pudding. The village string band strummed and sang until past midnight. Celebrants danced and sipped from a bottle of wine and half bottle of whiskey bummed from me. Natis, the next day, quietly joined Tio in his newly built house.

When I returned to Vanuatu two years later, Tio and Natis had left Samaria and were living up in Port Vila with their first child. Tio found work at Bellevue plantation, and he and Natis occupied a shack atop the cement foundations of the US Navy Base Hospital #2 laid during the Pacific War. Independent Vanuatu undertook to improve children's educational opportunities, and Tio's younger sister, and then his younger brother, had been admitted to new secondary schools. But village families then faced paying several hundred dollars in school fees and travel expenses each year. Tio's sister would become a schoolteacher, his brother a Presbyterian pastor. Tio's earnings mostly paid their school fees, and he has continued to work in Port Vila to cover the educational expenses of his own children, and then his grandchildren.

In 1983, the family moved briefly to Kakao settlement, and then took up the Ifira Island politician's invitation to occupy a part of the old Ohlen plantation. Port Vila's population boomed with new urban migrants. Incoming families from Samaria improvised shacks in several swelling squatter settlements, including Ohlen, Blacksands, and Prima. Tio improvised a sheet aluminum house at the north end of Ohlen, and he and Natis planted a garden of manioc, sweet potato, and banana on some unoccupied land, down the bluff near Tagabe Creek. Living in Ohlen, Tio and Natis had three more children. Over the years, the government has brought water standpipes into many settlement compounds. Outdoor latrines are easy to dig. Migrants occasionally access electricity by purchasing credit on prepaid meter cards, although many tap into pirate connections.

As Port Vila expanded, entrepreneurs invested in taxis and minivans (*bas*) that transport residents from settlements to town, and also serve increasing numbers of overseas tourists who arrive by air or cruise ship. Tio, drawing on his driving skills, found new work as a town taxi driver. He drove taxis for town businessmen until he saved enough money to purchase his own. Like most, this had no working meter. Customers negotiate fares upfront. Tio staked out his territory at the airport as overseas tourists reliably pay higher fares. Over the years, like many settlement pioneers, he also enlarged his original house to rent rooms to newer migrants who continued to arrive from Tanna and other islands. Eventually, he built three additional rental shacks income from which he supports his family.

Natis, like many settlement women, earns a little cash selling garden produce and cooked food, washing clothes, and babysitting. With other Ohlen women, she joined the VANWODS (Vanuatu Women's Development Scheme) microfinance organization. Sponsored by the government and the United Nations Development Program, the organization lends small amounts of money to groups of settlement women to support a variety of business endeavors, including trade stores, bakeries, catering, and handicraft production. Natis' company borrowed money for sewing machines and cloth to sew island dresses, church choir robes, and other clothing. The collective, however, often did not earn enough to make its monthly loan repayments. Tio's taxi earnings helped cover Natis' share of the shortage. What money Natis does make helps pay for the family's daily food.

Tio, by 2010, saved enough from taxi driving and from rents to acquire a National Bank loan to purchase a second taxi and a bus that one of his sons would drive. His profits, however, failed to cover monthly repayments and the bank repossessed both vehicles. He also ran unsuccessfully for Port Vila's City Council in the Tagabe Ward. More than a half dozen political parties, however, compete in the city's scrappy politics. People from every island across the archipelago populate the settlements, and it is difficult for candidates to build successful political coalitions.

In recent years, Tio gave up driving taxis and has worked in an automobile garage owned by a Fiji-Indian businessman. He lives much of the time on a piece of property at Erakor Hafbrij that he helped his sister purchase. Natis keeps the Ohlen family house open. Of their children, only their oldest son returned briefly to Tanna. He taught in several of the island's primary schools, but later moved to Williams Bay Secondary School on Erromango, where John Williams and James Harris met their sudden demise. Tio's other children, all grown now, live in town. His aged mother lives in Samaria. Whenever I hear her grumbles of loneliness, she quizzes me: "Have her children and grandchildren in Vila sent along any bread or fried cakes?"

City Life

Apart from old Isaac who left Samaria in the 1960s for plantation work on Efate Island, returning only to die fifty years later, Tio and Natis in 1981 were the first couple to leave the village behind. They were soon joined in Port Vila by most of their siblings and cousins, who come and go from Tanna to Efate, often staying in town for years. Port Vila offers both better schools and salaried employment to cover expenses for children schooled in town, or left back home in the village, which has dwindled. Or rather, Samaria has spread beyond Tanna as village families developed new trans-island connections.

Samaria's families have built town houses in several of the settlements that sprouted around Port Vila. Some, like Tio and Natis, live in Ohlen. Others found space in Blacksands, Freswin, Beverly Hills, Freswota, Bladiniere, or Prima. Sheet aluminum and junk lumber are favored building material, although over the years migrants have improved their houses, cementing floors and erecting cinder block walls. Those, however, who live uneasily on disputed lands hold back on home improvement, figuring that government bulldozers might arrive unexpectedly some early morning accompanied by police with court eviction orders.

Like Tio and Soarum, Tannese men in town work as drivers, in construction, in garages, and other jobs that do not require much education or significant

English or French language skills. Like Natis, Kusi, and Sivur women work as housegirls, seamstresses, and shop clerks. Those blessed with a family member elected to the National Parliament might find employment as government cleaners or drivers. Much work, however, is paid under the table as private employers evade business regulations and mandated employee compensation. Many migrants put in long hours, six or even seven days a week, for Vanuatu's minimum wage of 220 vatu/hour (about US$1.90). Village men also have moved into the growing security field, working as guards in stores, banks, and other establishments. One of Tio's cousins, for example, found a weekend job from dusk to dawn, guarding an ATM machine near a dance club. A nephew has a steadier, government job, providing night security for Vanuatu's National Museum.

Migrants, although they come to town to make money, complain frequently that town life instead costs money. Housing, food, water, transport—one must pay for everything. Some are particularly incensed that toilet attendants in Port Vila's main marketplace charge an entry fee. In counterpoint, people celebrate and remember their village home grounds, where life is free, although many can afford only an occasional trip back to Tanna, typically around Christmas and the New Year. To augment low and often erratic wages, most migrants establish kitchen gardens on scraps of available land within or near their settlement yards. Expert horticulturalists, they bring to town farming skills along with the range of island staples, particularly manioc that is easy to grow on marginal ground. Urban garden products supplement the store-bought rice and baked bread that people often cannot afford.

Urban migrants nostalgically evoke village tranquility. Samaria is calm, Port Vila noisy. The village is a haven, the town is dangerous. In Samaria, where everyone is closely related, life is secure. In settlements, migrants live with extended families as additional relatives continue to arrive in town and move in with kin already there. But settlements are jumbles of compounds, and one's near neighbors may have come from anywhere in the country. Town merchants and businessmen fret about security, but so do nervous migrants. They readily adopted the Bislama term *sekiuriti* and also *wajman* and *gadman* (watchman, guard). Older urbanites, too, are critical of youthful use of marijuana, and they point out lazybone layabouts who grow, smoke, and sell the drug in the settlements. Marijuana enthusiasts have brought the plant back to Tanna and smoke it there too. Many parents are convinced that its use leads to urban madness and folly. Like Kwatia on Tanna, migrants grouse often about *respek,* or rather the lack of this, wishing for more but expecting less.

Settlement sorcery fears have multiplied as migrants struggle with the everyday challenges of urban life. Sorcery offers explanations for worrisome illness, madness, and other misfortune, and disease and economic uncertainties are ordinary and widespread in town. Tanna's migrants particularly worry about *nakaemas, masing, su,* or *posen* (poison), sorcery techniques from northern Vanuatu. Tio warned me to take care where I drink kava in Port Vila. A cunning sorcerer might kill me by slipping a *neirapin posen* bundle into my drink. Settlement gossip circulates about obscure vampires who suck the blood of the unwary, about child-killing mothers, criminal rapists, and mysterious deaths. Settlement sorcery disputes sometimes escalate into violent confrontation, as happened in 2009 when Blacksands migrants from Tanna and Ambrym Islands battled one another and then the police, burning down a number of houses.

As urban settlements expanded, migrants created a new sort of community leader, the *taon jif* (town chief). These are older men who command at least some respect. Most settlements have a number of these, as each represents his home community. Tio is one of these, looking after migrants from Samaria and its environs in Ohlen. When disputes and problems occur, town chiefs summon one another to sit and talk. Tio complained to me that he "talks until he is tired." Common disruptors of settlement peace include drinking, fighting, adultery, sorcery, swearing, and gossip, problems aggravated if disputes break out between migrants from different island communities. Nervous settlement life encourages new sorts of urban etiquette and politeness. Mary Matheson in 1860 grumped that the Tannese have no word for gratitude, and William Watt, translating the New Testament in 1890, also found no Nafe equivalent for "thank you." Nowadays, however, people have invented the interjection *tanak,* assuring their neighbors of their appreciation, and lubricating often delicate settlement relationships.

Urban life is anxious and hard, but need for money remains intense even though the government has progressively waived its school fee requirements. More than this, Port Vila offers various attractions. Yes, everyone needs cash to afford school expenses and travel, but this is also a handy and socially acceptable excuse. Some come to town to trade their often-monotonous village lives for the city's brighter lights. Electricity, stores, civic events, television broadcasts, and Port Vila's system of minibuses and taxis make life easier and more vibrant than what Tanna can offer, at least for people with vatu in their pockets. "Will you miss electricity and your television if you go home to Samaria?" I asked Tio and Natis. "No, no, no," or so both replied.

Voyages

Islanders care deeply for home ground. Men especially, whose personal names embed them in the landscape, identify themselves with island soil. Women do so, too, although marriage often moves them from their parents' village to their husband's village. But places and people are gridded into networks that stretch across Tanna and beyond. Everyone has a home, but travel abroad creates and maintains useful new relationships and desirable larger unities. Despite rooted identities, Islanders appreciate mobility that encourages connection, prestige, and enlarged personhoods. In 1979, to celebrate the ending of the Iquaramanu Primary School year, parents hired two trucks to drive children up and down the road. Almost all had not yet traveled farther than they could walk. The gift, here, was motion.

The circular migration that once characterized the New Hebrides offered young men, and some brave women like Kusi, temporary respite from Tanna and fresh experience abroad, either appealing or alarming. Some considered these briefer voyages a sort of rite of passage, an oats-sowing, after which youth should return home, get serious, and get married. After Vanuatu's independence, urban migration patterns bent toward one-way journeys as previous circling from island to town and back slowed. Most migrant men began bringing their wives and children along to live with them in Port Vila.

Families have responded to extended residences in Port Vila in several ways. As they can, they fashion urban settlements after villages. Tanna's cultural landscape is concentrically conceived. Circular kava-drinking clearings, where people dance, debate, and exchange, are the focus of home space. Houses and hamlets encircle these clearings, with gardens and the forest farther afield. In town, migrants cleared urban versions of island-style kava-drinking grounds, where these can be squeezed into settlement geography, and they convene on these to prepare and drink kava for family exchanges, for debate, and for dispute settlement, much as they do when home on Tanna. Migrants mark unfamiliar city places with island names, as did Soarum and others who brought new place names back from Australia. Tio's cousin, for example, named his Blacksands kava-drinking ground Kraisun, after one of Iasur's volcanic vents. In Ohlen, the nearest kava bar is named "At the Banyan tree trunk."

Village families, split between Tanna and Efate, have remade themselves as trans-island units. They maintain connections to both places. Migrants return to Samaria during the Christmas and New Year's holiday seasons. They send some children home to be cared for by grandparents, aunts, or uncles. Village and town relatives ship garden produce and store-bought goods (bolts of cloth, for example) to one another, as contributions to family exchange responsibilities either in town or on Tanna. Messages pass regularly, and the spread of mobile telephones after 2008 has made possible daily communication.

On Tanna, trans-island families have bolstered celebrations of a boy's first shave. Old Tio's kinsmen, including the new Tio, marked shaving off a year of mourning's beard growth with a small feast and kava libation. Tannese families similarly organize exchanges between a boy's father and his mother's brother to mark the first time he shaves his whiskers. I saw few of these celebrations back in the 1970s but, today, they have become common. The mother's brother (or his son) shaves off his nephew's fuzzy chin hair, and he drinks kava and spits *tamafa* praying for the boy's success wherever in future he may go. Kin and friends line up to shake hands with the boy and his parents, and they pile up gifts of store-bought goods including sheets and towels, soap, basins, plates, and the like. This ceremonial recognition of a young man's approaching adulthood, which pointedly celebrates his enduring familial connections and responsibilities, strengthens family ties. Most boys soon will move to Port Vila taking with them the memory of their enduring duties to kin back home, reinforcing the ties that connect the village and urban branches of their trans-island families.

Circular labor migration has returned, within an enlarged sphere. Both Australia (with its Seasonal Worker Program) and New Zealand (Recognized Seasonal Employer Scheme) recruit ni-Vanuatu men and women to pick fruit and grapes, work in packing houses, and undertake other sorts of farm work. Workers must return home after six months in Australia, or seven in New Zealand. Just as thousands of Tannese men and women, beginning in the 1860s, signed up to work on plantations in Australia, New Caledonia, Fiji, and Samoa, so are they going abroad again. Rudely denigrated as "blackbirds" during the nineteenth century, Tanna's overseas recruits today are welcomed as seasonal guest workers. Most return home with savings to improve their houses, buy land on Efate, or pay more school expenses. Soarum several times has followed his ancestral namesake abroad, as has his wife. They invested their overseas earnings in a taxi truck, shipped down to Tanna. The renamed young Nasu, now grown with a family of his own, along with others from Samaria have several times voyaged back-and-forth to New Zealand and Australia.

Some long-term urban migrants from Samaria have lived abroad now for more than forty years. A respected town chief, Tio tells me he has retired from business. Where next, then? Everyone promises to return home to Samaria before they die, beating, so they hope, death back to the island. Whenever a migrant dies in Port Vila, families attempt to collect enough money to fly the body back to home ground. Refusal to bury ones dead in town is an important marker of vital trans-islandism. Those few villagers who have returned home to Tanna always leave grown children to occupy the family's settlement compound in town. So long as a family remains situated in both Port Vila and Samaria, its places and persons are thereby amplified. Every year that I find Tio and Natis still living in Ohlen, I ask them when they are going home to Samaria. "Soon, soon," they say.

Further Readings

Tanna Migrants in Port Vila

Lindstrom, Lamont. "Vanuatu Migrant Lives in Village and Town." *Ethnology* 50 (2011): 1–15.

———. "Urban(e) Tannese: Local Perspectives on Settlement Life in Port Vila, Vanuatu." *Journal de la Société des Océanistes* 133 (2011): 18–29.

Settlement Life

Eriksen, Annelin, and Knut Rio. "Demons, Devils, and Witches in Pentecostal Port Vila: On Changing Cosmologies of Evil in Melanesia." In *Pentecostalism and Witchcraft: Spiritual Warfare in Africa and Melanesia,* edited by Knut Rio, Michelle MacCarthy, and Ruy Blanes, 189–210. Cham, Switzerland: Palgrave Macmillan, 2017.

Mitchell, Jean. "'Operation Restore Public Hope': Youth and the Magic of Modernity in Vanuatu." *Oceania* 81, no. 1 (2011): 36–50.

Rio, Knut. "Handling Sorcery in a State System of Law: Magic, Violence and *Kastom* in Vanuatu." *Oceania* 80, no. 2 (2010): 182–197.

ni-Vanuatu Agricultural Laborers in New Zealand and Australia

Bailey, Rochelle. "Ni-Vanuatu in the Recognised Seasonal Employer Scheme: Impacts at Home and Away." *SSGM Discussion Paper* 2013/4. Canberra: Australian National University, 2013.

Hammond, J., and J. Connell. "The New Blackbirds? Vanuatu Guestworkers in New Zealand." *New Zealand Geographer* 65 (2009): 201–210.

CHAPTER 13

Reuben

REUBEN IS A COMPUTER whiz. In 2010, I found him living in Ohlen. Reuben's family, leveling the slope, had crowded several houses at the cliff edge of Tio's Ohlen compound. A few steps beyond the land falls away to Tebakor Creek and, across this, to the national airport. Reuben was in Port Vila to attend secondary school. An old desktop computer anchored his small room. Scraps of cloth disguised sheet aluminum walls and roof (figure 12). A long extension cord ran up the hill, pirating electricity from his uncle's better-equipped shack. Reuben and his family paid a little money for this though electric service was sporadic. With no Internet connection, Reuben and his friends traded computer files on floppy disks and, later, flash drives. He liked burning popular and gospel music. When electricity flowed, compound residents squeezed in to watch his video files. In years since, I bought Reuben two smaller laptops. He has tended these carefully in Port Vila and back home on Tanna. Settlement dust and Tanna's acidic volcanic soils are rough on equipment of all sorts. Computers, and books, have short lives in these islands.

Like Tio and Natis, Reuben's parents struggled to find money to send their sons to secondary school. Pita and Natumwi married a few months after Tio and Natis. Natumwi, although Natis' aunt, was about her age. She came along to support Natis when her niece returned to Samaria, and she too would balance a marriage exchange from a generation before. It looked at first that Natumwi would marry Kasu, Tio's father's brother's son, but she had her eye on Pita instead, another Tio cousin. The families organized a small feast of two small pigs, several kava roots, a taro pudding, a few blankets, mats, and lengths of cloth in that marital exchange, here, was between two brothers. Tio's father, who managed Natumwi's marriage futures, passed her along to his brother, Pita's father, to marry Pita.

Natumwi chose well as Pita proved to be a devoted husband and affectionate father. Kasu later would marry another girl and move to Port Vila where mostly he has lived since. Urban migration undoubtedly worsened his diabetes. Eating

FIGURE 12. Reuben and his computer, 2010. Photo by author.

more sugar and fats, ni-Vanuatu increasingly suffer from this and other diseases of modernity, like old Tio's deadly stroke. When diabetes affected Kaso's blood circulation, doctors amputated his feet. He stayed up in Vila until he passed away, as wheelchairs ambulate poorly back on home hamlets' rougher terrains, even Kaso's that is located on the relatively level coastal plain.

Although Pita and Natumwi worked sporadically in Port Vila and have left several grown children living there, they are one of a few families to make do in Samaria, minding the interests and property of relatives who have migrated north. Pita served on the valley's Nepraineteta Area Council of Chiefs and sought out several other government appointments. He follows his ancestral namesake, looking after the village's historic Presbyterian affiliation. A church elder, he worked diligently to raise money to build a new church in the village to celebrate and restore the first Samaria chapel that his grandfathers built in 1910. The church is open to all including Kwatia's Apostolic congregation.

Tanna is an island of generalists. Most everyone knows how to farm, fish, reef gather, build houses, make bark skirts and previously to engineer penis wrappers, drink kava and pray, and to contact God and the spirits. Alongside their shared occupational abilities, however, Islanders are keen to specialize. Tanna boasts two different chiefly titles. Personal names endow men with rights to manage particular stones that control this or that plant or animal species, as well as natural phenomena like the winds, rain, earthquakes, and volcanic eruptions. Farmers seek out new and unusual crops to plant. Men command exclusive chronicles about past doings of ancestors and culture heroes. Women plait distinctive family designs into mats and baskets. Almost everyone knows ways to cure, but they differ in which illnesses they treat, and how. Such specialization, which typically is inherited from one's ancestral namesakes, confers some distinction, respect, even, on those who otherwise share much in common.

Typically, then, where Pita pursued religious leadership, his older brother James specialized in *kastom*. In 1982, I recommended him to the Vanuatu Cultural Centre's Local Fieldworker Program. This well-regarded endeavor recruited dozens of island men, and then women, who work as culture experts, studying and documenting their own customs and traditions. This at least partly obviates need for sometimes bothersome foreign ethnographers. James took part in annual Fieldworker workshops convened in Port Vila and he found work as a National Museum security guard, a job he passed on to his son when he brought his family home to Samaria. Back on Tanna, he worked with a museum outpost, the TAFEA (Tanna, Aneityum, Futuna, Erromango, Aniwa) Cultural Centre, when this was better funded. He guided visiting archaeologists and other researchers around the island assisting their research projects, including two of mine focused on Pacific War history and urban migration. Retired to Samaria, like many he considers going into the tourist business. I wired him money to buy aluminum sheeting for a new tourist bungalow roof, although this has yet to materialize.

Pita and Natumwi found enough money to pay Port Vila school expenses for Reuben and his brother. When neither was accepted into a state high school, they scrimped to send both to a private academy. Reuben moved in with his family in town, walking to school either from the Ohlen compound or from Sivur's house in Blacksands settlement, by the sea. Both brothers did well and graduated with secondary school degrees. Reuben's brother registered for coursework in legal studies at Vanuatu's University of the South Pacific branch campus. Reuben decided to be an elementary school teacher. He enrolled in Vanuatu's Institute of Teacher Education, the country's main teacher training college. I helped with tuition so he could board at the college. Taking after his father and his commitment to the church, Reuben does not drink kava or use tobacco. Instead, he filled his school nights with studying, unlike some college friends who failed their coursework. Reuben completed the three-year program with good marks. He excelled particularly with technology, setting up computers, projectors, speakers, and other equipment that left his professors flummoxed. During his final year, Reuben practiced teaching skills as a trainee in a Pango village primary school, just outside Port Vila.

Pita and Natumwi booked passage on an interisland boat to attend Reuben's graduation. Ni-Vanuatu have adopted Fijian *salusalu,* flower garlands that bedeck honorees, and Reuben's face peeks out beneath a dozen of these in his official graduation photograph. With his diploma, the Ministry of Education posted Reuben to teach at Iquaramanu, the Nepraineteta valley primary school below Samaria. Home in the village, as should young unmarried men, he built a new house up the ridge from his parents. From here, he walks to work. It took the ministry nearly a year to put Reuben on its payroll, but he loyally met his class daily, working for free he told me, "like a slave." He teaches a mixed third-and fourth-grade class. When I visited him in 2018, forty-three rambunctious nine and ten-year olds belted out a welcome song before Reuben led them into a lesson. The ministry has developed a new vernacular education program for its primary schools. Children begin schooling in their local language and shift gradually into English and French as they progress. Reuben, that day, calling out for student responses bounced from Nafe, to Bislama, to English. He worries, though, that not much of the latter language soaks in.

Comfortable dealing with outsiders, Reuben manages money donated by a Christian college in Queensland that his school used to build and furnish a new *kinda* (kindergarten) building. On my way to the airport, I treated him to lunch at one of the better equipped tourist resorts on Tanna's west coast. He immediately struck up a conversation with a talkative visitor, a member of an Australian mission campaign. Missionaries of many sorts continue to wander around Tanna no matter that most island families converted a century ago, and even John Frum supporters pivot back and forth between religious affiliations. Our fellow diner looked friendly. An ambitious young man, Reuben likes to make connections, new roads. Thinking ahead, he imagines several possibilities. He could return to the Teacher Education Institute for a second degree that would qualify him for a better-paying secondary school teaching position. Or perhaps he could become a pilot. Or, like his uncle James, he thinks hard about all those new tourists.

Several valley families living just south and east of the volcano in the Nepraineteta valley have gone into the hospitality business. Island entrepreneurs have been quick to learn the ropes. What do tourists eat? How do they sleep? What do they demand? Water, electricity, toilets? Wifi, maybe? Samaria families, up on their ridge, enviously look down on these valley enterprises. Next door to his new house, Reuben built a second shelter, a possible tourist bungalow. In 2017, a government bulldozer widened the narrow footpath that connects Samaria to the valley floor road, and village tourists now are a more likely possibility. Previously, only the hardiest visitor would scramble up that steep path. Leaning over too far, one could fall off the cliff. Now, taxi trucks with four-wheel drives could haul them easily up the mountainside. Reuben purchased a hundred yards of plastic pipe to link his bungalow into the community's spring-fed reticulated water supply system, although this often runs dry. I helped him write a blurb, a potential bungalow advertisement that he could upload to Bookings. com and Airbnb.com. Beautiful and hospitable Tanna awaits!

Tourists

Before there were tourists, there came travelers. Overseas visitors began to call at Tanna toward the end of the nineteenth century, arriving on personal sailing vessels and, later, as passengers on Burns Philp or Messageries Maritimes cargo steamers. Tanna's volcano, and its missionaries who were obliged to host these sightseers, were main attractions. Travelers then came in search of savage thrills, cannibals, and new territory for colonial exploitation. They were conventionally critical of the island's inhabitants. Freelance journalist Julian Thomas, writing as "Vagabond," stopped off in 1883 on a ship that brought plantation workers back home from Australia. He enjoyed William and Agnes Watt's hospitality at Kwamera. He complimented Tanna's farmers and was taken by cute island children, but in his account he conveyed typical stories of island savagery: The Tannese "were jealous, and sudden and quick in quarrel, bloodthirsty and vindictive, with less respect for human life than any other race in the Pacific. They are still cannibals."[1] No matter, Islanders he met borrowed his names Vagabond and Julian, and their descendent namesakes have continued to recycle these down to the present.

Beatrice Grimshaw, another wandering journalist and Irish-Australian lady traveler, booked passage in 1905 on a Burns Philp steamer for the "island of murderers." Her mordant account of Tanna's charms did admit Islanders' cheerful and helpful character: "Indeed, the Tannese, when not actively engaged in murder or cannibalism, is not at all a bad sort of fellow." Islanders even promised to train into a "fine race," one day, when they could be "induced to clean their houses and themselves, and live decently and quietly." Grimshaw quizzed an amiable elder about his cannibalistic proclivities. He responded: "He had never heard of cannibalism, not he."[2] Grimshaw didn't believe him. She collected a human thigh bone as a souvenir. With two local guides, the intrepid Beatrice climbed the volcano at dusk to journal its explosions. Apart from herself, she found tourists to be "rare birds in the islands."[3] Britain, she advised, should best annex the archipelago.

Various oddball travelers followed journalists to Tanna. Proto-hippie and artist Charles Gordon Frazer, "the first white man to penetrate into the wild interior of Tanna," found his way to Port Resolution in 1888. He survived to produce a seven-foot long oil painting, *Cannibal Feast on the Island of Tanna*. This, still esteemed in 2004, sold for more than $59,000. In 1894, Austria-Hungarian Count Rodolfe Festetics de Tolna and his rich American wife, on a honeymoon cruise across the Pacific, moored their newly built yacht in Port Resolution. Countess Festetics would later abandon the voyage and sue for divorce, but Rodolfe ("the Cannibal Count") got a book out of it. He opened his Tanna ("The Cannibal Island") chapter with usual sensationalist keynotes: The savages "were truly appalling, with a fierce animalistic expression, of craven cunning and cruelty."[4] Adventurer John Voss in 1902 also found shelter in Port Resolution. The *Tilikum,* Voss' modified Nootka (northwest coast) red cedar dugout canoe, surprised Islanders, and the Watts, when it sailed into the bay. William and Agnes treated Voss to "a very nice dinner." Voss, of course, was eager to find cannibals and copra trader Wilson, a fellow guest at the Watt's table, assured him that a man had been eaten only a few days previously. Voss admitted that the Tannese were hospitable and generous, but he scorned shabby island villages where huts reminded him of dog kennels.

More distinguished literary travelers also visited Tanna, including Jack and Charmian London, assisted by Martin Johnson. Johnson with his wife Osa would return a decade later to film the archipelago's first silent movies, released as *Cannibals of the South Seas* (1918) and *Head Hunters of the South Seas* (1922). The Londons, in 1908, navigated into Port Resolution on Jack's yacht, the *Snark.* They also leaned on the Watts' hospitality. Charmian found Port Resolution's Christians to be "individuals of one kind or another of striking personality." One elder even "proved a lovable chap." Yet, she too pushed cannibal stories: "five miles back in the bush, the savages are unreclaimed ancestor-worshippers who eat one another to this day."[5] Watt assured Charmian that everyone was perfectly safe. This news, however, spoiled her storyline. Johnson more crudely burlesqued the Islanders he met: "They were the most savage, heathenish looking folk I have ever looked upon."[6] He didn't like William Watt, either, who refused to let him use the mission darkroom on the Sabbath. Jack and Charmian with Martin and other *Snark* crew members trekked along the valley and scrambled up Iasur's fiery summit. Eighty years later, visitor stories haven't much budged. Travel writer Paul Theroux in the 1990s, describing the Tannese channeled Martin Johnson's earlier snubs: "They were not much bigger than pygmies, and they were blacker and more naked . . . they looked like cannibals."[7]

Tourists on Tanna are no longer Grimshaw's rare birds. Visitors today are hard to miss. In 2003, I was astonished to run into a pack train of portly German tourists on horseback heading for the volcano. They, migratory birds, quickly have become commonplace. Tafea, Vanuatu's southern province, attracts 40 percent of the overseas visitors who travel outside Port Vila. In 2017, 10,700 tourists went south, and most of these headed for Tanna for a three or four day stay. These numbers increase annually. Iasur remains the principal draw, but tourist entrepreneurs also market the *nakwiari* dance festival and other elements of Tanna *kastom,* even John Frum spectacles like the movement's annual 15 February anniversary celebration.

Several expatriate businessmen were early boosters of island tourism. They developed a tourist lodge or two and composed initial blurbs to attract visitors. In years since, however, island entrepreneurs, particularly in the valley underneath Iasur and also at Port Resolution, jumped into the business. An enlarged airport at White Grass served by larger planes arriving twice daily from Port Vila facilitates tourist arrivals. Occasional cruise ships crammed with seagoing holidaymakers, some tipsy, call at the island and vague plans circulate proposing new boat docks and wharves. In the 1980s, the government bulldozed a road up the southeast side of Iasur. Visitors no longer need to hike up 1,184 feet of gritty volcanic ash to reach the caldera. Taxi trucks chug up the rutted trail that Grimshaw, the Londons, Martin Johnson, and even I once struggled to climb.

In the late 1970s, Samaria families on average eked out little more than US$500 each year, mostly from drying and selling copra and working casual jobs. After independence, almost everyone abandoned copra making. Oil palm plantations elsewhere in the tropics undercut copra's price, and interisland shipping dwindled. Villagers instead turned to urban migration, seeking work in Port Vila and beyond to earn cash. Today's tourists present new, potentially lucrative opportunities for those like Reuben and James now back home in Samaria. Most tourists book accommodation in several west coast lodges that offer electricity and running water. Increasing numbers, however, find their way to the bungalows that village entrepreneurs have constructed in the valley below the volcano, and eastward toward Port Resolution. The foundations of William Watt's Workers Memorial Church, Agnes' grave still nestled nearby, now support the Yacht Club Resort. Beer is on sale inside. Bungalow keepers also have tapped into an odd tourist taste for sleeping in treehouses, throwing up a half dozen of these around the volcano.

As they did a century ago, most visitors today come to Tanna to do Iasur, particularly at night when its magma and lava bomb explosions glow orange-red. Promoters advertise Iasur as "the world's most accessible volcano." Visitors pay upward of US$100 to truck up to the crater's lip. A second trip up to the caldera comes with a 50 percent discount, and a third is free. The volcano is spectacular, but how might tourists stay longer and spend more? Upselling, promoters now also boost the island's unspoiled nature and its age-old *kastom:* Tanna Island, boasts one tourist brochure, is renowned for its "active volcano, custom villages, potent kava, cargo cultists, strong traditions, exciting festivals, gigantic banyan trees, magnificent wild horses, long black and white beaches, velvet nights, and much more."

Before the John Frum movement fell on hard times in 2000, splitting into three factions, entrepreneurs also tried promoting cargo cult: Tourists will "learn about the fascinating John Frum cult." Daring visitors found their way down to Sulphur Bay's Friday night "cargo cult dances," there joined by crew members from occasional visiting yachts. Air Vanuatu's in-flight magazine, for example, in several of its issues celebrated Tanna's "ancient culture" and "untouched waterfalls" but also promised tourists that

> there are also cult tribes to learn about, including the Prince Philip cult and the John Frum cargo cult. If you visit on a Friday, you will be privy to the weekly ceremony when John Frum members conduct rituals such as raising flags and marching in unison, holding the belief that mimicking these American acts will lead to the delivery of magical cargo like radios, jeeps, fridges and other manufactured items owned by American visitors during WWII.[8]

Tourism marketers also have moved along to feature island *kastom,* particularly village exchange ceremonies. Promoters everywhere convert exotic dance festivals into touristic spectaculars. The *nakwiari* is certainly stunning but is irregularly organized. *Nieri* feasts, village exchanges of garden produce, are more common but also irregular. However, during the cool harvest season from April through September, one family or another is certain to organize a *tamarua,* a circumcision exchange. Entrepreneurs also hire relatives and neighbors to stage dance performances for tourists if no actual *kastom* ceremony is on hand. Numbers of tourists nowadays wander into these family circumcision exchanges, cameras clicking, as they also drop into first shave, first menstruation, and other occasional village ceremonies. Islanders are welcoming and generous, but some think strategically about how to monetize their *kastom*. *Nakwiari* organizers typically demand visitor admission fees, and they charge extra for picture-taking.

Then there is cannibalism. Islanders are rightly incensed at previous generations of visitors who came to Tanna, looked into people's faces, and saw savage cannibals, or at least so they claimed when they wrote up their travels. But cannibalism still sells. The Jungle Cultural Tour, located just down from Samaria, promises that tourists will "experience the past in the present." An entrepreneur in the valley under the volcano charges tourists to attend cannibal dances, guaranteed to raise goosebumps. Another, at Port Resolution, cleared a cannibal trail charging about US$10 to walk along this. Promoters elsewhere in Vanuatu offer similar cannibalistic thrills, including man-eating tours on Malakula and cannibal encounters on Efate. Elau's Erromangans ceremonially have apologized for killing and eating John Williams and James Harris.

It is a tricky business when one's culture goes on sale in the global tourism marketplace as primitive and peculiar. Connections between tourism and identity work both ways. Primitive or romantic nature attracts tourists, but tourism then feeds local identity as Islanders find it profitable to sell themselves as living primitives, jungle natives, cargo cultists, and even as erstwhile cannibals. Everyday life is colored by the themes that situate Tanna within the overseas touristic marketplace. When sightseers arrive, Islanders learn something about who they are, or what they are within global circuits. The touristic gaze is a sort of surveillance that transfigures the everyday into spectacle. Culture is no longer a lifeway, but a product. A dance is no longer a dance, it is a performance. A house is now a bungalow. A basket a commodity. Those beneath the gaze come to look back at themselves as tourists see them. Although most Islanders repudiate John Frum, and certainly deny any cannibal appetite, despite their protests Tanna is framed as the island of cargo cult and cannibal. Still, Reuben, his uncle James, and many other island businessmen are happy to host.

Digital Island

Creeping infrastructural buildup of airline and airport, roads and trucks, and village water supply systems has made tourism possible on Tanna. The mobile telephone, after 2008, also brings tourists to the island as entrepreneurs use smart phones to check their Internet bookings. Islanders have come to rely on their cell phones, *mobael* in Bislama, to do much more. As soon as two telephone companies pierced Tanna with cell towers, including one looming over Samaria on

Nukwaneinupum peak, everyone wanted a mobile. Within a year, 76 percent of households had access to a phone and this number has approached 100 percent. Mobiles quickly became expensive necessities. They require prepaid credit that people purchase from local trade stores, or from company kiosks in Lenakel (Blackman Town) on the other side of the island. With no electricity, villagers find ways to recharge their phones, bringing these over to Blackman Town where they pay storekeepers 100 or 200 vatu to plug in, tapping into automobile batteries, or using their own generators and solar panels. Everyone much appreciates cheap SMS text messaging. When out of credit, needy friends text free "please call me" messages. Linguists note that these fresh waves of text messaging, and also Internet postings, are transforming Bislama's orthography in extraordinary ways.

Reuben, in Samaria, charges up his mobile phone more often than he does his laptop. While Blackman Town boasts an Internet café that sometimes is open for business, a youth center with computers, and outposts of the University of the South Pacific and the Vanuatu Institute of Technology that offer occasional courses in information technology, mobiles are more versatile devices than computers. Many have upgraded to smart phones (*dak skrin*, "dark screen" in Bislama) that connect into the World Wide Web and also function as cameras and as handy flashlights at night, easier to light up than burning coconut fronds.

When mobiles first came into the market, Vanuatu buzzed with nervous urban, and rural, legends. Microwaves and computers sparked parallel anxious tales when these devices originally appeared in the USA, as elsewhere. Island friends warned me not to pick up at night if I didn't recognize a number. They feared a new form of sorcery where enchanters hijack one's brain through the phone. Young telephoners quickly figured out prank calling. One midnight caller asked me if I smoked marijuana and if I could please send over a young girl. I hung up. He called back. Boys trade girls' numbers. They dial randomly, aiming to flirt with any girl who might answer. Teenagers (and adults, too), with mobiles, appreciate digital possibilities to escape incessant family surveillance of their romances and other affairs. No one can ask "where are you going?" if one can't be seen going (or relating). Parents complain of these digital devils that eat money and deprave their children. However, mobiles lubricate and expand people's social networking in approved as well as deprecated directions. Trans-island families notably live online.

Mobiles are even more powerful mechanisms and objects of criticism as Islanders increasingly go online. Many who can afford dark screens, and enough phone credit, sign onto Facebook. Here, they vigorously engage with many popular Vanuatu Facebook Groups and Pages that feature island news, religious affirmations, sport commentary, critique of politicians and government, climate change and other worries, advertisements, and much more amidst all sorts of gossip, local rumor, and salacious tidbit. Facebook groups Yumi Toktok Stret, Whu i Luk, Yu Save Seh!, Living in Vanuatu, Mi Harem Se, and Mi Laekem Yu are contemporary digital kava-drinking grounds where people gather to discuss and debate, if often anonymously. Some shelter behind clever usernames that only their friends recognize. Many online, like Reuben, like to post selfies. They also recirculate popular memes, both local and global. Before mobile phones, Islanders tapped only occasionally into global frenzies and scams including chain letters, dubious baldness cures, pyramid marketing schemes, and other money-making swindles as these arrived in the sluggish mails. Now, all sorts of doubtful fiddles pop up daily onscreen.

Despite widespread technological worry and doubt, few will surrender their mobiles. These devices sustain today's trans-island families. People regularly text and call from Samaria to Port Vila and beyond, sharing family news, making plans, and tendering appeals. Growing numbers of family members, like Soarum and his wife when working abroad in New Zealand or Australia, likewise use their mobiles, and Facebook Messenger or WhatsApp, to stay in touch economically. Felina, Sivur's daughter and Reuben's cousin, messaged me from Australia. She's employed there in a mango-packing house at the Top End, near Darwin. She's okay but misses home. Take care, I told her. Next time I buy a mango I'll think of you. And my dark screen.

Notes

1. Julian Thomas (Vagabond), *Cannibals & Convicts: Notes of Personal Experiences in the Western Pacific* (London: Cassell & Company, 1886), 229.

2. Beatrice Grimshaw, *From Fiji to the Cannibal Islands* (London: Eveleigh Nash, 1907), 284, 285, 293.

3. Grimshaw, *From Fiji*, 319.

4. Rodolfe Festetics de Tolna, *Chez les Cannibals: Huit Ans de Croisière dans l'Océan Pacifique a Bord du Yacht "Le Tolna"* (Paris: Librarie Plon, 1903), 186 [my translation].

5. Charmian London, *The Log of the Snark* (New York: Macmillan, 1915), 324.

6. Martin Johnson, *Through the South Seas with Jack London* (New York: Dodd, Mead, 1913), 277.

7. Paul Theroux, *The Happy Isles of Oceania: Paddling the Pacific* (New York: G. P. Putnam's Sons, 1992), 196.

8. Air Vanuatu, "Around + About," *Island Spirit* 51 (July–September 2010), 19.

Further Readings

Vanuatu Cultural Centre's Local Fieldworker Program

Bolton, Lissant. "The Vanuatu Cultural Centre and Its Own Community." *Journal of Museum Ethnography* 6 (1994): 67–78.

Early Island Visitors

Ahrens, Prue, Lamont Lindstrom, and Fiona Paisley. *Across the World with the Johnsons: Visual Culture and American Empire in the Twentieth Century.* Farnham: Ashgate, 2013.

Langton, Joy. *Cannibal Feast.* London: Herbert Joseph Ltd, 1937.

Voss, J. C. *The Venturesome Voyages of Captain Voss.* Yokohama: Japan Herald Press, 1926.

Tourist Statistics

Latest Tourism News, Port Vila: Vanuatu National Statistics Office.

Tourists (and Cannibals)

Alexeyeff, Kalissa and John Taylor, eds. *Touring Pacific Cultures.* Canberra: Australian National University Press, 2016.

DeBlock, Hugo. "Cannibals in Paradise: The Exotic, the Familiar, and the Strange in Ritual and Performance in Vanuatu." *Journal of Anthropological Research* 74, no. 4 (2018): 541–557.

Lindstrom, Lamont. "Culture, Politics and Tourism on Tanna." In *Pacific Alternatives: Cultural Politics in Contemporary Oceania,* edited by Edvard Hviding and Geoffrey M. White, 180–199. Canon Pyon, UK: Sean Kingston Publishing, 2015.

Mobile Telephone in Vanuatu

Kraemer, Daniela. "'Do You Have a Mobile?' Mobile Phone Practices and the Refashioning of Social Relationships in Port Vila Town." *The Australian Journal of Anthropology* 28, no. 1 (2017): 39–55.

Taylor, John P. "Drinking Money and Pulling Women: Mobile Phone Talk, Gender, and Agency in Vanuatu." *Anthropological Forum* 26, no. 1 (2016): 1–16.

Vandeputte-Tavo, Leslie. "New Technologies and Language Shifting in Vanuatu." *Pragmatics* 23, no. 1 (2013): 169–179.

CHAPTER 14

Last Island

PEOPLE ARE CONVINCED, TANNA is the center of the world. Go Ipare: Up toward the mountain, to the middle. Tied into global grids for nearly 250 years, the island is well connected. Traffic and travel are constant. Captain Cook and crew came ashore, Elau shanghaied to London, Manehevi jailed in Port Vila, Soarum wandered a Queensland plantation, Nouar and his team shipped north to work on Efate's American military bases, Sivur, Kusi, and the rest of the family migrated to town, Soarum and Felina flew overseas to pick grapes and pack mangoes, and Mwatiktiki and other spirits continue to rove. Islanders worry, though. Perhaps Tanna is only the center of *their* world. Maybe they are only the tail of the fish, not the fish. Ipare, sometimes, looks to be at the outer edge of the grid, the last stop along the road. Some, ruefully, call their home the Last Island, and tourist brokers have marketed the place as such. But yet—with *kastom,* the volcano, John Frum, pig exchange feasts—the world keeps coming.

Those on the Last Island sometimes predict that the Last Day will soon arrive. Evangelical missionaries cultivate the expectation of the world's end, but Tanna time concepts also presume sudden earthly disturbances and transformation. John Frum predicted a new day and, so some say, a new island. The Prophet Fred foresaw volcanic Lake Siui's vanishing. Many village families, on 31 December 1999, decamped to sleep in bush hidey-holes. Rumors of impending world calamity and catastrophe had amplified fiercely as the third millennium approached.

Whether first or last among islands, villagers fret uncertain aspects of the future even as they draw strength from the past. Although linked since 1774 into global networks, Tanna remains distinct, its own place, although this is a place deeply figured and shaped by local and global forces alike. Islanders zealously cultivate *kastom,* but they also welcome strangers and novelty if these promise advantage and esteem, leading to respect—the converse of shame. They hop ships and board planes for destinations overseas, but keep in mind future homecomings even though these returns may be years away. Tanna endures as a refuge, an island sanctuary, where wayfaring villages root their identities and, when need be, return to find shelter.

Home Ground

Nafe language has no generic verb or noun for "work," although it offers words for particular tasks like farming, fishing, and making things. Missionaries (and plantation recruiters), who aimed to inculcate an appreciation of honest labor among the converted, struggled with this verbal gap. William Watt, in his 1890 Nafe *New Testament,* sometimes defaulted to the English loan "work," sometimes opted for Nafe *tafaga* (behavior), sometimes an invented paraphrase *narimnarime ikamo* (things you do), and sometimes he omitted "work" altogether from a translated verse.

Islanders discovered *wok* when they learned Bislama, and they have worked ever since on plantations, mission and colonial roads and gardens, American military bases, in Port Vila's settlements, and again overseas in New Zealand and Australia's farms and orchards. Money drives them. Those employed abroad express powerful nostalgia for island life, where everything is free, although of course people must work at home, too. The island, though, offers a haven when things go bad. When overseas relocation and employment become troublesome or impossible, people retreat to their village homes, gardens, and pigs. Almost no island land has been lost or alienated, unlike on Efate and Espiritu Santo Islands where overseas investors have leased large tracts. On Tanna, land remains in the hands of its *kastom* owners. And land is more than real estate. It is home ground. The island's given name after all, thanks to James Cook, means ground, earth, or soil.

Anthropological theories of the dividual argue that single persons incorporate within themselves elements of others, notably their close kin, and also traces of material elements including the land and food that nourished them. On Tanna, persons profoundly identify themselves with places. When abroad, they pass as *Man Tanna,* associated with the island as a whole. On Tanna, they distinguish themselves according to their villages, their home grounds. This is particularly true of men whose personal names embed them in landscape, but home places come to define women as well. When someone is distressed or ill, home food is the best cure. Old Tio's kin brought food grown on home ground to sustain him during his final days in hospital. Pita and Natumwi insisted that a sickly granddaughter, born in Port Vila, come straight home to Tanna where local foods would heal. Families on Tanna ship home-grown food to kinfolk living in Port Vila's settlements. This local food both nourishes and sustains their island personhoods.

Globalization, however, unsettles us all. Surging flows of people, goods, and ideas reach even out-of-the-way, last islands like Tanna. In response, nationalism, xenophobia, and chauvinism spark around the world. People romanticize home values in the face of the strange and the unfamiliar. Islanders, thanks to John Frum, turned once before to *kastom* to resist the world and they may well do so again: Banish outsiders and ditch their money. But what are the chances here? Pavegen's line of wild cane stuck into Port Resolution's sands didn't deter those alien sharks for long. The lighthouse of the Pacific continues to attract its sight-seeing moths. Several thousand new Chinese have moved into Vanuatu, opening trade stores and petty businesses, although the Tannese so far have kept them off their island renaming Lenakel, pointedly, Blackman town. Tanna's population has recovered from deadly nineteenth-century epidemics and probably exceeds its 1774 numbers. Island ground has filled up. Most personal name stocks currently are bestowed and enlivened. New possibilities abroad, however, increasingly beckon. Trans-island families today root themselves at home and away. Children find overseas spouses. Grandchildren in town may or may not learn much Nafe language.

Climate change, too, keeps people on edge. There are, nowadays, about as many global warming missionaries wandering the island as there are Christian. Armed with munificent resources these, too, preach visions of dark and dismal futures. Salvation is possible but demanding. Some on Tanna seize on global warming messaging to explain passing drought and threatening cyclones, but also common colds, unruly pigs, and mischievous winds. The world is increasingly dangerous. Yet the good life as most imagine this, including travel, education, cement brick houses, solar electric systems, mobile phones, and even Reuben's computers, requires at least some cash and this pulls people away for work in Port Vila and beyond.

Educational opportunity and urban migration have loosened Tanna's gender roles and expectations. Women in town enjoy new possibilities to relax familial surveillance. Many now speak for themselves; they choose their own spouses. Some ignore masculine kava-drinking prerogatives. The island's *kastom* pattern of peripheral women who cleave to a core of men in the center is eroding as women find ways to live independently, particularly in town. People elsewhere in Vanuatu figuratively describe men as banyans, with deep roots sunk into their home grounds, and women as birds who flit from tree to tree. A few of the birds now have flown the forest altogether, nesting on their own in Port Vila or beyond.

FIGURE 13. Kaha Monty, 2018. Photo owned by author.

Kwatia, reflecting on his life and times, urged everyone to mind their home ground. Uri, his homesick brother-in-law who left Tanna for Port Vila years ago, also longs for the island's peace and harmony. In perilous times, home ground remains a refuge, but it too needs protection. How might village justice systems be remade in order to address and resolve novel problems brought by sharp increases in tourism, possible land leasing and alienation, conflicted urban settlements, global appropriation of island cultural property, and more? Will future lease holders of island lands, when disputes erupt, be convinced to take part in all-day moots that culminate in mutual gift giving? Sorcery fear may work to deter neighbors from violating one's *kastom* privileges on Tanna and in town settlements, but how far will this fear extend? Can *nakaemas* or Tanna's power stones reach beyond Vanuatu's borders to bump off outsiders who misbehave?

Land disputes are a particularly vexing issue and Islanders actively reach out to councils of chiefs, island and state courts, and the Ministry of Land hoping that these official bodies might solve home-ground rows that local dispute-settlement systems fail to handle. Villagers take land squabbles to court where previously they would have dealt with these in local moots. Three of Samaria's families have enrolled sons, including Reuben's brother, in legal studies at the University of the South Pacific maneuvering to protect home ground from future mischief-makers.

Tanna's entwined persons, home grounds, and its embedded personal and place names have sustained island *kastom* since 1774 despite much coming and going. Vibrant island *kastom,* though, entices even more overseas visitors who pay to experience sizzling volcanic eruptions and romantic, sometimes savagely romantic, cultural spectacles. This traffic brings novelty and change to the island, but it also firms up people's insistence to remain themselves. Villagers travel down many roads leading abroad, but Tanna's ground calls many back home. Globally networked, Tanna's places and people have endured. The island, although in the world, is greater than that world.

Kaha Monty

The last day has nearly arrived for me, too. I found my way luckily to Tanna several decades ago and the island has pulled me back many times since. Not quite twenty-five, I wasn't yet feeling old and it was then disconcerting when new friends instructed their children to call me Kaha Monty, *kaha* "grandfather," and Monty my island-ish name. This grandparental kinship title, of course, signified good village manners, an effort to ease an awkward stranger into ordinary island relationships. Many years later, I happily embrace my grandfatherly status (figure 13). Age and grey hair on Tanna command respect, deserved or not. Village grandchildren, my *mwipuk,* continue to find and reach out to me, on Facebook, as their *kaha.*

Kaha I am, but maybe also a *Kout Kasua.* Kout Kasua belonged to neither of the two island moieties, Numrukwen and Koiameta, which united families across Tanna. Instead, they passed messages between the two sides and, when disputes flared, opened negotiations between them. *Kasua* derives from the verb *asua,* which means "paddle, travel by canoe" but also "be alert" or "be knowledgeable or wise." Kout Kasuas were useful characters when nineteenth-century feuding intensified with imported firearms. People's appreciation of their mediating and communicative functions, though, is always tinged with suspicion. Kout Kasuas also tell stories behind one's back, spilling the beans to island rivals. Anthropologists, too, like to tell other people's stories. We carry these from one place to another. And we, too, hope that this cultivates new understandings and deeper mutual appreciation among those living on last, or first, islands.

As my last day on the last island approaches, village friends eye my *kwanakwevur,* that grey hair. Tanna's places, persons, and their relationships ideally never go away. They are, rather, actively and persistently replaced. Yesterday's named personages living on their designated home grounds should recycle and reappear, come tomorrow. Islanders carefully maintain good connections and valued roads. I followed instructions and brought two of my daughters along to Samaria so that they will know how to find the village and replace me when I'm gone, when I transform into a *kaha eraha,* a departed grandfather spirit.

Until then, I say *tanak asori* as do Islanders today, having now found a Nafe phrase that is expressive of gratitude, as earnest missionary Mary Matheson once put this. Or, more aptly, I echo Agnes Watt's gravestone epitaph at Port Resolution: *In rapi nakur Ipare.*

Further Readings

Place, Ground, and Personal Identity in Vanuatu

Hess, Sabrina. *Person and Place: Ideas, Ideals and the Practice of Sociality on Vanua Lava, Vanuatu.* New York: Berghahn Books, 2009.

Jolly, Margaret. *Women of the Place: Kastom, Colonialism and Gender in Vanuatu.* Chur, Switzerland: Harwood Academic Press, 1994.

Taylor, John P. *The Other Side: Ways of Being and Place in Vanuatu.* Honolulu: University of Hawai'i Press, 2008.

The Anthropologist on Tanna

Lindstrom, Lamont. "Surprising Times on Tanna, Vanuatu." In *Change and Continuity in the Pacific: Revisiting the Region,* edited by John Connell and Helen Lee, 55–68. New York: Routledge, 2018.

INDEX

ABOUT THE AUTHOR

LAMONT LINDSTROM is Kendall Professor and Chair of Anthropology at the University of Tulsa. He has also taught anthropology and sociolinguistics at Rhodes College (Memphis), the University of Papua New Guinea, and the University of California at Berkeley. He has long-term research interests in Vanuatu and other Melanesian countries and is the author of *Cargo Cult: Strange Stories of Desire from Melanesia and Beyond* (1993), *Knowledge and Power in a South Pacific Society* (1990), and *Kwamera Dictionary* (1987), co-author of *Kwamera* (1994), *Island Encounters: Black and White Memories of the Pacific War* (1990), *Kava: The Pacific Drug* (1992), and *Across the World with the Johnsons: Visual Culture and Empire in the Twentieth Century* (2013), editor of *Drugs in Western Pacific Societies: Relations of Substance* (1987), and co-editor of *Chiefs Today: Traditional Pacific Leadership and the Postcolonial State* (1997), *Culture, Kastom, Tradition: Developing Cultural Policy in Melanesia* (1994), and *The Pacific Theater: Island Representations of World War Two* (1989). His recent publications focus on urban migration and personhood in Vanuatu, nineteenth-century missionary wife Agnes C. P. Watt, bark belts and Tanna masculinity, and early imagery of Tanna Islanders.

Printed in the United States
by Baker & Taylor Publisher Services